Internet TV Systems

2nd Edition

By Lawrence Harte
Roger McGarrahan

DiscoverNet Publishing
2474 Walnut Street, Suite 105
Cary NC 27518 USA
Telephone: +1.919.301.0109
Fax: +1.919.557.2261
email: books@DiscoverNet.com
web: www.DiscoverNet.com/books

DiscoverNet

First Printing

Printed and Bound by Lightning Source, TN.

International Standard Book Number: 9781932813265

About the Authors

Lawrence Harte is the president of DiscoverNet media which publishes Social TV Magazine, runs Internet TV Plus conferences, and develops tech and business courses on emerging technologies. As of 2016, he authored 113+ books on communication technologies (more than 20 on TV systems and technologies). Lawrence is a technical and marketing advisor to several TV show and movie production companies. Between 2005 and 2016 he interviewed over 3820 companies that produce TV products and provide services. Mr. Harte has designed, setup, managed products, and invented patents on communication technologies. He has worked for companies including Ericsson/General Electric, Audiovox/Toshiba and Westinghouse and consulted for hundreds of other companies including Google TV, Samsung, Sony, Rovi, and Others. Mr. Harte holds many degrees and certificates including an Executive MBA from Wake Forest University (1995) and a BSET from the University of the State of New York, (1990).

Roger McGarrahan is co-founder and President/CEO of PathFinder Digital LLC which provides complete satellite communications systems to state and federal government agencies and the US military; inclusive of satellite terminal hardware, satellite data services, field installation and support services. Roger was also the co-founder and COO of StreamVu (PathFinder TV) which provides Internet based digital video streaming solutions including Over-the-Top IPTV and multi-platform live video streaming. Prior to that, Roger was CEO of Thomson Broadcast & Multimedia, Inc. (Thomson/Grass Valley) in charge of North America operations and previously its General Counsel. Earlier Roger was legal counsel for COMSAT RSI which specialized in the design and delivery of satellite communication systems. In total, Roger has twenty five years experience as executive management, operations management, and corporate counsel in the broadcast, satellite and telecommunications industries.

Acknowledgements

Many smart people have helped us to create this book. Some of them gave substantial amounts of time to share their experience, answer many questions, and invite us into their businesses and onto their production sets.

TV and Movie Production leaders and on air talent including Mike Davis from Uptone Pictures, Alisha Ramsey with AM Raleigh, Tracie Clark with WCAP TV News, Jerry McGlothlin from Moving Visions Entertainment, John Demers with Rusty Bucket kids TV show, John Draughon of iMedia Foundation, Ross Cooper from Channel Islands, Tim Bell from Blackett Bell Films, Konrad Arnold with Mighty K Bot Creative, Billy Lewis from Orange St Films, Drew Becker with Convey Media, and John Clark from ABC 11.

TV Technology and Business Professionals including Christine Gallen at ABI Research, Michael Lantz from Accedo Broadband, Dean Kashlan of AcumenLink, Ric Brovedani at Alcatel Lucent, Jeremy Deaner with Amberfin, Carl Walter Host with Appear TV, Rick Ducey from BIA, Juan Carlos Rivero at Broadcom, Arthur Drevnig of Broadview, Don Gordon from Bulldog United, Scott Puopolo with Cisco, Alex Terpstra with Civolution, David Kaiser with Coincident, Drew Becker from Convey Media, Mike Nann with Digital Rapids, Ben Weinberger at Digitalsmiths, Doug Sheer at DIS Consulting, Raj Jaswa at Dyyno, Natalla Psakhie with Elecard, Ameer Karim from Entone, Anton Monk from Entropic, Kirk Edwardson at Espial, Alexander Iliev from Gracenote, Peter Maag from Haivision, Mark Reinhardt with Hargray, Sanjay Raman with Howcast, Scott Burnett with IBM, Toni Leiponen with Icareus, Isaac Calderan at IGuGu, Kirk George with IneoQuest, Jeff Heynen and Kimberly Peinado from Infonectics, Steve Outridge from Informa Telecoms and Media, Michael Sommer from Information Technologies, Jennifer Hicks and Alexandra Crabb with Ink Communications, Chris Moon from Innodigital, Timothy Downs with Interwork Media Inc., Todd Schuelke from Iomega, Yariv Erel at JustAd.TV, Joseph Wang with Lookee TV, Kimberly Sauceda with Looxcie, Thomas Hughes from MGM, Jerónimo Macanás Candilejo with MGMedia,

Ted Malone at Microsoft, Mauro Bonomi from Minerva Networks, Rob Gelphman with MoCA Alliance, David Grubb with Motorola, Bob Saffari from Mozaik, Rick Brown with NC State University, Chris Wagner from Neulion, Slava Levin and Konstantin Salenkov of NexTV, Scott Brown from Octoshape, Ted Miller from Opera, Angela Scheller from Packet Video, Rich Tarpley, Joel Suttles and Austin Snow of PathFinder TV LLC, David Bramley, Ian Westover, and Gay Bell with Platform PR., George Wehmann from Raleigh Television Network, Todd Cochrane at Raw Voice, Feng Chen from Rockchip, Jim Funk of Roku, Joe Ledlow at Scheduall, Dave Allred from Sezmi, Robert Saunders from Skitter TV, Paal Huff at Snap TV, Dennis Nugent and Steve Popper from STB Advertising, Frans Blommestein of Telergy, Mark Myslinksi and Thomas Carey of Televue, Andy Tarczon with The Diffusion Group(TDG) Research, Tom Weiss from TV Genius, Yonatan Sela with Tvinci, Tom Rosenstein from Verivue, Francois Saint-Martin with Viaccess, Roy Kirsopp at Vidiom, Jeff Cody from Vidtonic, Brad Bitterman and Eric Berman of VTilt Digital, David Netz at Wall Street Communications, Charles Herring from Wealth TV, Dave Stubinvol from Wowza, Greg Fawson from XMediaResearch, Ron Jocaby of Yahoo!, Dan Eakins from Zeitera.

Table of Contents

About the Authors III
Acknowledgements V
Table of Contents VII

WHAT IS AN INTERNET TV SYSTEM? 1

Internet TV Content Sources 1
Internet TV Service Providers 2
Internet TV Distribution Systems 2
Internet TV Viewing Devices 2
TV Channel Types 3
Linear Channels 3
On Demand Channels 4
Public Channels 4
Private Channels 4
Internet TV Content Types 5
Movie Studios 5
Network Television 6
Independent Producers 6
Organizational Content 6
User Generated Content (UGC) 7

INTERNET TV SERVICES 9

Broadcast Services 10
Linear Channels 10
Sponsored Programming 10
Advertising Funded 10

SUBSCRIPTION SERVICES 12
Subscription Accounts *12*
Premium Channels *12*
Tiered Services *12*
ON DEMAND SERVICES 13
Switched Video *13*
Live Streaming *14*
Download and Play *14*
Pay Per View (PPV) *14*
Pay Per Period (PPP) *14*
ADVERTISING 15
Interstitial Advertising (Interruption) *16*
Overlay Advertising *16*
Skin Advertising *16*
TELEVISION COMMERCE (T-COMMERCE) 17
Direct Sales *17*
Affiliate Sales *18*
Third Party Sales *18*

INTERNET TV CONTENT SOURCES 21

Content Producers *21*
Network Television *21*
Community Content *21*
Original Programming *22*
CONTENT PRODUCERS 23
Movie Studios *23*
Syndicates *24*
Production Companies *24*
TELEVISION NETWORKS 25
Network Affiliate Distribution *26*
Network Content Types *26*
Network Feeds *26*
Ad Spots *27*

CONTENT AGGREGATORS . . . 28
Content Brokers . . . *28*
Media Ingestion . . . *28*
Media Adaptation (Transcoding) . . . *29*
Content Distribution . . . *29*
LOCAL PROGRAMMING . . . 30
Local News . . . *31*
Local Events . . . *31*
Local Weather . . . *31*
INTERNATIONAL PROGRAMMING . . . 32
Foreign Networks . . . *33*
Foreign TV Stations . . . *33*
Foreign Programs . . . *33*
SPECIALTY CONTENT PRODUCERS . . . 34
Independent Filmmakers ("Indies") . . . *34*
Companies . . . *35*
Groups . . . *35*
COMMUNITY CONTENT . . . 37
Public Broadcasting . . . *37*
Shared Media . . . *38*
Social Media . . . *38*
PUBLIC DOMAIN (PD) . . . 39
Expired Copyrights . . . *40*
Government Content . . . *40*
Abandoned Content . . . *40*
ORIGINAL PROGRAMMING . . . 41
Remote Interviews . . . *41*
Web Seminars . . . *42*
Event Coverage . . . *42*

INTERNET TV VIEWING DEVICES . . . 45

Cloud Pairing . . . *46*
Firmware Updates . . . *46*
Digital Media Adapter Compatibility . . . *47*
Backdrop Display . . . *47*

INTERNET TV SET TOP BOXES (I-STB) 47
Network Data Interface 48
Media Decoder 48
Device Storage 48
TV Outputs 49
Application Platform 49
TV MEDIA STICK (DONGLES) 50
WiFi Connection 50
Media Connector (HDMI) 51
Power 51
Remote Control 51
HYBRID TV BROADCAST SET TOP BOXES (HSTB) 52
Broadcast Connection 52
Internet Access 53
Application Platform 53
MULTIMEDIA PERSONAL COMPUTERS (PCS) 54
Soft Client 55
Operating System (OS) 55
Media Decoding 56
Security 56
PC Video to TV Converter 56
MULTIMEDIA MOBILE TELEPHONE 58
Broadband Access 58
Microplayer 58
Mobile Operating System 59
Security 59
Human Interface Capabilities 59
CONNECTED TELEVISIONS (SMART TVS) 61
Internet Connection 61
Media Processing 61
Connected TV Operating System 62
Application Processing 62

Networked Gaming Devices 63
Internet Connection *64*
Media Processing *64*
Application Processing *64*
Connected Media Players 65
Network Connection *66*
Media Processing *66*
Java Scripts *66*
Application Platform *66*
Store Media Applications *66*

INTERNET TV TECHNOLOGY 69

Media Capturing *69*
Compression *69*
Packetization *70*
Packet Transmission *70*
Packet Reception *70*
Decompression *71*
Decoding *71*
Rendering *71*
Switched Digital Video (SDV) 72
Physical Connection *72*
Logical Connection *73*
Sessions *73*
Unlimited Number of TV Channels *73*
Communication Protocols 74
Application Protocols *75*
Session Protocols *75*
Network Protocols *75*
Link Protocols *76*
Protocol Suites *76*
Audio Digitization 77
Analog to Digital Conversion (Digitization) *77*
Sampling Rate *78*

Bits per Sample *78*
Fidelity *78*
Audio Channels *79*
Surround Sound *79*
Dolby Noise Reduction *79*
VIDEO DIGITIZATION 80
Video Components *80*
Resolution *81*
Aspect Ratio *81*
Frame Rate *81*
MEDIA COMPRESSION 83
Display Resolution *83*
Lossy Compression *83*
Spatial Compression *84*
Time Compression (Temporal Compression) *84*
DIGITAL MEDIA FORMATS 85
Container Format *85*
Stream Format *86*
VIDEO COMPRESSION FORMATS 87
MPEG-1 . . . . *88*
MPEG-2 . . . . *88*
MPEG-4 . . . . *88*
Windows Media (VC-1) *90*
Flash Video (FLV) *90*
DivX *90*
Motion JPEG (MJPEG) *90*
AUDIO COMPRESSION FORMATS 91
MPEG Layer 1 (MP1) *91*
MPEG Layer 2 (MUSICAM – MP2) *91*
MPEG Layer 3 (MP3) *92*
MPEG Layer 3 Pro (MP3Pro) *92*
Advanced Audio Codec (AAC™) *92*
Advanced Audio Codec Plus (AAC Plus™) *93*

MUTLIMEDIA 94
MPEG *94*
Elementary Streams (ES) *94*
Transport Streams (TS) *94*
Media Synchronization *95*
TV PROGRAM METADATA 96
TV Program Metadata *96*
Program Metadata Sources *96*
Interstitial Metadata *97*
TV Metadata Standards *97*
PROGRAM GUIDES 97
Barker Channel List *98*
Electronic Program Guides (EPG) *98*
Interactive Program Guides (IPG) *98*
TRICK MODE (VIDEO PLAYER SPEED CONTROL) 99
Multiple Bit Rate Formats *100*
Timing Index *100*
Streaming Control *100*
Reference Key Frames *100*
GEOGRAPHIC TARGETING 101
Location Registration *102*
IP Address Geocoding *102*
Delivery Restrictions *102*
PACKET TRANSMISSION 103
Packet Addressing *103*
Packet Routing *104*
Packet Control *104*
PACKET LOSSES 105
Packet Congestion *106*
Packet Corruption *106*
PACKET TIMING 107
Transmission Time *107*
Packet Sequencing *108*
Time Stamping *108*
Packet Jitter *108*

Transmission Types 110
Unicasting *110*
Multipoint *110*
Multicasting 111
Group Addressing *112*
Multicast Routers *112*
Mirror Sites *112*
Peercasting (Gridcasting) 114
Peer Relaying *114*
Striping *114*
Peercasting Protocols *114*
Packet Reception 115
Demultiplexing *115*
Packet Buffering *116*
Retransmission Requests *116*
Rendering 117
Video Rendering *117*
Audio Rendering *117*
RF Output *118*

INTERNET TV SYSTEMS 119

Contribution Network 119
Headend 120
Distribution System 120
Viewing Devices 120
Contribution Network 121
Connection Types *122*
Program Metadata *123*
Program Transfer Scheduling *124*
Headend 126
Receivers *126*
Media Decoders *126*
Switching System *126*
Media Encoders *127*

CONTENT MANAGEMENT SYSTEM (CMS) 128
Content Acquisition 128
Metadata Management 129
Content Storage 129
Media Encoding 130
PLAYOUT SYSTEM 132
Scheduling Server 132
Streaming Servers 133
Media Gateways 133
AD INSERTION 134
Insertion Opportunities (Avails) 134
Cue Tones 135
Ad Splicer 135
DISTRIBUTION NETWORK 137
Content Sources 137
Core Network 137
Access Networks 138
Home Media Servers (HMS) 138
HOME MEDIA NETWORK 139
Home Multimedia Service Needs 140
Home Media Network System Types 141
DEVICE MANAGEMENT 145
Device Capabilities 145
Communication Protocols 145
Software Versions 146
Configuration 146

INTERNET TV SYSTEM OPERATION 149

CONTENT ACQUISITION STRATEGY 149
Single Channel Services 149
Multiple Channel Services 150
INGESTION 151
WORKFLOW MANAGEMENT 151
Projects 151
Production Tasks 152

Resources *152*
Workflow Systems *152*
Workflow Automation *152*
CONTENT MANAGEMENT 154
Online (Real Time) *154*
Nearline (Short Time) *154*
Offline (Long Term) *154*
PROGRAM SCHEDULING 155
Channel Lineup Schedules *155*
On Demand Programming *155*
Automatic Scheduling *156*
CONTENT DELIVERY NETWORK 156
MONITORING AND MAINTENANCE 157
Monitoring *157*
Back-up Systems *157*
SUBSCRIBER MANAGEMENT 158
New Subscribers *158*
Customer Profiles *159*
Service Plans *159*
Customer Care History *159*
ADVERTISING SALES 160
Sales Prospecting *160*
Advertising Proposals *161*
Advertising Contracts *161*
Insertion Reporting *161*
ORDER PROCESSING 162
Services *163*
Products *163*
Third Party Sales *164*

INTERNET TV SYSTEM OPTIONS ... 165
Internet TV Hosting ... 165
Integrated Internet TV System ... 165
Custom Internet TV System ... 166
HOSTED INTERNET TV SYSTEM ... 167
Hosted Media Ingestion ... 168
Content Management ... 168
Playout System ... 168
Subscriber Management ... 169
Broadcaster Service Packages ... 169
INTEGRATED INTERNET TV SYSTEM ... 170
Integrated Turn-Key System ... 170
Pre-Configured Equipment ... 171
Broadcast Software Package ... 171
Support Services ... 171
CUSTOM INTERNET TV SYSTEM ... 172
Media Encoders ... 172
Playout System ... 173
Media Production System ... 173
Billing System ... 174
Software Programs ... 174
Systems Integrators ... 174

CONTENT PRODUCTION ... 177
PROGRAM DEVELOPMENT ... 177
Program Concept (Topic Idea) ... 177
Feasibility ... 177
Preproduction Plan ... 178
Shooting (Recording) ... 178
Post Production ... 178
Program Packaging (for Distribution) ... 178
STORYBOARDING ... 180
Program Theme ... 180
Scenes ... 180
Scripting ... 180

Content Sources 182
Original Content *182*
Stock Media *182*
Program Archives *183*
Talent 183
Directors *184*
Actors *184*
Production Staff *184*
Studio Production 185
Television Studios *186*
Studio Rental *186*
Virtual Studios *186*
Remote Sites *187*
Video Editing Systems 188
Media Components Formats *188*
Timeline Editing *188*
Effects *189*
Remote Editing *189*

LIVE INTERNET TV 191

Location Preparation *191*
Live Content Acquisition *191*
Real Time Production *191*
Live Broadcasting *192*
Live Event Preparation 193
Shoot Plan *193*
Site Review *193*
Staff Introductions and Permissions *193*
Lighting Requirements *194*
Acoustics *194*
Equipment Positioning *195*
Live Media Acquisition 195
Daily Call Sheet *195*
Live Video Cameras *195*
Microphones *196*
Production Crew *197*

Live Media Production Console 197
Console Inputs *197*
Switching *198*
Effects *198*
Live Broadcast Communication Links 200
Wired Internet Connection *200*
Wi-Fi Internet Connection *200*
Leased Line *200*
Mobile Data *201*
Satellite Links *201*
Intercoms *201*
Live IP Broadcasting 203
Media Uplink *203*
Media Encoding *203*
Streaming Sessions *203*
Backup Plans 205
Connection Loss *205*
Backup Image *205*
Alternate Sources *205*

INTERNET TV BILLING 207

Subscriber Database *207*
Services List *208*
Rate Plans *208*
Advertising Campaigns *208*
Sales Transactions *208*
Revenue Sharing Agreements *208*
Rating System *209*
Invoicing *209*
Payment Processing *209*
Customer Support *209*
Subscriber Account *211*
Subscriber Profile *211*
Subscriber Services *211*

Subscriber Communication History 212
Service Items 213
Service Types 214
Service Provisioning 215
Periodic Charges 216
Transaction Rates 216
Packages (Bundles) 217
Advertising Contract Terms 218
Insertion Orders 218
Insertion Events 218
Insertion Rating 219
Sales Commissions 219
Product Cost 221
Leasing Rates 221
Activation Fees 221
Service Contracts 221
Online Account Presentation 223
Pending Transactions 223
Online Invoicing 224
Payment Gateway 224
Billing Pre-Authorization 225
Payment Information 226
Payment Processing 226
Content License Types 227
License Fees 228
Revenue Assurance 228
Hosted Billing 229
Mediation Devices 229
Billing Interfaces 229

INTERNET TV MARKETING 231
INTERNET TV MARKETING OBJECTIVES 231
Viewership 231
Sales Revenue 232
Advertisers 232
INTERNET TV PROMOTION 233
Network Advertising 233
Channel Advertising 233
Program Advertising 234
AFFILIATE MARKETING 235
Affiliate Partners (Publishers) 235
Affiliate Promotion 235
Affiliate Networks 236
Affiliate Content 236
Affiliate Guidelines 236
Affiliate Compensation 236
DISPLAY ADVERTISING 238
Display Ads 238
Display Ad Development Tools 238
Banner Ad Networks 239
SEARCH PAY PER CLICK (PPC) ADVERTISING 240
PPC Keywords 241
PPC Ads 241
Quality Score (QS) 242
VIRAL MARKETING 243
Viral Content 243
Seed Distribution List 243
Copy Tag Line 244
Referral Incentives 244
DIRECT MAIL PROMOTION 245
Direct Mail Content 245
Direct Mail List 246
Mail Stuffing 246
Tracking Codes 246

PUBLICITY PROGRAMS . . . 247
Press Releases . . . 248
TALK SHOWS . . . 250
Publicity Agent (PR Agent) . . . 252
Program Manager . . . 252
Talk Show Host . . . 252
Talk Show Guest . . . 252
Question List . . . 253
Radio Talk Shows . . . 253
Podcasts . . . 253
SPONSORSHIPS . . . 254
Events . . . 254
Contests . . . 255
Social Media Sites . . . 255
BLOG MARKETING . . . 256
Blog Posting . . . 256
Blog Post Title . . . 257
Blog Post References . . . 257
Tags . . . 258
MICROBLOGGING (TWEETS) . . . 259
Account Name . . . 259
Hashtags . . . 259
Shortening URL Links . . . 260
Review Requests . . . 260
Availability Announcement . . . 260
DISCUSSION GROUPS . . . 261
Topic Research . . . 262
Discussion Engagement . . . 262
Earned Media . . . 262
Internet TV Content References . . . 263
REVIEW PROGRAMS . . . 264

Email Broadcasting 266
Targeted Lists 267
Email Service Provider (ESP) 267
Internet TV Program Announcement Message 268
Email Testing 268
Promotional Videos 269
Storyboarding 269
Video Production 269
Embedded Videos 270
Video Titles 270
Video Captions 271
Video Transcriptions 271
Shared Video Networks 271
Promotional Video Optimization (PVO) 271

INTERNET TV CONTENT LICENSING 273

Entertainment Law 273
Licensing Aggregator 274
License Types 274
Transport License 274
Use License 275
Type of Use 276
License Scope 276
License Elements 276
Free-to-Air Content License 277
Distribution Systems 277
Open Distribution Systems 277
Closed Distribution Systems 278
Use Period 279
Release Windows 279
Distribution Time Period 280
Use Frequency 280
Geographic Limitations 281
Access Network Restriction 281
Geo-Filtering 281

Authorized Media Formats 283
Sub-Licensing 283
Fee Structures 284
Revenue Assurance 285
Content Protection Methods 285
Transport 286
Indemnification 287

INTERNET TV ADVERTISING 289

Advertisers 289
Internet TV Broadcasters 289
Viewers 290
Video Ad Networks 291
Interstitial Ads (Standard TV Ads) 291
Linear Ads 291
On Demand Ads 291
Long Form Advertisements 292
Bumper Ads (Pre-roll and Post-roll) 292
Pre-roll Ads 293
Post-roll Ads 293
Pause Ads 293
Overlay Ads 294
Logo Insertion 295
Image Placement 295
Transparent Overlay 295
Scrolling Text 296
Squeeze Back (Squeezeback) 297
Foreground Display Resizing 297
Background Video Display 297
Product Placement 298
Product Integration 298
Dynamic Product Placement (DPP) 298
Interactive Product Placement 299

Skin Ads 299
Window Viewing *300*
Player Skin Ads *300*
Addressable Advertising 301
Location Based Advertising (LBA) 303
IP Address Geographic Coding (IP Geocoding) *303*
Ad Slot Identification *303*
Ad Insertion *304*
Interactive Advertising 305
Enhanced Ads *305*
Dedicated Ads *305*
Hosted Ads *305*
Program Guide Advertising 306
Interstitial Ads *306*
Graphic Ads *306*
Preview Ads *307*

APPENDIX 1 - ACRONYMS 309

APPENDIX 2 - SAMPLE RELEASE FORM 315

APPENDIX 3 - INTERNET TV MARKETING PLAN SAMPLE 317

INDEX 323

What is An Internet TV System?

An Internet TV systems is a transmission system that provides video and audio (television) information on a communication channel that is delivered through the public Internet. These television signals can be viewed in computers, standard televisions (using an adapter), or other types of multimedia devices that can receive streaming video signals (such as game consoles). Internet TV is sometimes referred to as over the top television (OTT) because the TV signals travel over the top of the Internet rather than through a broadcast television system.

Because Internet TV signals can reach many types of connected devices located almost anywhere, virtually any company or person can become a global television provider. Internet TV systems are similar to regular broadcast television stations, except they send TV signals through the Internet. This book describes the way Internet TV operates, the types of equipment needed, and how to run an Internet TV system.

Internet TV systems can provide TV broadcast quality services with additional content customization and user interaction features - TV+.

Internet TV Content Sources

Internet TV content sources can range from live TV networks (such as CNN) to niche, on-demand content from micro-producers. Internet TV systems can deliver an unlimited number of channels as each television set only requires one TV channel connection, which can be linked to any other TV source the Internet TV service operator (broadcaster) can provide.

Internet TV Service Providers

Internet TV service providers obtain the rights to transmit media programming to people that they allow to view their signals (free and/or paying subscribers). While Internet TV service providers may focus on providing TV services in geographic areas (such as where they own or control TV distribution rights), they can technically provide programming anywhere they can reach customers through a broadband data connection.

Internet TV Distribution Systems

Internet TV distribution systems transfer media programs from content sources to viewing devices. There are many types of systems that can distribute IP data packets, including telecom, wireless, cable TV systems, power companies (data over power line), and competitive access providers (such as new optical networks).

Internet TV Viewing Devices

Internet TV viewing devices can receive media in IP form and convert it into media that can be viewed by users. IP viewing devices range from standard televisions that use digital media adapter boxes to convert IP video signals, to mobile telephones with digital video viewing capabilities.

Figure 1.1 shows that Internet TV systems are composed of content providers, broadband Internet connections, video viewing devices and Internet TV service providers. The content providers include existing television networks, on demand content providers (content aggregators), and independent content provider companies. This example shows a distribution networks that uses many types of systems to transfer IP video packets from the content source to the viewing devices. IPTV viewing devices include standard televisions (with adapters), multimedia computers and multimedia mobile devices. The Internet TV system operator manages how customers can connect to the system and which services they can receive.

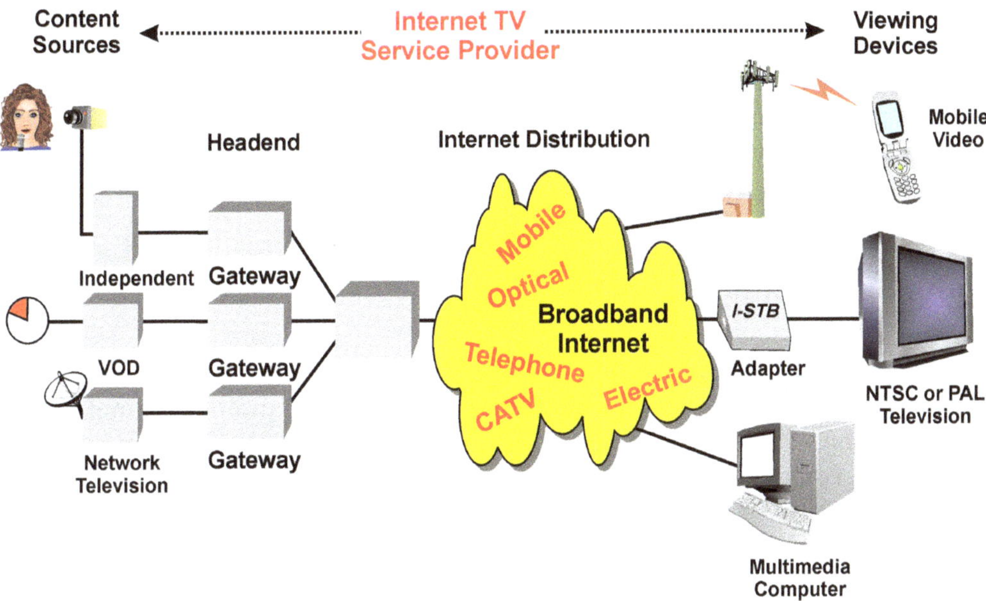

Figure 1.1, Basic Internet TV System

TV Channel Types

The types of TV channels that an Internet TV systems can provide include linear (scheduled) channels, on demand channels, public channels and private channels.

Linear Channels

Linear channels are programs that are sent in a defined time sequence. Linear channels can be a mixture of live content and scheduled content. They are controlled by a playout system that identifies and selects the programs to play or stream during predetermined time slots.

On Demand Channels

On demand programming is providing or making available programs that can be interactively requested and received by users. On demand content may be provided in continuous (streaming) or downloaded formats. Viewers (or their intelligent devices) control the selection and request of the playout of on demand programs and content.

Public Channels

Public channels are a source of media that contains programs or content that is made available to any person. An example of a public channel is the broadcasting of television coverage of an event to any person who can connect to the content source.

Private Channels

Private channels are a source of programs or content which are made available to people who have been authorized to receive the content. An example of a private channel is the broadcasting of television coverage of a company event to employees of the company that have registered to receive access.

Figure 1.2 shows some of the types of TV channels that are available on Internet TV systems. Linear channels are prescheduled into time slots (some are live events and others are stored programs). On demand channels are programs that are available for the viewer to choose and view. Public channels can be viewed by any person who can connect to the signal source. Private channels are only available to people who have been authorized to receive and view the content.

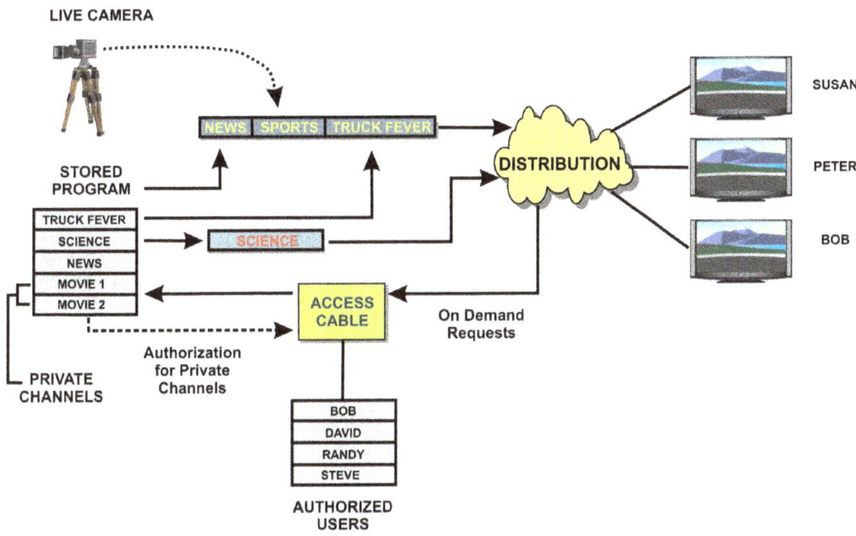

Figure 1.2, Types of Internet TV Channels

Internet TV Content Types

The types of content that are provided through Internet TV channels can range from traditional TV content (rebroadcasted TV programs) to highly specialized (niche) programs that only appeal to a small group of viewers.

Movie Studios

Movie studios are companies that produce long form programs (typically one hour or longer). Movie studio productions tend to have high budgets (millions of dollars), and have tightly controlled distribution channels. Distribution of movie studio content is commonly divided into release windows such as movie theaters, pay per view, premium TV channels (such as HBO), stored media (such as DVD or Blu-Ray), and other distribution channels. Movie studios may limit the distribution of their premium content to more controlled, higher profit channels before allowing the content to become available on Internet TV systems.

Network Television

Television networks are organizations that create and provide programming to local broadcast distribution systems (TV affiliate networks). While local broadcasters may contribute to the cost of developing or acquiring network program content (such as TV shows), most of the network television content is primarily paid for by advertisers. While the redistribution of network television programs through Internet TV channels may benefit advertisers, network television operators may not allow their live or recent content to be distributed through Internet TV channels because it is difficult to earn advertising revenue on channels that cannot be measured, and the distribution may compete with existing Internet TV channels already provided by the network television systems.

Independent Producers

Independent producers are companies or people that produce programs or content that can be sold or licensed to other companies. Independent producers tend to create specialty content in varying lengths. The content created by independent producers may be shown at film festivals as a way to attract potential buyers or distributors. Independent producers may be highly motivated to have their content distributed on Internet TV systems as a way to gain publicity for their programs.

Organizational Content

Organizational content is media that is produced by companies or groups to help promote their products or services, or to communicate messages. Until recently, organizations had limited distribution options for organizational television content. Organizations such as manufacturers, business groups and other types of companies are highly likely to be willing to develop and provide content for distribution on Internet TV systems.

User Generated Content (UGC)

User generated content is information that is produced by users of similar content (such as YouTube). A portion of user generated content may be suitable for Internet TV distribution. The cost to acquire the rights to such content may be low. However, creators of UGC are commonly unskilled in media production, and they may not have obtained the necessary rights, which may include location rights, release forms and music rights, to use the content that they have created.

Figure 1.3 shows some of the content types that may be broadcasted by Internet TV systems. Movie studios produce high value content that has controlled distribution channels. Television networks produce popular content that is primarily paid for by advertisers. Independent producers create specialty programs. Organizations produce content related to the products or services that they provide. User generated content (UGC) is produced by the sample people that watch the content.

Content Type	Description	Notes
Movie Studios	Produce long form programs (1 to 4 hours)	Commonly restrict the distribution of new release and premium content.
TV Networks	Produce popular programs paid by advertising.	May not want to compete with their own Internet channels.
Independent Producers	Produce specialty content.	Looking for ways to get exposure for content.
Organizational Content	Create content related to their products or services.	May be willing to pay to create and to broadcast content.
User Generated Content (UGC)	Content that is produced by the users who view the content.	Some excellent content but may not have the necessary usage release documents.

Figure 1.3, Internet TV Content Types

Internet TV Services

Internet TV services include broadcast (free) and subscription services (controlled access), pay per view (on demand), advertising (video and other forms), and television commerce (direct sales).

Figure 2.1 shows that Internet TV services can include a mixture of subscription, broadcast (advertising based), on demand (transaction based), and television commerce (t-commerce) services. Subscription services allow customers to pay a monthly fee for access to television content sources. Advertising services can range from traditional one-way insert services to interactive advertising services. Pay per view programming may charge customers or sponsors a fee for the viewing of programming. Television commerce produces revenue from the direct sales transactions that occur through the Internet TV system.

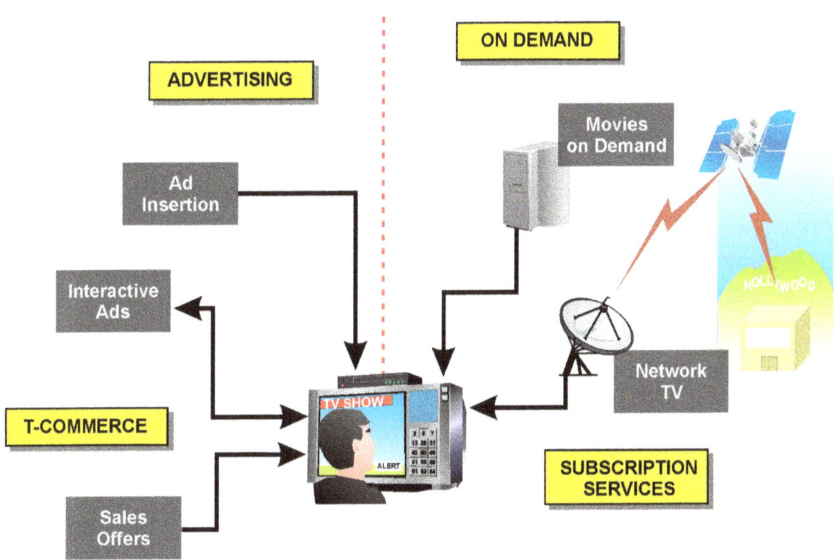

Figure 2.1, Internet TV Services

Broadcast Services

Broadcast service is the transmission of an information signal to devices or people that can receive or connect to the broadcast source. Broadcasting allows the same information to be viewed by all customers that can successfully receive and decode the information (such as within a geographic area that can receive a radio broadcast signal).

Internet TV provides broadcast services by allowing devices to connect to video servers that are providing the same media to other users.

Linear Channels

Linear channels are programs that are sent in a defined time sequence. Linear channels may contain previously recorded media or live content. Live content may actually be broadcasted on a short delay (such as a few seconds) to allow for the censoring of content (muting of inappropriate words).

Sponsored Programming

Sponsored programs are media items, such as movies or games, which are provided to consumers and paid for by other people or companies. Companies may pay to sponsor the creation of programs that reference or use their products or service. For example, a car manufacturer may pay to sponsor a sports utility vehicle program that regularly or exclusively uses cars that they manufacture.

Advertising Funded

An advertiser funded program is broadcasted or downloadable media content that is paid for by companies or people other than the broadcasting entity that is transmitting the content. Some Internet TV broadcasters may require their viewers to watch advertisements prior to granting access to the programming.

Free view is a service that provides media content to viewers at no cost. The development and broadcasting of free view content may be paid for by advertising or grants.

Figure 2.2 shows that a broadcast service transmits programs at scheduled times. Linear channels may consist of a mixture of stored content and live content. Broadcasting may be paid for by sponsors, or through the insertion of advertising into the programming.

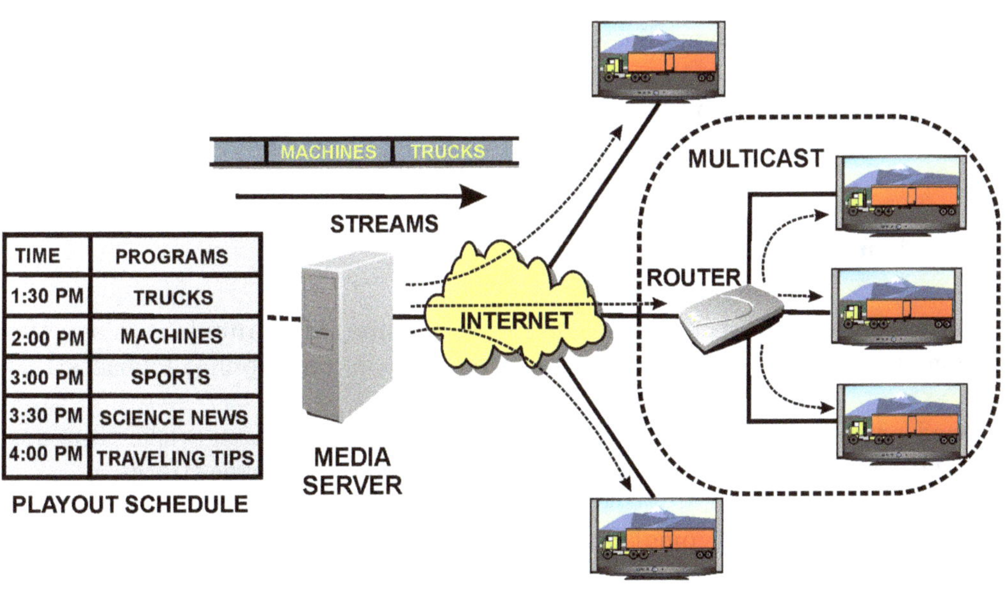

Figure 2.2, Internet TV Broadcast Services

Subscription Services

Subscription services are value-added services that provide or entitle a customer to receive or gain access to services. Paid subscription services may be provided on a periodic basis (such as monthly), and different rates may be charged for groups of services (tiered programming).

Subscription Accounts

A subscription account is a unique identifier that designates a customer or company that has been established (subscribed), allowing them to continue to receive products or services that are billed or posted to their account.

Premium Channels

Premium channels are media services (such as television programs) that are offered as a supplement or upgrade to other services. Premium channels may be provided as a bundled package (multiple channels), on a per channel subscription basis, or on a pay per view (PPV) basis.

Tiered Services

Programming tiers are the grouping (partitioning) of channels into specific category levels that have similar service offers or content characteristics.

Tiered pricing is the assignment of value to products or services that are offered for sale, that vary with specific characteristic ranges (tiers).

Figure 2.3 shows the typical rate plan for a TV system. This example shows that a typical rate plan for TV service consists of several free local and regional channels, which are paid for through monthly subscription services, as well as many pay per view channels.

	Per Month
Basic television – 28 Channels.............................	$15
-News – Weather – FreeTV	
Upgraded Television – 42 Channels.......................	$22
-3 Movie Channels – Sports – Music	
Premium Television – 36 Channels........................	$24
-HBO – Showtime – Starz – Cinema	
Pay Per View Movies...............Appx. $1- $6 (per movie)	
-Thousands of movies to choose from	
Installation and Set-up.......................................	$99
Equipment Rental..................................$4 (per box)	

Figure 2.3, TV Subscription Services

On Demand Services

On demand programming is the provision or availability of programs that can be interactively requested and received by users. On demand services may be provided using a switched video service that connects to the viewer to a live stream or to content that can be downloaded and viewed at a later time. On demand services may be billed on a pay per view or pay per period basis.

Switched Video

Switched video service (SVS) is a process that can dynamically setup (on demand) video signal connections between two or more points. SVS can range from the setup of data connections that allow for video transfer to the organization and management of video content and the delivery of video programs.

Live Streaming

Live streaming is the process of transferring audio or video streaming whereby users have no control over the playback time of the media. That is, the clients may not control when the stream starts, pause the stream, skip to a different time within the presentation, and so on. Live streaming is often used for the broadcast of an event happening in real time.

Download and Play

Download and play is a process of downloading a media program (an audio or video file) and, once the file has completely downloaded, starting playback.

Pay Per View (PPV)

Pay per view service is the provision of television programming, such as sports, movies and other entertainment video, which customers may view on a per event basis for a fee. PPV services may allow end users to interactively request and receive television channels or programs. These services may range from previously stored media (entertainment movies or education videos) to accessing live connections (news events in real time). PPV services may also allow other companies (sponsors) to pay for the services in return for branding opportunities or the sharing of viewing data.

Pay Per Period (PPP)

Pay per period is the authorization to obtain a program or access to a program over a defined period of time. An example of pay per period is the authorization to watch a movie or a group of movies for a fee, such that access to the content is authorized for a specified period of time (such as 24 hours). A pay per time period may begin immediately, after the viewing of the program begins, or by some other defined time period.

Figure 2.4 shows how Internet TV can allow a viewer to request control of the presentation of television programs on demand. This diagram shows that a television on demand viewer can browse through available television channels. In this example, this Internet TV service provider informs the viewer of which programs they have already viewed and the length of time each program will run. When the user selects a potential program to view, a short description of that program is shown at the bottom of the screen, along with the cost for viewing that particular program.

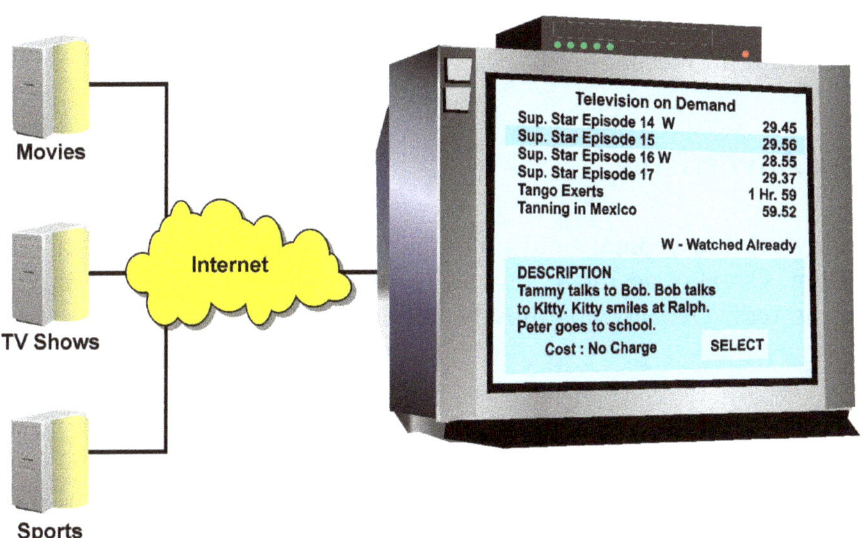

Figure 2.4, Internet TV On Demand Services

Advertising

Internet TV advertising combines traditional television advertising (one-way video commercials) with interactive Internet advertising (two-way marketing).

Internet TV can offer advanced advertising services through the use of targeting (specific viewers and number of repeated views), ad customization (branding and offer changes), and interaction (ability for viewers to directly respond to ads).

Interstitial Advertising (Interruption)

An interstitial ad is the temporary display of advertising messages in between the requesting and opening or closing of a web page. The interstitial ad is usually setup to display for a short period of time (usually 5 seconds). Some interstitial ads include a link that allows the viewer to bypass the interstitial ad message.

Overlay Advertising

An overlay ad is a promotional message that is inserted on top of another media item. Overlay ad insertion can include the insertion of logos, images or scrolling text. Overlay ads may be solid or transparent.

Skin Advertising

Player skin ads are promotional messages or images that appear in the area surrounding the viewer's media player window.

Figure 2.5 shows how Internet TV advertising messages can be presented in the form of interstitial broadcast messages, mixed media messages or interactive ads. In example A, a network operator provides a program with advertising messages already inserted within (interstitial). Example B shows how an advertising message may be overlapped or merged into the underlying television program. Example C shows how an advertising message may change based on the selections of the viewer.

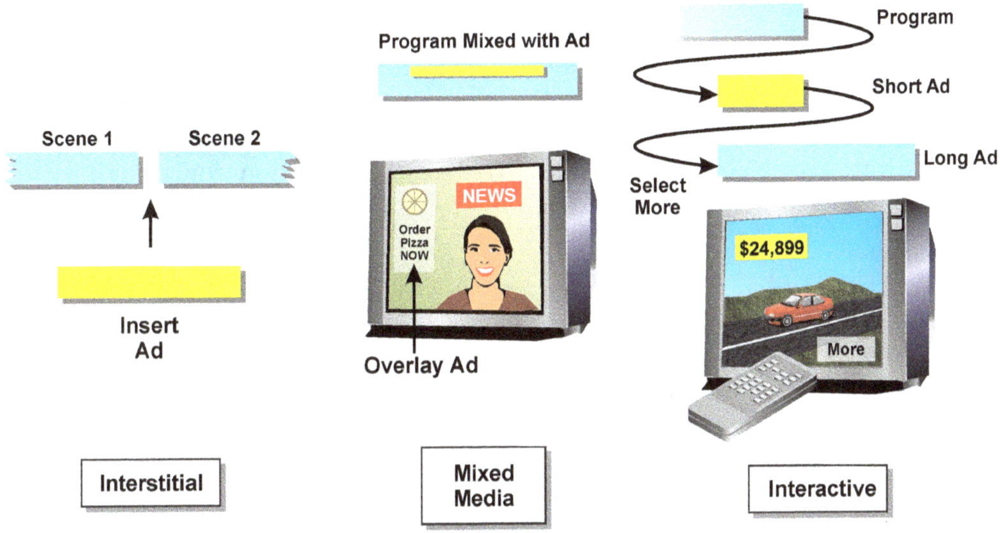

Figure 2.5, Internet TV Advertising Services

Television Commerce (T-Commerce)

Internet TV television commerce (t-commerce) is the provision of order processing services directly through the Internet TV system. T-Commerce transactions can range from the sale of products provided directly by the Internet TV broadcaster (such as movie DVDs) to the processing of orders for other companies which provide a revenue share compensation for the sales.

Direct Sales

Direct sales are the values that are received (usually in sales dollars) as a direct result of a marketing effort, which is setup, and can be controlled by a person or company.

Affiliate Sales

Affiliate marketing is the process of sharing marketing and sales programs between companies that want to sell products (merchants) and companies that are willing to promote these products to their customers (affiliates). The affiliate merchant compensates the affiliate partner for their role in customer communication and sales.

Third Party Sales

Third party sales are transactions that are performed for the exchange of goods or services, which are facilitated or overseen by a third party. In some cases, vendors may be allowed to promote their products or services directly on television channels and broadcasters may provide the transaction mechanisms (e-commerce) through which direct sales and payment processing occur. In return for processing third party sales, the TV broadcaster may receive a sales commission and/or transaction fee.

Figure 2.6 shows how a vendor may receive a television commerce (t-commerce) order report. This example shows that a t-commerce vendor may receive payment from a customer directly by a cash or credit card transaction, the customer may be able to place the order on their television bill, or the customer may use a 3rd party such as PayPal to complete the transaction.

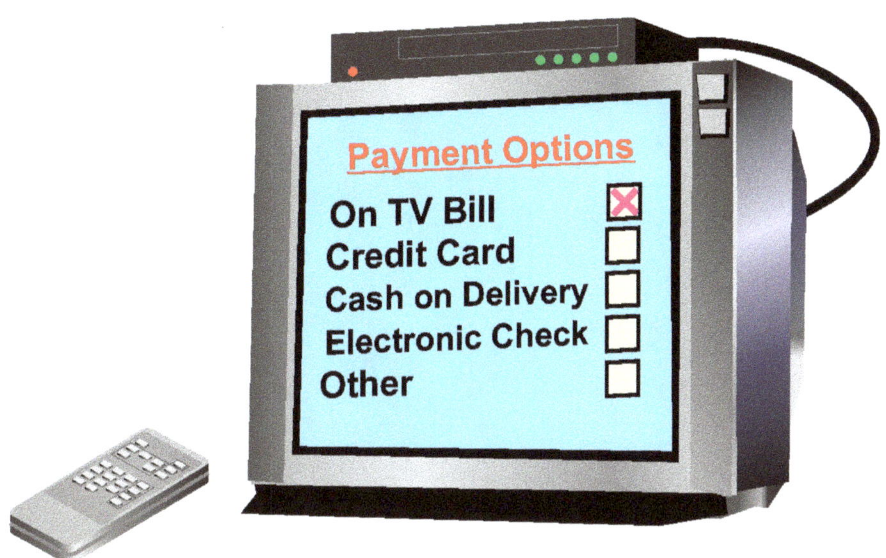

Figure 2.6, TV Commerce Payment Options

Internet TV Content Sources

Internet TV content sources include a mix of traditional content (movie studios, network programming) and new types of content (specialty and user generated content).

Content Producers

Professional content producers include movie studios, syndicates and production companies. Traditional content producers create high value content that is released in a controlled distribution environment (release windows).

Network Television

Network television systems produce and distribute TV shows, movies, sports programs and other content that is usually distributed to affiliate broadcasters located over large geographic areas. Content aggregators distribute programs from studios and other sources such as movies and event programs. Local programming sources include TV news stations, educational and government media programs. Studios may provide content directly to broadcasters instead of using TV networks or content aggregators.

Community Content

Internet TV broadcasters provide new opportunities for content distribution including international television distribution. Specialty producers are evolving to provide content for niche audiences such as specific types of sports. Internet TV broadcasters may fill some of their programming slots with content that is created by viewers (community content) as is the case with YouTube. Internet TV broadcasters may also produce some of their own content, such as live event coverage or developing programs, which their subscribers find highly appealing.

Original Programming

Original programming is content that is owned, developed and controlled by a network operator that provides the media to its viewers. Original programming may be in the form of news, documentaries and education, or it may include other types of programming that is created specifically for the network. While the creation of original programming may reduce the cost of content, it may still involve the payment of fees or royalties for the use of brands, actors or other images.

Figure 3.1 shows some of the types of Internet TV content sources which include traditional television content and new sources of media. Traditional sources of content include television networks, content aggregators, local programmers and studio provided media (movie producers). New types of Internet TV content include global television channels, specialty producers, community content and original programming.

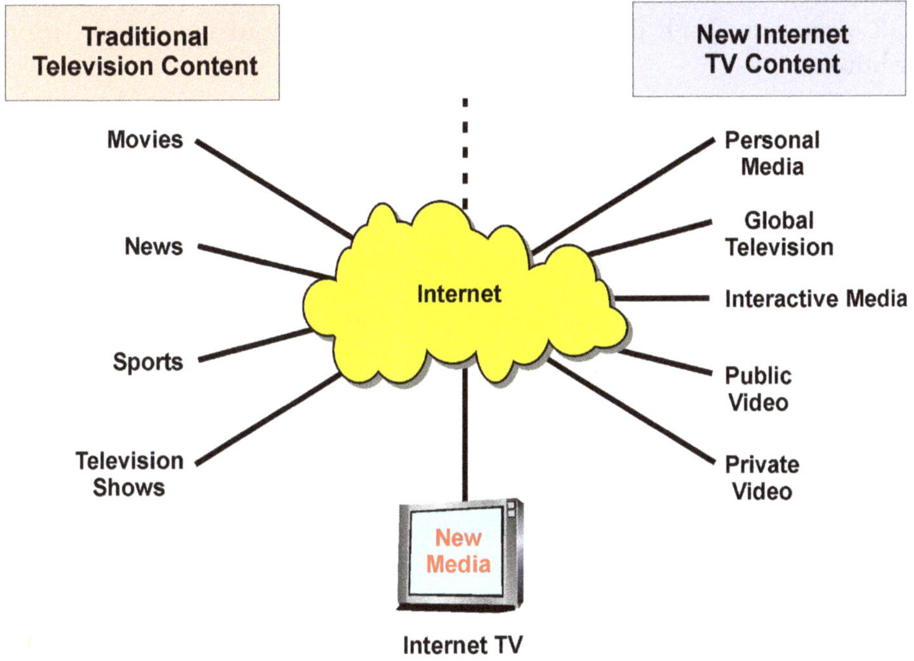

Figure 3.1, Internet TV Content Sources

Content Producers

Content producers are companies or developers that create professional (high-value) media content. The tightly controlled release schedules used by content producers are designed to maximize the revenue potential of the content that is produced. These include distribution to high value restricted channels first such as movie theaters and new TV seasons.

Movie Studios

A movie studio is a company or facility that is used to produce long format programs (1+ hour movies). A move studio is composed of one or more rooms or sets that are designed for the recording of video and audio.

While movie studios may use scheduled release windows for their content, they are eager to find new, high value distribution channels and tightly controlled, premium (high profit) early releases of content via secure Internet distributors.

Syndicates

A syndicate is a company or organization that is formed to represent a common interest to multiple parties. Initial programs created by syndicates may be exclusively licensed to distributors, such as TV networks that can limit their interest and ability to allow their content to be distributed on Internet TV systems. Syndicates may be very willing to provide older syndicated programs for distribution, as they have little value to TV networks due to a niche audience appeal. The same niche audience may have specific desirable demographics (such as older TV shows that appeal to an older, more affluent audience) that advertisers find highly valuable.

Production Companies

Production companies are organization that create content when they are contracted to provide services. The production company identifies and performs tasks to produce products or services. Production companies may scout locations, plan shoots, cast talent, supply crew and film equipment for shootings, supply and obtain props, shoot programs and provide footage. The content that is created by production companies tends to be exclusively owned by the company that contracted production.

In some cases, content ownership or distribution rights may revert back to the production companies after a period of time, or if the company that contracted the production is no longer in business.

Figure 3.2 shows some of the producers of professional movie and television content. Movie studios produce high-value content in long formats (1+ hours) which have structured distribution schedules. Syndicates produce content for multiple distributors such as television series. Production companies are contracted to created specific types of content such as special effects.

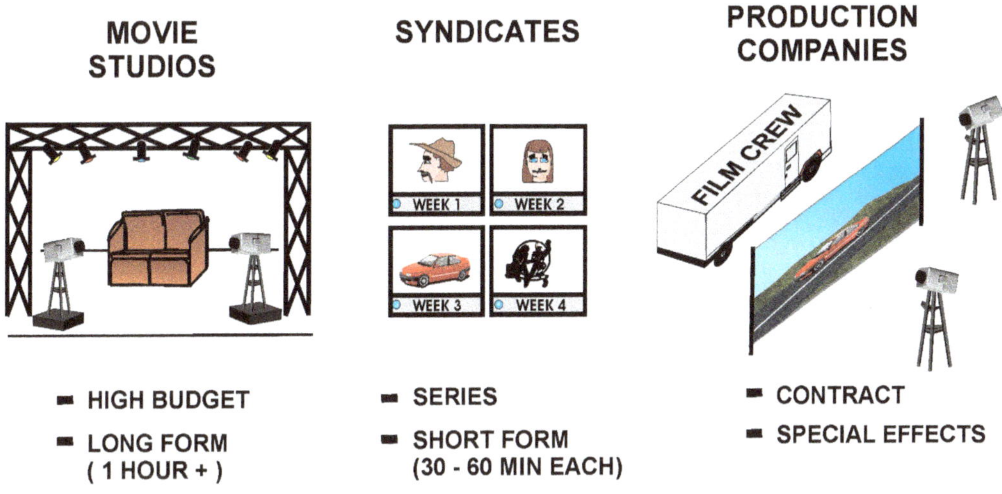

Figure 3.2, Movie and TV Content Producers

Television Networks

Television networks are systems that provide multiple channels of programming to affiliate distribution partners (local broadcasters). The content that television networks provide tends to be produced by other companies. TV networks select and schedule the content for broadcast on TV channels (network feeds) that are provided to local broadcasters (affiliates). TV networks sell ads that are included in the TV channels.

Network Affiliate Distribution

A network affiliate is a broadcasting company that has a content distribution relationship with a network. A network affiliate may receive content from a network provider in return for a combination of money and advertising time. Some Internet TV access providers have managed to become distributors for TV networks (such as NeuLion and Hulu).

Network Content Types

TV networks commonly provide a mixture of rebroadcasted content and original programming, as well as series programs (TV shows) that appear at scheduled times.

Network Feeds

Network feeds are communication lines from TV networks that carry multiple channels of content (programming) throughout the day. Local broadcasters rely on networks to provide programming content that will be of value to their local viewing audience.

TV networks may already provide direct Internet access to their network feeds (simulcast Internet streams). TV networks may desire to limit the redistribution of their network programming to protect the viewership of their affiliates and keep viewers who directly connect to their streaming sources to themselves.

Ad Spots

TV network content is provided with television commercials (ad spots) already inserted. The TV network may allow the local broadcaster to replace some of the national ads with local commercials (about 10% to 20% of the ad slots).

Distribution agreements (carriage agreements) commonly define that the distribution networks and local broadcasters are not allowed to alter the content that is provided by the TV network. Internet TV broadcasters may not be authorized to replace or insert ads (such as overlay ads) in the TV network content.

Figure 3.3 shows that TV networks commonly provide multiple channels of content in different content areas. TV network channels are provided (network feeds) to local broadcasters (affiliates) for transmission to viewers. These network TV channels (network feeds) contain ads that are sold by the TV network. TV network channels do contain some time periods that the local broadcaster can use to insert (sell) local TV commercials.

	7:00 AM	7:30 AM	8:00 AM	8:30 AM
NETWORK 1 (FAMILY)	TRAVEL TIME	MONEY TIPS	PARTY PLANNER	
NETWORK 2 (SPORTS)	FOOTBALL REVIEW		FOOTBALL REVIEW	
NETWORK 3 (DRAMA)	SOAP STAR CENTRAL		ONE MORE DAY	
NETWORK 4 (NEWS)	WORLD NEWS	TRENDS	NATIONAL REVIEW	
NETWORK 5 (ENTERTAINMENT)	STARS GOSSIP		MOVIE REVIEWS	

Figure 3.3, TV Network Content

Content Aggregators

A content aggregator obtains the rights from multiple content providers for the resale and distribution of content through other communication channels. A content aggregator typically receives and reformats media content, stores or forwards the media content, controls and/or encodes the media for security purposes, accounts for the delivery of media and distributes it to the systems that sell and provide it to customers.

Content Brokers

The content aggregator serves as middleman (content broker) between the content producers (such as movie studios) and distributors (such as Internet TV providers). Content producers may not have the ability to provide and control content to many thousands of distributors. Distributors (such as Internet TV service providers) may not want to negotiate and setup thousands of agreements with different content sources.

Content aggregators tend to specialize in specific content areas such as movies, sports, international content, documentaries and other areas. Content aggregators are likely to be excellent sources of specialized content and knowledge to Internet TV providers.

Media Ingestion

Content aggregators gather and import media from multiple sources that range from TV networks to specialty content providers. There are many types of media formats available for content, ranging from film to highly compressed media files. Internet TV providers may not have the capability to ingest some forms of content (especially older formats).

Media Adaptation (Transcoding)

Media adaptation (transcoding) is the conversion of digital signals from one coding format to another. Transcoding is necessary to convert a master media format (high resolution) into a form that can be displayed by specific types of devices and their displays. Content aggregators may convert media into forms that can be used for distribution. This may include the addition of descriptive information (metadata).

Content Distribution

Content aggregators setup systems that allow them to transfer media to distributors (such as Internet TV broadcasters) when and where they want it. Because broadcaster have a limited amount of storage capacity (several days worth of content), the content distributor may provide access to the content shortly before it is scheduled for broadcast. The transfer of content may also be scheduled during non-peak data transmission time periods (late at night) when costs are lower.

Figure 3.4 shows that a television content aggregator receives media from multiple content providers, processes this media and distributes it to companies that sell and provide it to end users. This example shows that the content aggregator may receive the information in a variety of formats including via digital satellite channels, leased communication lines, data networks (such as the Internet), or in DVD, CD or tape formats. The content aggregator will reformat this information into a form that can be delivered to TV broadcasters which may include Internet TV distributors, mobile video over cellular, television over DSL lines, or programs to private systems such as hotel video systems.

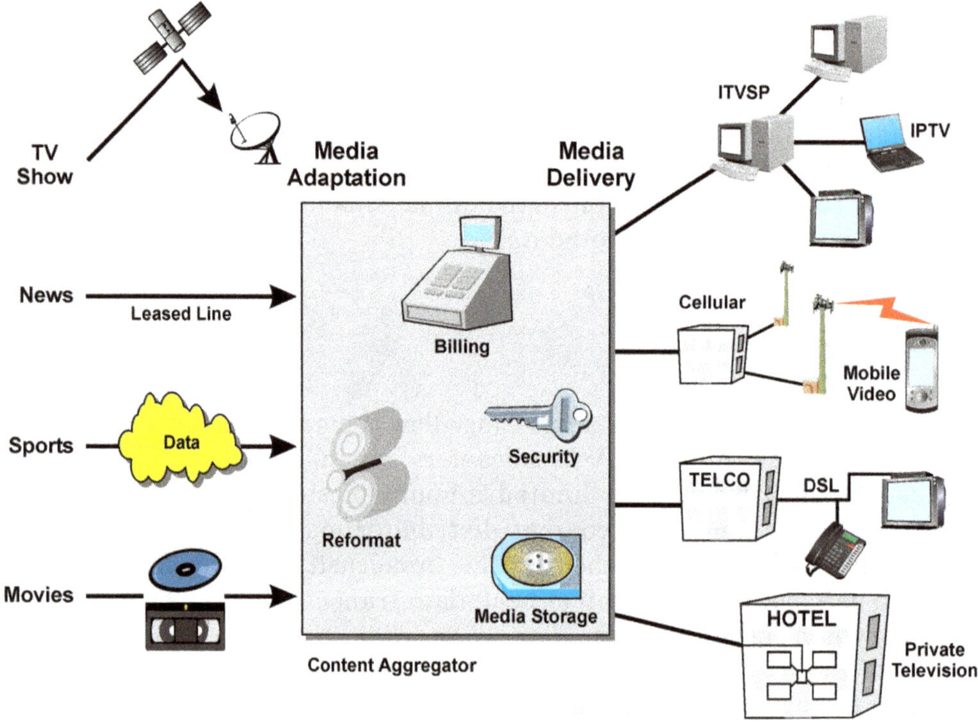

Figure 3.4, TV Content Aggregators

Local Programming

Local programming is the selection of shows and programs that are offered by a television network provider that is located within close proximity. Local broadcasters tend to produce local news stories, cover local events, and provide localized weather information.

Local News

Local news stations have reporters in the community that receive calls and emails about news topics and select some of the more important and interesting topics to cover. The news organization may have mobile equipment (vans and cameras) that can be dispatched to cover breaking stories.

Internet TV broadcasters may use a combination of staff (reporters) and citizen journalists to cover stores. The combination of trained reporters, citizen journalists, and social media systems may be a very effective (and low cost) method of covering local news.

Local Events

Local TV stations may cover events such as sports events, state fairs, conferences and other group activities. Internet TV stations may send local reporters (who may be volunteers) to interview people and companies that participate in the event.

Event organizers commonly desire co-marketing partnerships with media and may provide press passes and free space for Internet TV staff at the events. Interviewing companies with equipment that displays the channel logo can be effective in promoting a TV station and gathering interesting content.

Local Weather

TV stations may broadcast local weather information which adds local content to weather data that has been provided by the National Weather Service. Internet TV broadcasters may provide weather related information by gathering and reporting on images sent in by viewers (from their mobile phones) or from web cams that are located throughout the community.

Figure 3.5 shows some of the content that is produced by local television stations. News reporters (mobile) and anchors (at the studios) gather and present stories of interest to the local community. Local TV stations may cover events such as local sports (high school games), conferences and gatherings. Local weather may add local information to national weather forecasts.

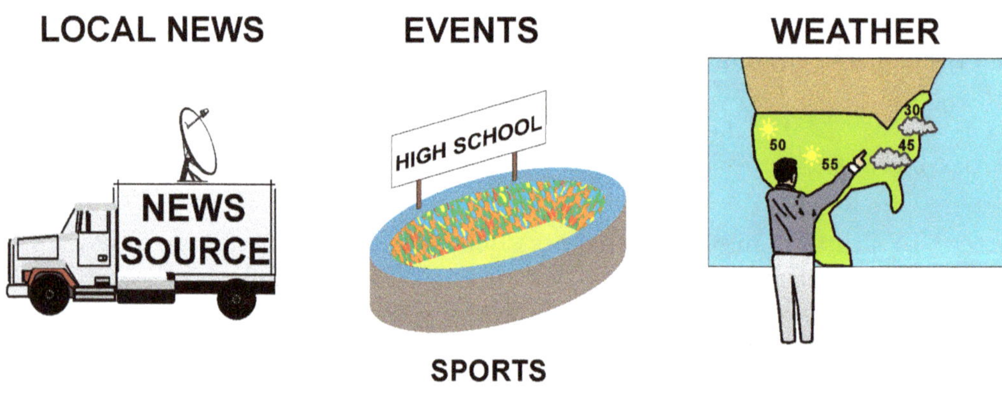

Figure 3.5, Local TV Station Content

International Programming

International programming is the selection of shows and programs that are offered by a television network provider that offers media channels to multiple countries. An example of an international program is a television program that is created by a network operator that is broadcasted by many television systems which are located in multiple countries.

Foreign Networks

Foreign networks are TV network providers that distribute their content to broadcasters in other countries (such as a China broadcaster distributing content in the United States).

Foreign TV networks may be willing to provide real time access to their network feeds because they may not have any competing distribution agreements.

Foreign TV Stations

Foreign TV stations are producers of local content who distribute their media to broadcasters in other countries. Foreign TV stations may already provide a live stream on the Internet that can be received and rebroadcasted. Foreign TV stations may be willing to make their live and stored content available in higher resolution format.

Foreign Programs

Foreign programs are media programs that are created in other countries. Foreign producers may be excited about distributing their content in other countries. This content may be sent in stored format (DVD) or transferred through the Internet.

Figure 3.6 shows some of the sources of international programming. Foreign TV networks offer one or more continuous channels of media which may be provided by satellite distribution. Foreign TV stations provide locally produced content such as news, events and weather, which may be streamed through the Internet to a local Internet TV broadcaster. Foreign programs from studios may be provided in various forms including stored media (tapes, DVDs).

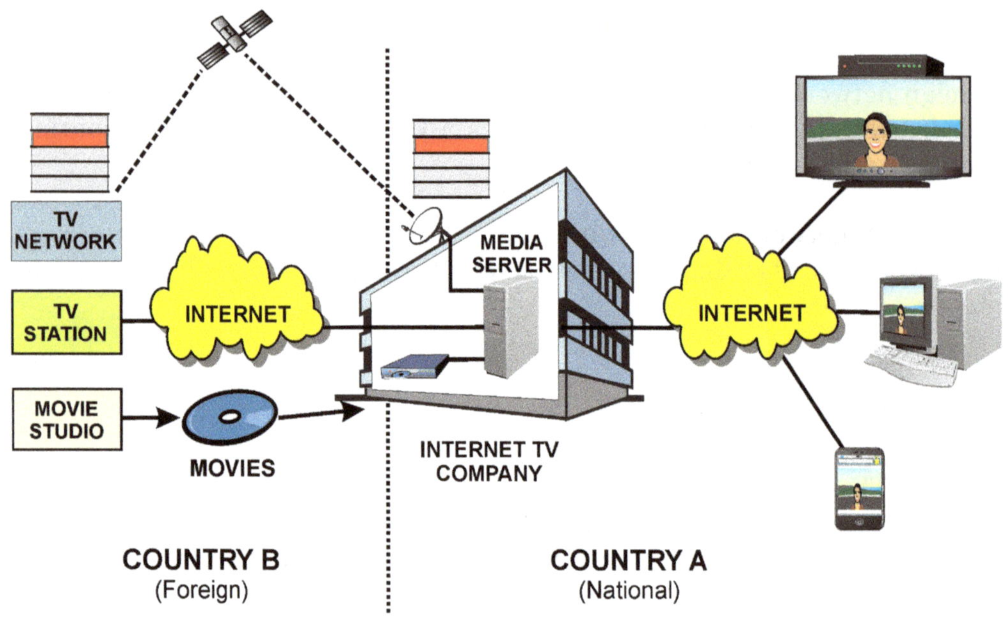

Figure 3.6, Internet TV International Content

Specialty Content Producers

Specialty content producers are studios, companies or groups who produce content that appeals to a relatively small (niche) audience. Specialty content producers include independent filmmakers, companies or groups.

Independent Filmmakers ("Indies")

An independent film is a media program that is produced without funding or backing from a network or media group. Indies tend to produce films on low budgets which are not accepted by traditional channels.

While much of the programming produced by independent content may have questionable quality, there are some that produce excellent programs. Indie producers may be anxious to promote their content so it may be possible to obtain distribution rights for some excellent and unique content at low cost.

Companies

Company content is media that is created by or for companies. Company content may be created for public (potential customers) or private distribution (company staff). Company content can include entertaining programs that include the use of products or services produced or provided by a company. An example of a company program is a travel program that is hosted by an airline (such as the one created by Southwest Airlines). While the viewers may be interested in watching travel experiences, the entire program features the airline jets and brands.

Companies may be willing to pay for the development and broadcasting of their content. This is a reversal of the traditional media distribution channels where local broadcasters pay networks for content. An Internet TV provider may get companies to pay for program creation, and also pay for the broadcasting of their programs.

Groups

Group content is media that is created by or for organizations such as business groups (Rotary), religious groups or fan clubs. These programs can include educational sessions, documentaries and events.

Groups are often passionate about their causes and may be willing to pay for the development and broadcasting of their content. Some groups restrict advertising, such as religious groups, and educational and documentary programs may be an excellent promotional tool for these groups.

Figure 3.7 shows some of the sources of specialty TV content. Independent filmmakers create films that they promote (try to sell) at independent film festivals. Companies (such as airlines) produce organization content that may be valuable to viewers while promoting their company. Groups (such as business clubs) may produce content that covers and promotes their activities.

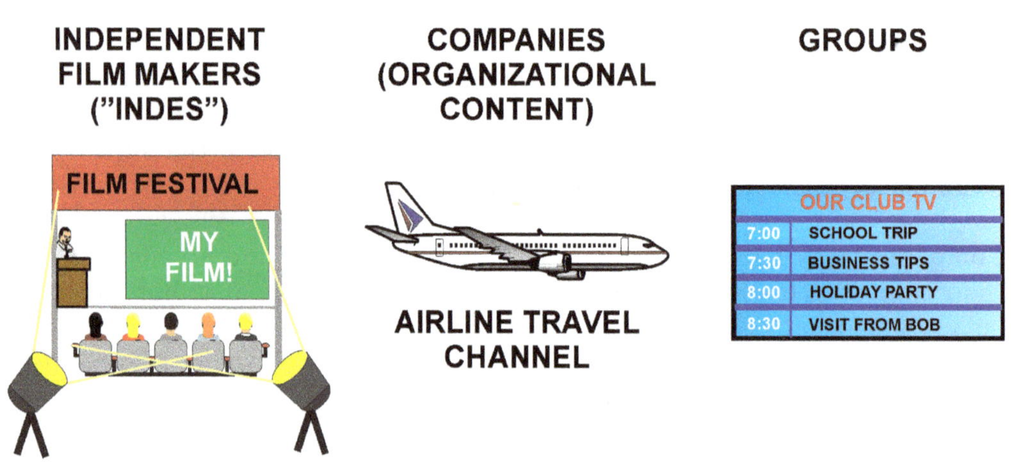

Figure 3.7, Specialty TV Content

Community Content

Community content programming is media that is created and managed by members of a community or a group that can be viewed by others who are interested in community content. Examples of community content include school, sports and local events that members of a community have an interest in. Community members are commonly interested in assisting in the creation, management and delivery of the community content with or without direct compensation.

Public Broadcasting

Public broadcasting is the use of a broadcast station by any nonprofit institution engaged primarily in the production, acquisition, distribution or dissemination of educational and cultural television or radio programs. Some directors and producers begin their careers by creating content that is broadcasted on public broadcast channels.

TV broadcast stations may provide training and certification programs for PBS producers. This means that the content may have all the necessary production releases. Some of the content that is created on public broadcasting channels may be rebroadcasted on Internet TV stations. Producers of PBS content may be highly motivated to find new places (such as Internet TV) where their content can be broadcasted.

Shared Media

Shared media is content (such as a video or audio program) that may be accessed and used by systems or people. Shared media systems may identify and coordinate access to the media (such as YouTube).

Shared media content may be available for rebroadcasting on Internet TV channels without significant (or any) costs or fees. Contributors to shared media sites (including companies and corporations) may define the terms under which their content may be used, such as the inclusion of a web address or a link to the original source within the content.

Social Media

Social media is information (voice, data or video) from related users (within a social network) that may be stored or transmitted to other users. Social media content may be created by the combined efforts of members of groups.

While there can be substantial amounts of interesting content produced and distributed on social media systems, the producers of shared media content tend to be unskilled, and the necessary authorizations and release forms may not have been obtained (a bit risky to rebroadcast).

Figure 3.8 shows that community content can come from public channels, shared media sources and social media sites. Public broadcasting is created by the community where the production is overseen by a broadcaster. Shared media is content that may be produced and uploaded along with an explanation of the rights required to use it. Social media content is produced by one or more members of the community.

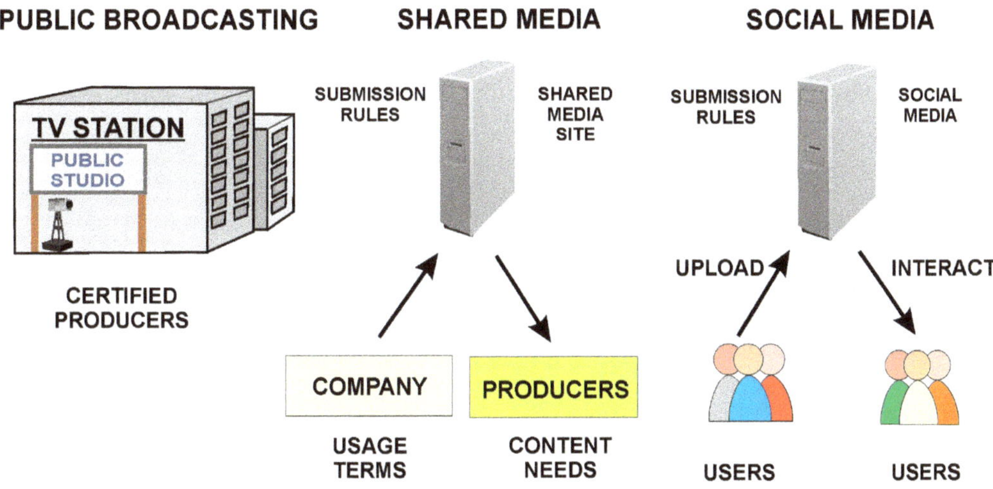

Figure 3.8, Internet TV Community Content

Public Domain (PD)

Public domain is media content, including books, audio and video, which has its ownership transferred to any user (the public). Some media items, such as published government documents, may immediately become part of the public domain. Other protected media items, such as movies, may be automatically transferred to the public domain after their copyright term has expired, making them accessible to and usable by the public.

Expired Copyrights

Expired copyrights are content protection rights that are no longer applicable because a defined amount of time has elapsed since their creation. An excellent source of valuable content for Internet TV systems can be older movies.

Government Content

Media that is produced under government contract (such as video that is recorded by NASA) may be available for use by anyone.

Abandoned Content

Content that is produced where there is no owner or the owner is no longer in business may be available for public use.

Figure 3.9 shows several sources of public domain content. Content that has expired copyright (such as old movies) has passed the time limits for copyright protection. Media that is produced under government contract (such as NASA video) may be free for use. Video that has been abandoned, or no longer has an owner in business, may be available for use.

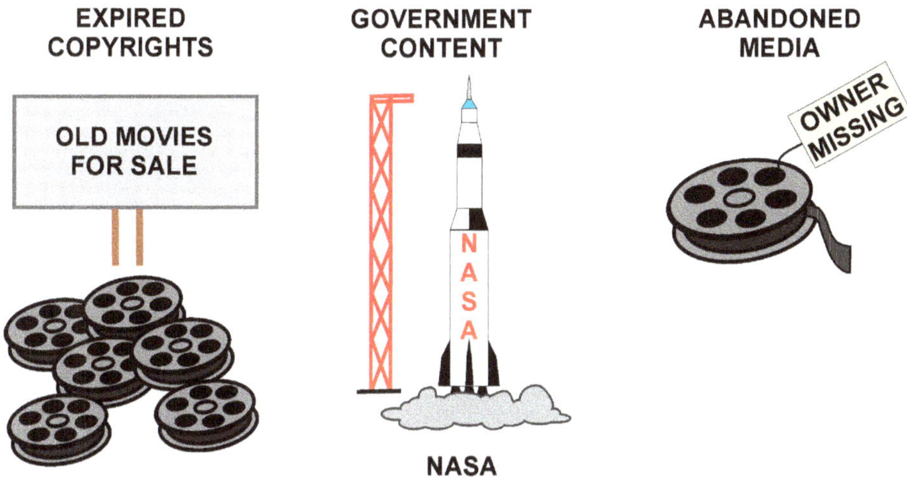

Figure 3.9, Public Domain Content

Original Programming

Original programming is content that is owned, developed and controlled by a network operator who provides the media to its viewers. Some of the common forms of original programming created by Internet TV stations include remote interviews, web seminars and event coverage.

Remote Interviews

Remote interviews are the interaction of a person with a reporter or media agent who is communicating at a different location. Remote interviews can be performed using web cams and an Internet connection.

Companies and their staffs are often very willing to be interviewed for television programs. Remote interviews can be simple to setup, performed at times that are flexible to the person being interviewed, and can be a very low cost source of valuable content. The person being interviewed may also become an avid spokesperson for the TV broadcaster.

Web Seminars

A web seminar (webinar) is an online instruction session that uses the Web as a real time presentation format along with audio channels (via web or telephone) that allow participants to listen and possibly interact with the session. Webinars allow people to participate in information or training sessions from any location that has Internet and audio access.

The content that is presented on a web seminar can be recorded in video format. This video content, or portions of it, can be converted into a TV program.

Event Coverage

Internet TV stations can cover events by purchasing or renting a relatively small amount of equipment such as portable cameras, microphones and basic lighting.

Internet TV stations may cover specialized events such as seminars, group meetings and other types of events that are of interest to their viewers but do not have enough of a following to attract traditional broadcasters.

Figure 3.10 shows some potential sources of original programming for Internet TV stations. Remote interviews can be setup from a small office where the person being interviewed connects a web cam. Web seminars can be hosted, streamed live and/or converted into video for later broadcasting. Members of the Internet TV station, or volunteers, may take a small amount of recording equipment to an industry event to perform interviews and cover key stories.

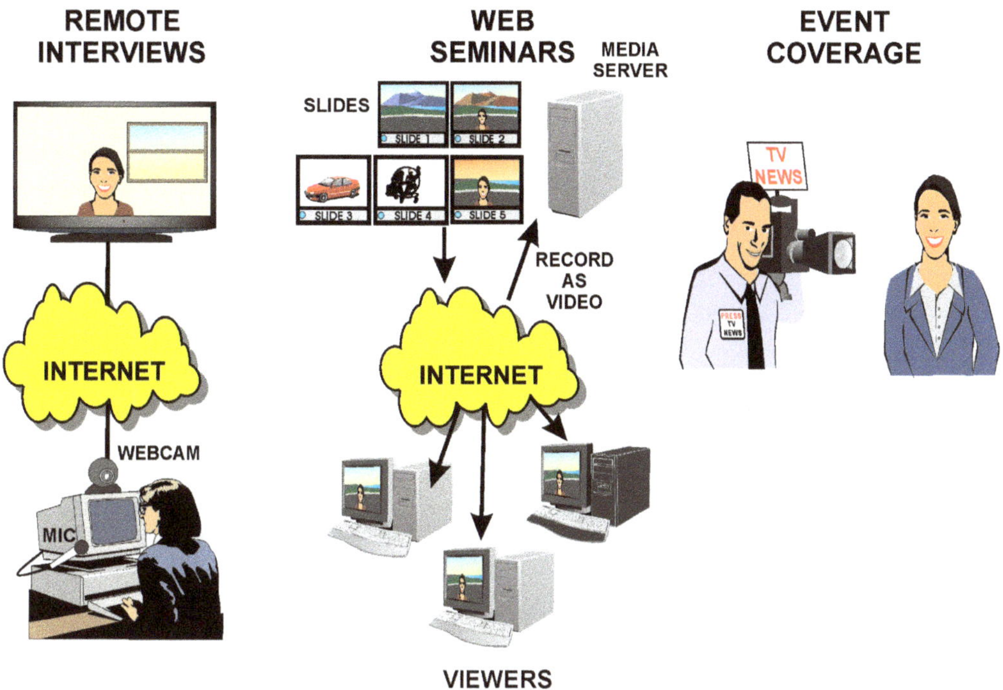

Figure 3.10, Internet TV Original Content

Internet TV Viewing Devices

Internet TV viewing devices allow a person to view or obtain and use content from an Internet TV system. Internet TV service providers will need to identify, possibly sell, and help viewers to get Internet TV access devices that are compatible with their system.

The key types of Internet TV viewing devices include Internet set top boxes (ISTB), TV media stick (Dongle), hybrid set top boxes (broadcast TV and Internet TV), multimedia computers, multimedia mobile telephones, connected televisions, gaming consoles, and media players (such as Blu-Ray).

Internet TV viewing devices are commonly called digital media adapters (DMA) or streaming devices. They require an Internet connection (wired or wireless) and a way to control network (Internet TV service providers) and channel selections (remote control or app on a smartphone or tablet.) To use the viewing devices, it needs to be setup (cloud paired) with an Internet TV service provider.

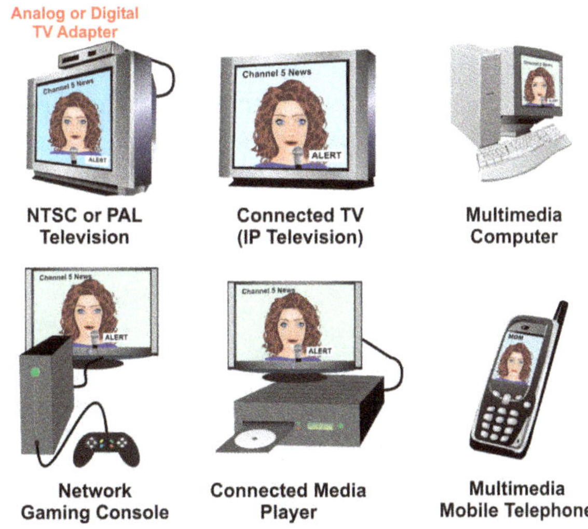

Figure 4.1, Internet TV Viewing Devices

Figure 4.1 shows several types of television viewing devices. Internet TV set top boxes are digital media adapters (DMAs) that convert Internet TV signals to TV signals (RF or HDMA). TV media sticks are streaming adapters that directly plug into the TV viewing device with either remote controls or app channel control on smartphones or tablets. Hybrid set top boxes allow viewers to receive both broadcast TV and Internet TV. Connected televisions include broadband Internet connections that can link the TV to an Internet TV server. Network connected gaming consoles can use their advanced graphics processing to receive Internet video. Media players (such as Blu-Ray) may include network connections (wired and/or wireless) that allow them to use media processing for Internet TV applications. Mobile telephones use microplayers to process video from broadband data connections (such as 3G or Wi-Fi).

Cloud Pairing

Cloud pairing is typically performed when a users device attempts to access the Internet TV system for the first time. Cloud pairing registers and associates a device to the Internet TV system. During the pairing process, identifying information that is unique to each device is stored in the paired device. After devices have been paired, they can automatically identify each other during future communication sessions.

Device pairing may be pre-established at the time of sale (customer data pre-loaded into the device), it may occur during the first attempted use of the device with the internet service, or it may be manually performed through use of a menu display or buttons on the device.

Firmware Updates

Firmware updates may be periodically required for TV viewing access devices to operate correctly. Firmware is the software program instructions that are stored inside the TV viewing access device that manages the user interface and processes media.

Firmware updates may provide access to new features (such as advanced navigation), update security processes and keys, and fix software errors (bugs) in the device. While the Internet TV platform provider may provide or automatically update the firmware in the device, the Internet TV provider customer care staff should be aware of the versions of firmware and what features they include and software errors they fix.

Digital Media Adapter Compatibility

It is important to note that not all I-STBs and streaming devices will work with all Internet TV systems. The reasons for incompatibility may be a result of business or technical differences. To make an I-STB compatible with an Internet TV system, some software is required. This can range from the addition to a generic TV app to customized user interface controls. Internet TV platforms and service providers may choose which devices they are compatible with. Some Internet TV service providers produce or distribute their own branded streaming devices and may choose not to support competing Internet TV service providers.

Backdrop Display

When no content is selected or an extended period of inactivity has been reached, a backdrop display may be shown. These can be photos or other media provided by the Internet TV service provider (attractive photos or promotional messages) or personal photos from the user. Ending streaming sessions can be important for saving streaming transmission fees for the Internet TV broadcaster.

Internet TV Set Top Boxes (I-STB)

An Internet set top box (I-STB) is an electronic device that decodes the Internet communications medium to and plays the content in a format that is viewable by a television or other video display devise. The output of an I-

STB can be a television RF channel (such as channel 3), analog video and audio, or media signals. I-STBs are commonly called digital media adapters.

Some of the providers of retail I-STBs include Roku, Apple and Western Digital. There are many manufacturers of generic or OEM branded Internet set top boxes.

The I-STB must include certain protocols and configuration settings that enable it to work with the broadcaster's system. These are usually determined by the application platform utilized by the I-STB.

Network Data Interface

The input to an Internet set top box is a data connection which can be a wired Ethernet, wireless local area network (WLAN), or other type of broadband access connection.

Media Decoder

The media decoder portion of an I-STB decompresses video and audio media. The media decoder section may be hardware or software based. I-STBs commonly contain multiple types of media decoding capabilities. Because license fees for technology and software are usually paid for additional capabilities, I-STBs that have multiple types of media decoding capabilities tend to be more expensive.

Device Storage

The I-STB may include a storage area for programs (hard disk and/or flash memory) which can allow the device to play media even when an Internet connection is not available.

TV Outputs

The output of an I-STB may be in multiple formats including composite video, RF channel, analog audio and video, and digital format such as HDMI.

Application Platform

The application platform for I-STBs is a combination of media servers, receiving devices, software programs and protocols that enable the user to select and connect to media sources. Some of the application platforms are based on Javascript or HTML text commands. Other application platforms use client software programs that communicate with media servers via application program interfaces.

Figure 4.2 shows a functional diagram of an Internet TV STB (I-STB). This diagram shows that an IP STB typically receives IP data packets that hold

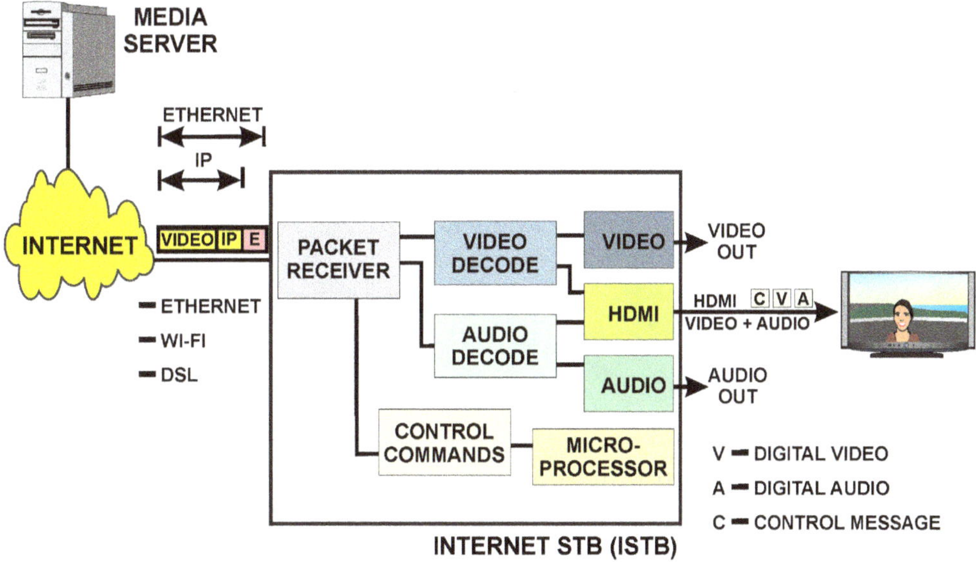

Figure 4.2, Internet TV Set Top Box

video and audio which are inside (encapsulated in) Ethernet packets. The I-STB extracts the IP packets to identify which packets hold video, audio and control messages. The I-STB then decompresses the video and audio messages (expands them to their original digital format). The digital video and digital audio are either converted into a video and audio output or they are processed to be sent on a HDMI cable (combined digital cable). The HDMI cable sends digital video, audio and a control packet to the viewing device (the television set).

TV Media Stick (Dongles)

TV media sticks (commonly called dongles) are small accessories about the size of a chewing gum pack that can be attached to a viewing device (typically a TV set). Some TV media stick manufacturers include Alticast, Tronsmart, and Ricomagic.

TV media sticks receive streams directly from either an Internet TV service provider (such as NetFlix, Google TV, or Amazon Prime) or may receive a streaming signal from a nearby device (such as a tablet or smartphone) which is called "Casting." When the casting contains the media on the device display it is called "Mirroring."

TV media sticks must be setup to enable it to work with the Internet TV system. The TV media stick provides a menu on the television that prompts the viewer to enter the setup mode when it is initially attached using a TV remote or an app on a smartphone or tablet.

WiFi Connection

The Internet input to a TV media stick is typically a WiFi connection. This connection must be setup when initially installed. The TV media stick provides a menu which shows the available WiFi connections are available and allows the user to select the WiFi network and enter passwords.

WiFi connections can experience limited data transfer rates due to distance from the WiFi router, location of the dongle (behind metal objects), or due to interference from WiFi and other signals. Users may have difficulty viewing their programs if the data rates are not sufficient. A simple solution may be to enable the viewers to select different WiFi channels or frequency bands (2.4 or 5 GHz) for their WiFi connection.

Media Connector (HDMI)

TV media sticks typically connect to an HDMI socket. The HDMI connection provides for security control and high quality digital media transfer.

TV media sticks can be several inches long making them difficult to install in the space available next to the TV viewing device and unattractive objects extending from the TV. Some media stick kits include short cables to allow them to be located in areas behind or around televisions.

Power

TV media sticks require power which is not provided by the HDMI media connection. The power can come from a power supply that plugs into a wall or from a USB cable that may plug into the TV or other nearby device that has a USB connector. The amount of power that is available from a USB connector is limited which may not be enough for some TV media sticks to operate.

Remote Control

Users select Internet TV networks and media channels by either using a remote control (provided with the TV media stick) or an app on a connected (e.g. Bluetooth) smartphone or web browser.

Hybrid TV Broadcast Set Top Boxes (HSTB)

A hybrid set top box is an electronic device that adapts multiple types of communication mediums to a format that is accessible by the end user. The use of HSTBs allows a viewer to get direct access to broadcast content from terrestrial or satellite systems in addition to accessing other types of systems such as Internet TV via a broadband Internet connection.

The hybrid broadcast and broadband television association (HbbTV.org) is an industry group that oversees standards on to mix broadcast media transmission with Internet connections. Hybrid broadcasting allows for the embedding of media and links in the broadcast signal which can be used to enhance the viewer's TV media experience. When a viewer interacts with the embedded objects (such as links), their TV can be redirected to other sources (such as Interactive ads).

Some of the manufacturers of hybrid set top boxes include EKT, Pace, and Humax. Because the set top box may be produced for or leased by a TV broadcaster such as a DTT or cable TV provider, it may be necessary to work with the broadcaster to gain access to the Internet TV portion of the set top box.

Broadcast Connection

The broadcast connection for a hybrid set top box can be digital terrestrial television (DTT), satellite system (SatTV), or a cable system (CATV). The broadcast signal contains multiple (simulcast) TV channels. When the set top box is in broadcast receive mode, it receives, selects and decodes a specific channel from a group of broadcast channels. Some or all of the broadcast channels may be protected (encrypted) by a conditional access system. To receive the protected channels (such as premium content), the STB may include a security system (such as a removable Cablecard or Smartcard).

Internet Access

The Internet access connection for a hybrid set top box can be from a wired data connection, wireless local area network connection (WLAN), or through an embedded cable modem (eCM). The Internet access channel may be used to connect to a streaming source (selected by the user) or to download content into a storage disk (hard disk) for future use (possibly automatically transferred to the STB).

Application Platform

Access to the application platform for hybrid set top boxes may be controlled by the broadcast company that provides the set top box to the consumer. This can allow the broadcast company to control which channels and applications the viewer can use (a walled garden).

Figure 4.3 shows some of the functions of a hybrid television set top box. This STB includes a receiver that accepts and selects channels from simulcast signals (multiple signals) from a cable television broadcaster. Some of

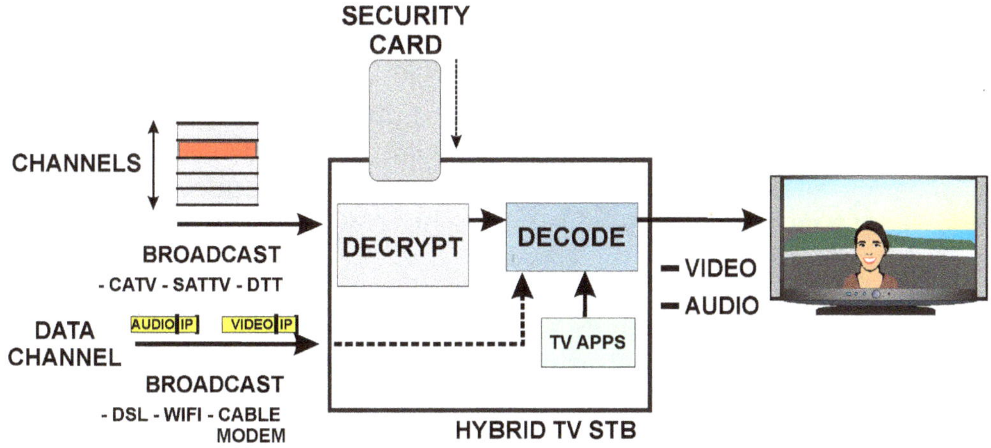

Figure 4.3, Hybrid Broadcast Set Top Box

these channels may be protected (encrypted) and a security card may be used to decode these channels. The Internet access portion allows for the selection of a single channel, from an unlimited number of sources, to be provided to the box. The compressed media (from broadcast or Internet) is decoded and converted into a form that can be connected to a TV display (such as analog video, audio or digital HDMI).

Multimedia Personal Computers (PCs)

Because many computers are already multimedia and Internet ready, it is often possible to use a multimedia computer to watch Internet TV through the use of a media player software program and some security processes (access control and content protection). Some of the advantages of using a multimedia computer to watch Internet TV include no cost for a set top box, more capability than an STB can offer, and a large, ready-to-use customer subscription.

Companies that are getting involved with Internet TV for the first time, and even TV broadcasters that are expanding into Internet TV, can start to provide services to Internet TV without the need to setup adapter boxes or relationships with other connected TV systems. If viewers insist on watching programs on televisions, Internet TV service providers can provide viewers with PC-to-TV adapters.

Internet TV signals may be displayed on a multimedia computer as long as it has enough processing power (processing speed) and the necessary media player protocols and signal decompression coders. Multimedia computers tend to have much more available processing power and memory for applications than traditional set top boxes.

To enable multimedia computers to work with Internet TV systems, viewers need to either download a software program (soft client) or use an existing media player.

The processing power of a computer may be a limitation for receiving and displaying Internet TV signals. This may become more apparent when IP television is taken from its small format to full screen video format. Full screen display requires the processor to not only decode the images, but also to scale the images to the full screen display size. This may result in pixilation (jittery squares) or error boxes. Using a video accelerator card that has MPEG decoding capability may decrease the burden of processing video signals.

Some of the newer operating systems include software security utilities that can allow the Internet TV system to validate identity (authenticate), authorize access, and secure (encrypt) the media that is sent to the multimedia PC.

Soft Client

A soft client is a software program that operates on a computing device (such as a personal computer) that can request and receive services from a network for specific applications. The soft client program communicates with the host computer to setup and manage video connections. To access Internet TV channels, a soft client software program may be downloaded into the computer or an existing software program may be used (such as an Internet browser).

Operating System (OS)

A personal computer operating system is a set of software functions that enable software programs to operate and communicate with the computer hardware. Multimedia computers tend to have large operating systems (such as Windows, Apple OS, and Linux) that include extensive media processing and security features.

Media Decoding

The media decoding process in a multimedia computer may be performed by software or hardware. Multimedia computers that do not have (or cannot use) media decoding hardware can perform digital video and audio decoding using software that uses the computer's microprocessor. Media decoding can require a substantial amount of processing capability and, if the multimedia computer has many services and applications running simultaneously, it may interfere with and reduce the quality of the video and audio of the Internet TV media.

Security

Security for multimedia computers includes access control, content protection and digital rights management. Access control for Internet video can be controlled during the setup of a connection request. Content protection can be provided by encrypting the transmitted data which is decoded by the receiving device. More recent versions of the computer operating systems tend to include advanced security capabilities, such as digital rights management, which involves the control of physical access to information, identity validation (authentication), service authorization and media protection (encryption). DRM systems are typically incorporated within newer computer operating systems.

PC Video to TV Converter

To display Internet TV from a computer to a standard television set, a video-to-TV converter can be used. The video-to-TV converter transforms the monitor video and audio into a signal that can be used by a television set (such as analog video or HDMI).

Figure 4.4 shows how a multimedia computer can be used to watch Internet television. The multimedia computer needs to have a software program that can communicate with a host service (a soft client). The client communicates with the media player which selects and decodes media (video and audio). The media player may use software to decode the media (such as MPEG decoding) using some of the computer's processing capability. The service may also use security mechanisms which are included in the operating system (certificates) to ensure that the media is being received and decoded by an authorized user. This example shows that the video output may be displayed on the computer monitor, or an optional video monitor adapter can be used to display the video on a television set.

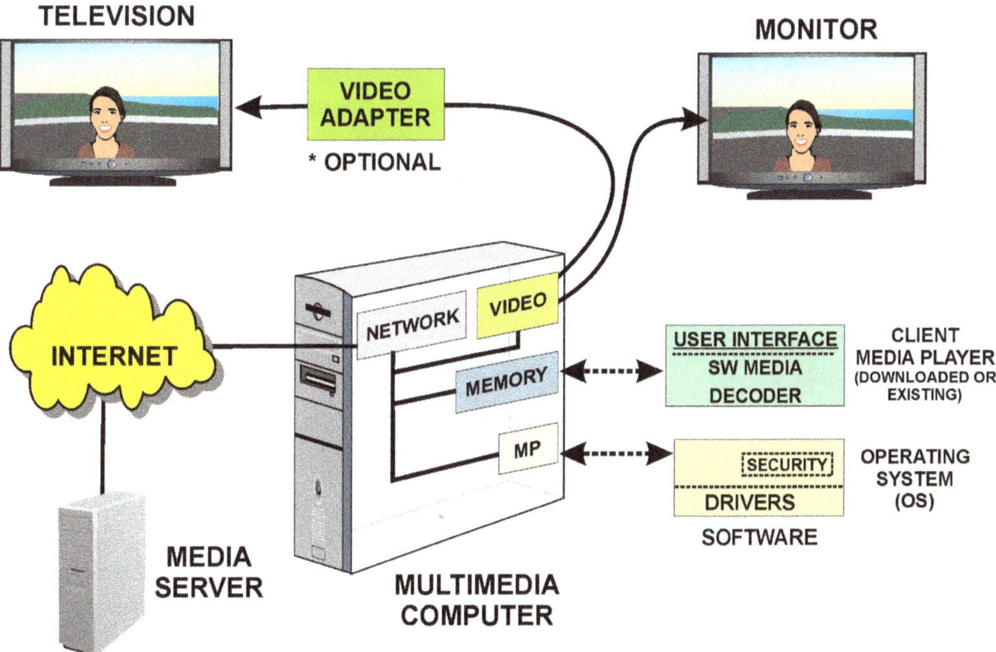

Figure 4.4, Internet TV on Multimedia Computer

Multimedia Mobile Telephone

Multimedia mobile telephones are wireless communication devices that are capable of receiving and displaying digital media such as digital video and digital audio. Multimedia mobile telephones usually contain one or more broadband data receivers such as mobile phone (3G) and Wi-Fi. Newer mobile phones include embedded software that allows them to receive and decode digital media (such as Internet video). Older multimedia mobile telephones may require the user to install a media player to receive and view Internet TV video signals. The operating system and the capabilities of the device (memory, display and processing power) may determine if and how well mobile devices can view Internet TV signals.

Broadband Access

The broadband connection to a mobile telephone may be provided from a mobile telephone system, wireless local area network, or some other form of broadband connection that can access the Internet. The user may desire to only connect to Internet TV using certain access connection types to avoid high usage costs (such as only watching Internet TV when a free Wi-Fi connection is available).

Microplayer

A microplayer is a media player that is designed for devices that have limited amounts of processing capability as well as small display screens (such as smart phones and other handheld wireless devices). Early multimedia mobile telephones did not include microplayers, so software client programs needed to be installed in the devices. Devices from different manufacturers required different types of drivers for media player adaptation. More recent mobile devices include microplayers that can be used to display multiple types of media.

Mobile Operating System

A mobile operating system is a group of software programs and routines that directs the operation of a mobile device in its tasks and assists programs in performing their functions. The mobile operating system software is responsible for coordinating and allocating device assemblies (keypad, display, memory) and communication resources (voice and data connections). The mobile operating system functions include transferring data to and from memory, processor and peripheral devices and communication channels. Software applications use the mobile operating system to gain access to these resources as required.

Older mobile telephones used operating systems that were unique to the manufacturer. Newer mobile telephones (smartphones) use more standardized operating systems including Symbian OS (open license), Android (open source), Apple iOS (proprietary), Blackberry OS (proprietary), and Windows Mobile (proprietary).

Security

Security on mobile devices may not be a significant issue because the media is only provided to specific users, is in a lower resolution form (less valuable), and it is generally difficult for a user to gain access to the media stream. As a result, content owners may be more willing to license good content for delivery to mobile devices than for delivery to other devices such as multimedia computers.

Human Interface Capabilities

The human interface capabilities for mobile telephones that are used for TV media commonly include small display, limited audio quality and reduced and mismatched buttons (keypad).

When the mobile telephone connects to the media server, it is usually able to transfer a list of its capabilities (media formats and controls). This can allow the media server to select and adapt appropriate formats and controls for that device (if the video hosting system is capable of this).

Figure 4.5 shows the basic structure of a mobile telephone that has a Java media player which can be used to display Internet video (such as Internet TV). This diagram shows that a mobile device contains a microprocessor (uP), memory that holds software program instructions, and data and display and data port adapter functions. The Java media player is a small program (Applet) that uses the standard Java programming language to provide media player functions on the mobile device. When media stream is received by the media player (such as Play or Stop), the Applet converts these media control commands into instructions the Java application can understand. The Java program then converts (interprets) these commands into a form that the operating system can understand, and the operating system sends information to the specific devices (such as the LCD display)

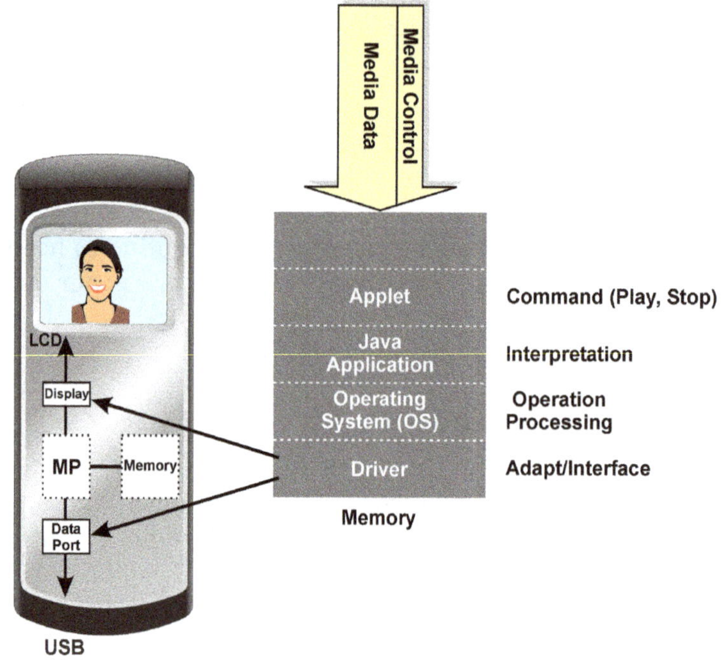

Figure 4.5, Internet TV Mobile Viewing

using driver software that converts the information into a format that can be used by the specific device (such as a small color LCD display).

Connected Televisions (Smart TVs)

A connected television set is a viewing device that is specifically designed to receive and display video digital television signals through the IP data networks (such as the Internet). Connected televisions may include other receivers (such as cable connection or DTT receivers).

Adding Internet TV connections to televisions enables the manufacturers to earn additional revenue on the installation and use of TV applications. Even applications that are free to the consumer (such as movies on demand applications like NetFlix, Vudu and Blockbuster) may generate sales revenue. An application activation incentive may be paid to the TV manufacturer ($10 for a movie rental application) and a percentage of sales and advertising revenue may be provided (residual income). This means that the small increase in cost for adding Internet connection capability can be recovered and even turned into a profit center.

Internet Connection

Connected televisions include broadband network data connections, which may be wired or wireless. To save cost, a connected TV may require an accessory for wireless network connection. Optionally, connected televisions may include an embedded cable modem (eCM).

Media Processing

Television sets already have video and audio decoding hardware that may be used to decode Internet TV media. While TVs include MPEG television media processing capability, additional types of media decoding capabilities may not be available (such as VC-1 or FLV).

Connected TV Operating System

Connected TVs tend to use proprietary operating systems that are not well publicized. To gain access to these operating systems, applications may be created on industry standard TV application or widget platforms such as Yahoo TV. After the applications are created, each TV manufacturer must review and approve them before allowing them to be downloaded and used on their television sets.

Application Processing

Television sets commonly have limited processing capabilities and available memory for other features such as applications and user interface programs. A typical television set (mid-range) in 2010 could hold approximately 50 to 100 TV apps. This is likely to increase in the future as more valuable connected television applications become available.

Figure 4.6 shows how a television may include the ability to display Internet TV services. This example shows a television that also has an Internet connection (wired or wireless). The media processing that is used (media decoding hardware) can also decode Internet TV content. The connected TV also includes memory for application programs that allow the user to view and select Internet TV channels and programs.

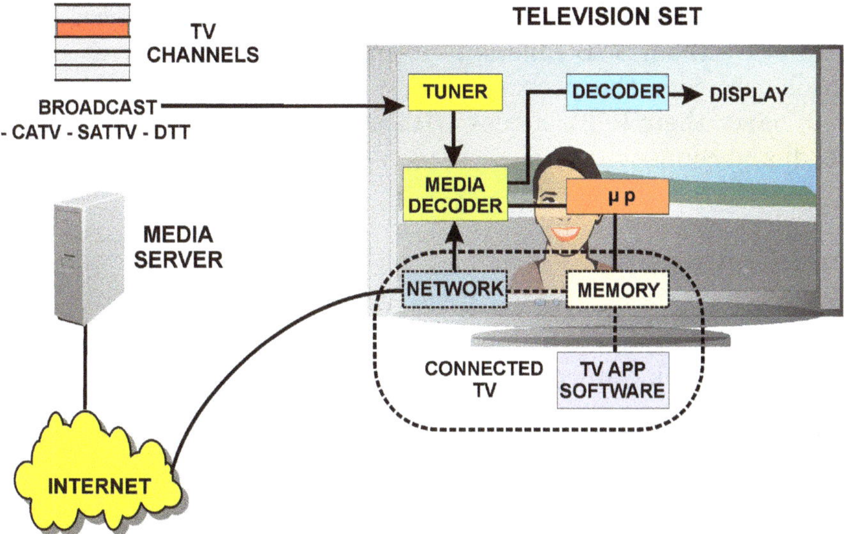

Figure 4.6, Internet TV Connected Television

Networked Gaming Devices

Networked gaming devices are data processing assemblies that can use and process multiple forms of media such as audio, data and video that are coordinated with removable, downloadable or online (hosted) software programs.

Because many gaming devices are already multimedia and Internet ready, it is often possible to use a gaming device to stream video (Internet television). Some of the network gaming devices that can be used to view Internet TV (such as NetFlix and Vudu) include Xbox (Microsoft), Wii (Nintendo) and Playstation (Sony).

The media player must be able to find and connect to Internet TV media servers, process compressed media signals, maintain a connection, and process television control features. Network gaming devices tend to have much more data storage and media processing capabilities than set top boxes or connected video devices. They commonly contain a hard disk that can hold many applications.

Boot disks and thumb drives can also be used to upload software to gaming consoles to give them STB functionality. This is a cost effective solution as the console provides the processing horsepower. It also enables the subscriber to carry their IPTV access with them, watching their channels on any broadband connected devise.

Internet Connection

Some gaming devices include Internet connections for networked services. To setup the network connection, the user may be required to join a network service.

Media Processing

Network capable gaming devices usually include hardware that includes multiple types of video, audio and graphics processing capabilities, which may be used for Internet TV services.

Application Processing

There are many application developers for gaming consoles. Applications are distributed through the companies that own the platforms (walled gardens), so Internet TV channel applications need to be reviewed and approved by the platform owners.

Figure 4.7 shows how a gaming device can be used to watch Internet TV programming. The gaming device has a wired broadband network connection. It already has several media processing capabilities (MPEG, VC-1) which can also be used to process Internet TV signals. Applications (such as video players) can be downloaded from the platform (walled garden).

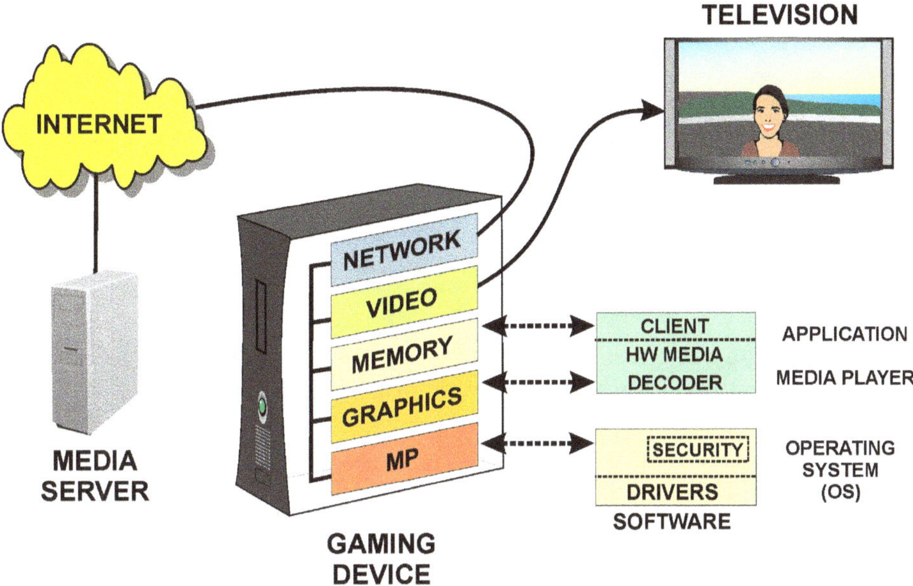

Figure 4.7, Internet TV Gaming Device

Connected Media Players

Connected media players are devices that can read, decode and play stored media (such as Blu-Ray players) which can also redirect a content source from the stored media device to an Internet connection.

Media players tend to be low cost devices and the same companies that produce televisions may produce media players. Some of the key manufacturers of connected media players include Samsung, Sony and Insignia. Media player devices may be designed to only work with application platforms that are controlled by the manufacturer (walled gardens).

Media players have the capability to decode media and more advanced media players (such as Blu-Ray players) have the capability to run text based scripting languages such as Java. In addition to allowing the users to request Internet TV channels and programs, media players have the added ability to encourage (prompt) users to obtain additional content via a connection through the Internet.

Network Connection

Media players may include a network connection, which may be wired or wireless. To save cost, some media players may require an accessory for wireless network connection.

Media Processing

Media players may use a hardware based media decoding (MPEG) process, which can also be used for the Internet TV decoding process.

Java Scripts

Advanced media players (such as Blu-Ray) are capable of running JavaScript programming. This allows applications to run on the media player regardless of the type of operating system being used.

Application Platform

The application platform may be directly controlled by and unique to the manufacturer of the media player. Because media players are commonly manufactured by the same companies, the application platforms tend to be the same as those used for connected TV systems. Unfortunately, media players are sold at much lower prices than connected TVs, so the amount of memory for applications may be limited.

Store Media Applications

Media players that have removable disks (such as Blu-Ray) are able to redirect the media source to an Internet connection. The viewer may be prompted with a message offering access to additional content (such as background on the actors in a media program), which connects them to an Internet TV media server.

Figure 4.8 shows how a media player may be used for Internet TV service. This media player has both a wired network connection (Ethernet data plug) and a built-in Wi-Fi wireless receiver. The media player has multiple types of media processing capabilities (MPEG, VC-1) that are hardware-based (dedicated circuits). It is designed to work with vendor-provided (proprietary) communication protocols that ensure that the manufacturer of the device (or their licensees) can control how the user can connect (walled garden). The stored media disks (Blu-Rays) can be created with redirect control options prompting the viewer to connect to additional content sources.

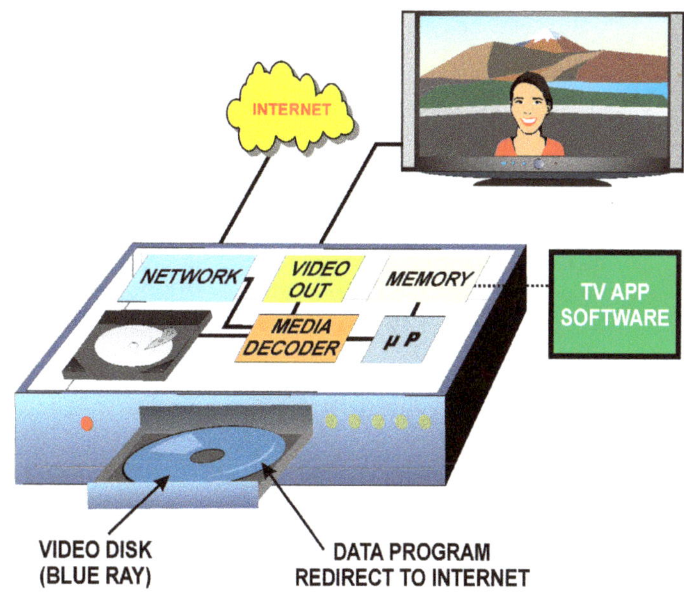

Figure 4.8, Internet TV on Media Players

Figure 4.8, Internet TV on Media Players <ag_Internet_TV_Media_Players>

References:

1. http://www.fierceonlinevideo.com/story/report-hybrid-stb-market-hit-1-3b-2014/2010-08-10
2. Lawrence Harte, personal interview, industry expert, November 8, 2010

Internet TV Technology

Internet TV systems transfer media by capturing media, data compression, packetization, transmission, packet reception, decompression, decoding, and converting (rendering) the media signal back into its original form.

Media Capturing

Media capturing is the process of gathering and processing signals or information. For Internet TV systems, media capturing can involve the conversion from analog video to digital video (A/D conversion). Because the digital video data rates are relatively high (270 Mbps for standard definition video and 3.0 Gpbs for high definition video), the digital video signal is compressed.

Compression

Compression is the processing of digital information to a form that reduces the space required for storage. There are several types of compression that can be used for video and audio. Some of the compression techniques replace commonly occurring sequences of characters by tokens that take up less space and others convert media segments to other formats that approximate the media to dramatically reduce the data rate (lossy compression). The higher the compression level (MPEG-4 video is approximately 200:1 compression), the more sensitive the media is to distortion (such as corrupted or lost data packets).

Packetization

Packetization is the process of dividing data files or blocks of data into smaller blocks (packets) of data. For Internet TV systems, packetization involves converting media into fixed size data packets (MPEG packets). Each MPEG packet only contains a certain type of media such as a video segment, audio segment, or clock reference message. These packets are relatively small so several MPEG packets fit into the data portion (the payload) of an IP data packet. This means that if one IP packet is lost during transmission, several MPEG packets may be lost (including timing reference information).

Packet Transmission

Packet transmission is the process of addressing, transferring, and controlling packets as they pass through switching points in a packet data network. A destination address is added to the header part of each packet before it is sent into the packet data network. Control information (such as the maximum number of transfers or hops that may occur) is also added to the packet header.

Packet Reception

Packet reception is the process of identifying and gathering packets with the correct destination address and routing them to the appropriate function or service within the receiving device (via the port number on the IP address). Packet reception may involve the requesting of retransmission of missing packets and filtering (elimination) of duplicate packets that are received.

Decompression

Decompression is the processing of compressed digital information to convert it into its original uncompressed format. Internet TV systems decompress multiple types of media such as video and audio.

Decoding

Decoding is the process of converting encoded data into its original signal format. For Internet TV systems, the decoding process may involve converting digital audio and video into forms that can be played or displayed to the user.

Rendering

Rendering is the process of converting media into a form that a human can view, hear or sense. Internet TV systems may convert digital media into analog or digital form that can be used by a variety of devices such as television sets, computer monitors, or mobile phones.

Figure 5.1 shows how video can be sent via an IP transmission system. This diagram shows that an IP video system digitizes (A/D) and reformats (codes) the original media (video and audio). The system analyzes and compresses the media. The IP address and transmission control information is added to each packet. The packets travel through a packet data network. The receiver gathers and assembles the packets. The media is decompressed back into its original video and audio data form. The data is then converted into its original video and audio forms.

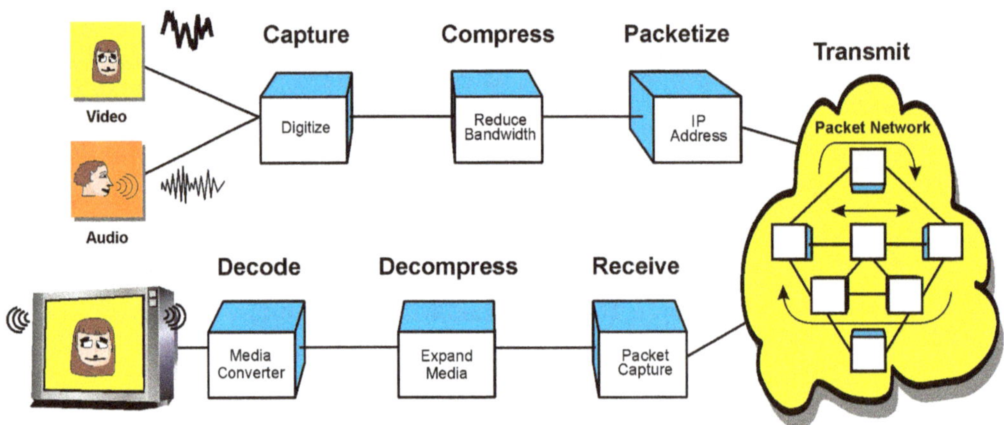

Figure 5.1, Internet TV Functional Operation

Switched Digital Video (SDV)

Internet TV channel selection is the process of finding and connecting to an IP address on a media server so it can receive and decode a television channel. This switched digital video process involves the use of physical connection, logical connections, and communication sessions. Because SDV can connect a viewing device to almost any video source, Internet TV systems can have an unlimited number of channels.

Physical Connection

Physical connections are the electrical, radio, or optical transmission channels that are connected between transmitters and receivers. Users commonly share physical connections (such as Cable Modem or DSL lines) with other users.

Logical Connection

Logical channels are a portion of a physical communications channel that is used to for a particular (logical) communications purpose. The physical channel may be divided in time, frequency or digital coding to provide for these logical channels.

Logical connections are setup as connection paths between two points. Several logical channels may share a single physical connection. For example, a TV program has a separate logical connection for a video channel and a separate logical connection for an audio channel.

Sessions

Sessions are the time and activity between the operation of a software program or logical connection between two communications devices. In communications systems, the session involves the establishment of a logical channel with configuration transmission parameters, operation of higher level applications, and termination of the session when the application is complete (such as connect to a TV channel, watch a TV channel, and disconnect from a TV channel).

Unlimited Number of TV Channels

To watch television programs, viewing devices (such as Internet set top boxes or connected TVs) connect to media servers or channels that are provided by other sources such as TV stations. Because the provider of the connection (the Internet TV) can have as many programs or streaming media sources, this allows the Internet TV to offer an unlimited number of TV channels.

Figure 5.2 shows how switched digital video allows users to have access to an unlimited number of channels. This diagram shows that a home has a single physical broadband connection to the Internet. Each user in the home creates one or more logical connections to communicate to other computers that are connected to the Internet. When a user requests to use Internet TV service, a session to a media server is setup. The user may be able to connect to many other media servers or video streams.

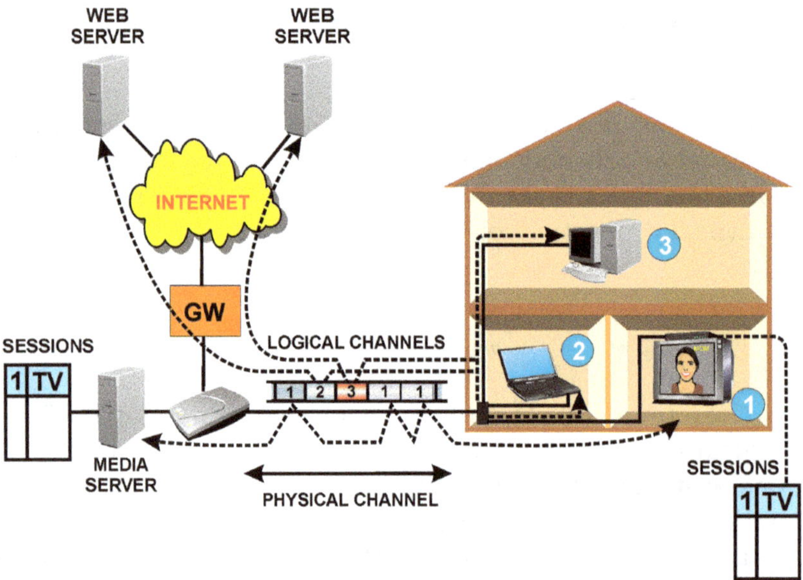

Figure 5.2, Switched Digital Video

Communication Protocols

Communication protocols are sets of rules and processes that manage how transmissions are initiated and maintained between communication points. Communication protocols define the format, timing, sequence, and error checking used on a network or computing system. Internet

Communication protocols vary in complexity, ranging from simple file transfer protocols to reservation protocols that setup and manage the reliability of connections through a network.

Protocol commands and processes tend to expand and change over time. This means that newer versions of protocols can have provide additional features and services that are not possible with other protocols. Protocols may be updated by downloading new software into devices (firmware upgrades).

Internet TV systems use a mixture of protocols including application protocols, session protocols, network protocols, and link protocols. Protocols that interact with each other may be combined into protocol suites.

Application Protocols

Application protocols are commands and procedures used by software programs to perform operations using information or messages that are received from or sent to other sources (such as a user at a keyboard). The use of well-defined application protocols (agreed commands and processes) allows the software applications to interoperate with other programs that use the application protocol independent from the underlying technologies that link them together (such as wires or wireless connections).

Session Protocols

Session protocols are a precise set of rules, timing, and a syntax that govern the accurate transfer of information between devices or software applications through a communication system.

Network Protocols

Network protocols are commands and process that are used to setup and manage network elements and transmission links in communication networks. Network protocols are used to setup connection between the viewing device and their content sources (media servers).

Link Protocols

Link protocols are the commands and processes used to coordinate the delivery of data between devices on a communication connection. Link protocols are designed to transfer data through a single connection (such as a cable modem line or a DSL line).

Protocol Suites

Protocol suites are a set of related protocols. Protocol suites are usually designed to allow reliable interaction between upper layer and lower layer protocols.

Figure 5.3 shows how a communication system functions can be divided into functional layers. This example shows a generic open system interconnection (OSI) protocol model and how it coordinates communication between an email client (user that is checking email) to an email server (computer providing the email information) independent of who controls each layer, provided the interfaces between each layer are specifically defined. This diagram shows that the application layer is the interface to the user that permits the user to request delivery of their email. The application layer presents this request to the transport layer as a data file. The data file is divided up into smaller blocks of data and presented to the session layer. The session layer determines a new session is required (communication link) between the client and the server and this session information is passed on to the transport layer that will oversee the transfer of data during the session. The transport layer sends the destination address of the email server to the network layer. The network layer sends this information to the data link layer that establishes and maintains a data link connection to the network. The data link layer sends information to the physical layer that converts to data signals to either radio, electrical, or optical formats suitable for transmission.

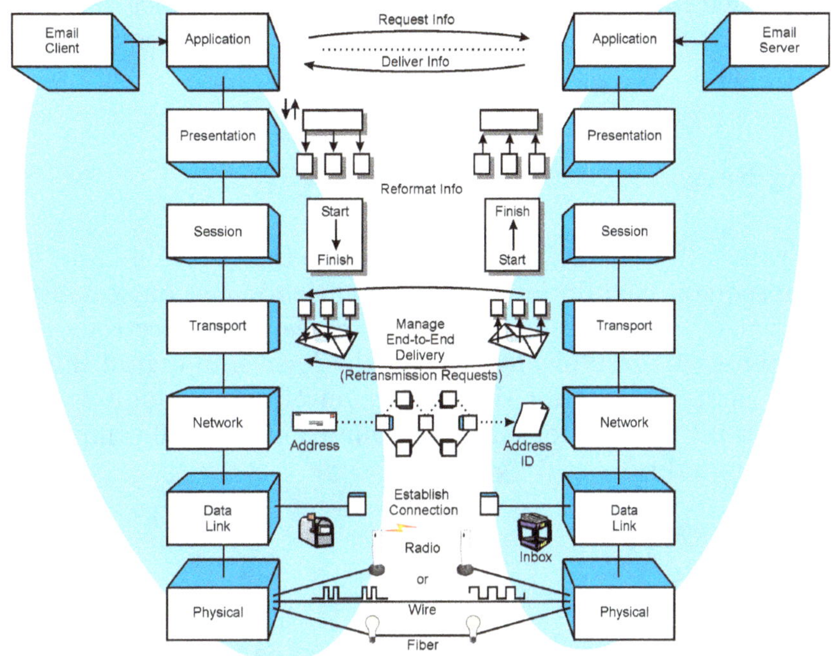

Figure 5.3, Communication Protocol Layers

Audio Digitization

Audio digitization is the conversion of analog audio signals into digital form. To convert an analog audio signal to digital form, the analog signal is digitized by using an analog-to-digital (pronounced A to D) converter. The A/D converter periodically senses (samples) the level of the analog signal and creates a binary number or series of digital pulses that represent the level of the signal.

Analog to Digital Conversion (Digitization)

Analog to digital conversion is a process that changes a continuously varying signal (analog) into a digital values. A typical conversion process includes an initial filtering process to remove extremely high and low frequencies that could confuse the digital converter. A periodic sampling section that at fixed intervals locks in the instantaneous analog signal voltage, and a converter that changes the sampled voltage into its equivalent digital number or pulses.

Sampling Rate

Sampling rate is the rate at which signals in an individual channel are sampled for subsequent modulation, coding, quantization, or any combination of these functions. The process of taking samples of an electronic signal at equal time intervals to typically convert the level into digital information. The typical sampling rate for the conversion of analog audio ranges from 8,000 samples per second (for telephone quality) to 44,000 samples per second (for music quality).

Bits per Sample

Bits per sample is the number of levels that can be represented by the sampling system. The higher the number of bits per sample (typically 8 or 13), the higher the data rate that is required to transmit the digital audio information.

Fidelity

Audio fidelity is the degree to which a system, or a portion of a system, accurately reproduces at its output the essential characteristics of the signal impressed upon its input. The higher the fidelity, the higher the data rate that is required to transmit the digital audio information. For high fidelity audio signals that are sent thorough digital TV systems, the uncompressed data rate for each audio channel is 1.5 Mbps.

Audio Channels

Each television channel has one or more audio channels. Stereo audio uses two channels. For Internet TV, there may be several audio channels available per video program for multiple languages. Only one of these audio channels needs to be selected and transmitted to the user (logical channels).

Surround Sound

Surround sound is the reproduction of audio that surrounds the listener with sound that is provided from multiple speaker locations. The use of surround sound can allow a listener to hear audio in a way that they can determine the relative position of sound sources around them (such as in front and behind).

To create surround sound, 5.1 or 7.1 channels of audio may be used. These are grouped into front left and right, back left and right, center, and a very low frequency. To provide surround sound, additional data transmission bandwidth is required.

Dolby Noise Reduction

Dolby is an audio signal processing system that is used to reduce the noise or hiss that was invented by Ray Dolby. The original Dolby noise reduction process that was developed in 1960s used compounding and expanding to adjust the dynamic range of the audio into a range that was more suitable for stored or transmitted medium. Since it original development, various enhancements to the Dolby system have been developed including Dolby A, Dolby B, Dolby C, Dolby S, Dolby SR and Digital Dolby.

Figure 5.4 shows the basic audio digitization process. This diagram shows that a person creates sound pressure waves when they talk. These sound pressure waves are converted to electrical signals by a microphone. When the microphone senses a large sound pressure wave (loud audio), it produces a large (higher voltage) analog signal. To convert the analog signal to digital form, the analog signal is periodically sampled (8,000 to 44,000 times per second) and converted to a digital code (number) that represents the level.

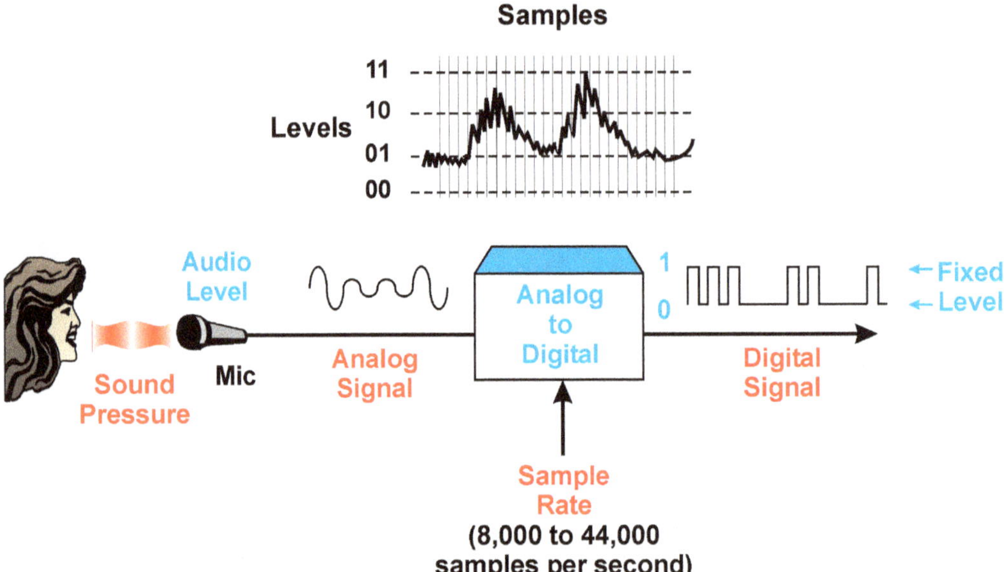

Figure 5.4, Audio Digitization

Video Digitization

Video digitization is the conversion of video component signals or composite signal into digital form through the use of an analog-to-digital (pronounced A to D) converter. The A/D converter periodically senses (samples) the level of the analog signal and creates a binary number or series of digital pulses that represent the level of the signal.

Video Components

Video components are separate electrical signals that represent the intensity and color of video signals. Video is separated into red, green, and blue components and each color has a separate intensity level.

Resolution

Resolution is the number of image elements (pixels) per unit of area. A display with a finer grid contains more pixels, and therefore has a higher resolution, capable of reproducing more detail in an image.

The conversion of standard definition (SD) video to digital format results in an uncompressed data transmission rate of 270 Mbps. The conversion of high definition (HD) video to digital format results in an uncompressed data transmission rate of 3 Gbps. Uncompressed ultra high definition video is 10 Gbps.

Aspect Ratio

Aspect ratio is the relationship of a number of items (such as pixels on a screen) compared to the width and height of those items. The aspect ratio determines the frame shape of an image. The aspect ratio of the NTSC (analog television) standard is 4:3 for conventional monitors such as home television sets, and 16:9 (widescreen) for HDTV.

Different versions of program are needed for different aspect ratios. This is a challenge for simulcast systems (such as cable television) where each channel uses the available bandwidth, Internet TV has one connection which can be switched to programs which different formats.

Frame Rate

Frame rate is the number of images (frames or fields) that are displayed to a movie viewer over a period of time. Frame rate is typically indicated in frames per second (fps). The higher the frame rate, the more data must be transmitted (higher bandwidth usage). For television, the minimum frame rate for a quality picture (no flickering) is approximately 15 frames per second (fps).

Some Internet TV adapters convert the frame rate of the stream to the frame rate used by the viewing device. This can be important for global distribution where some viewers have 25 fps devices (Europe) and others have 30 fps devices (North America).

Figure 5.5 shows the basic process used to digitize images for pictures from analog video. For color video, is separated (or filtered) into red, green, and blue components. Each element (pixel) for each image frame is converted into digital equivalent codes that represent levels. The digital color level information from each red, green, and blue pixel is combined and sent out.

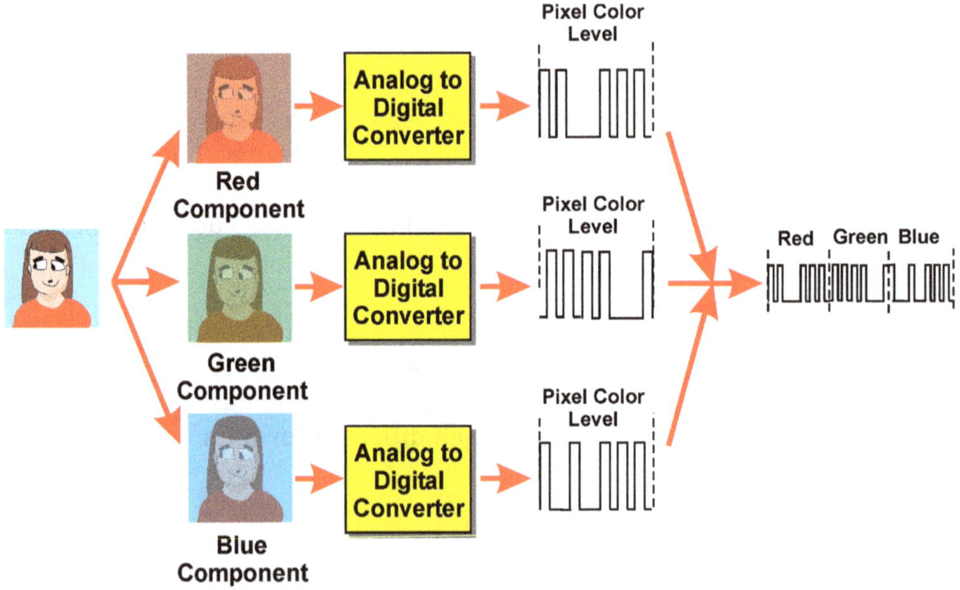

Figure 5.5, Video Digitization

Media Compression

Media compression is the process of transforming digital information into a form that requires a smaller amount of space for storage or lower streaming bit transmission rate. Uncompressed digital media files are much too large (270 Mbps to 10 Gpbs) to send through broadband Internet connections (1 to 100 Mbps). This means that the media must be dramatically reduced in size. This can be accomplished through the analysis and of each image (frame in a video sequence) and the sending of image change information between each image. The amount of media compression can vary based on the desired resolution and the willingness to lose exactness (lossy compression).

Display Resolution

Display resolution is the number of pixels per unit of area. The larger the display resolution (better looking image), the greater the number of pixels that are required to represent each frame image. Standard definition (SD) television has a display resolution of 640 x 480 which is approximately 0.3 megapixels per frame (image). High definition (HD) television has display of 1920 x 1080 which is approximately 2 megapixels per frame.

Lossy Compression

Lossy compression is a process of reducing an amount of information (usually in digital form) by converting it into another format that represents the initial form of information. However, lossy compression does not have the ability to guarantee the exact recreation of the original signal when it is expanded back from its compressed form.

Uncompressed SD video is approximately 270 Mbps and uncompressed HD is approximately 3 Gbps. By using lossy compression, it is possible to reduce the bandwidth required for video signals by approximately 200:1 (MPEG-4 or VC-1).

Spatial Compression

Spatial compression is the analysis and compression of information or data within a single frame image. Spatial video compression involves the use of a group of compression methods that identify graphic components within an image (areas of a certain color or shapes) which can be represented by relatively short codes. For example, an image that contains a white background could be replaced by code that indicates the color white and the area of the white shape (the background).

Time Compression (Temporal Compression)

Temporal compression is the analysis and compression of information or data over a sequence of frames, images or sections of information. Temporal video compression involves an analysis of the changes that occur between successive images in a video sequence so that only the differences between the images are sent, rather than all of the information for each image. To accomplish this, time compression can use keyframes and motion estimation.

Figure 5.6 shows how video compression may use spatial and temporal compression to reduce the amount of data needed to represent a video sequence. Video data is greater than 300,000 pixels per frame and each pixel also has color information. Inevitably, the compression process introduces loss of detail and distortion artifacts. In order to deliver the compression factors that are required, similar areas of video are treated as one, resulting in loss of detail. This diagram shows that a frame in a video sequence may use spatial compression by representing the graphic elements within the frame with objects or codes. The first frame of this example shows that a picture of a bird that is flying in the sky can be compressed by separating the bird image from the blue background and making the bird an object (group of pixels) and representing the blue background as a box. The next sequence of images only needs to move the bird on the background and record the difference in the group of pixels from the previous frame (temporal - time compression).

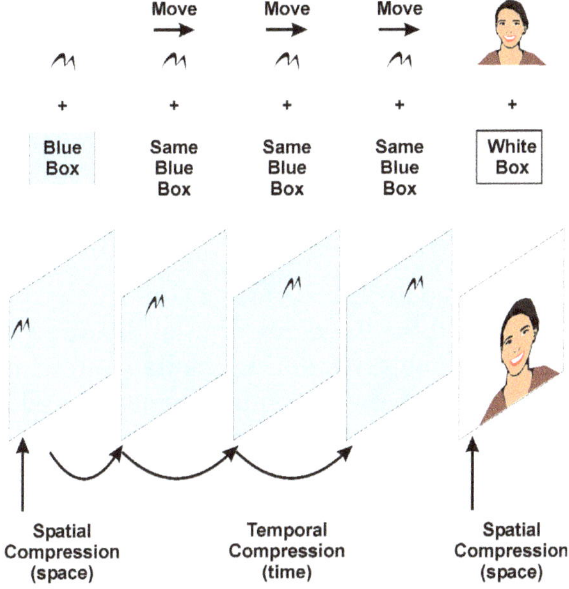

Figure 5.6, Internet TV Video Compression

Digital Media Formats

Digital media formats are the structures of audio, video, and/or other media segments within a file (container file format) or sequence of transmitted bits (a media bit stream).

Media formats are usually associated with specific standards like MPEG video format, or software vendors like Quicktime MOV format or Windows Media WMA format. In a few cases like MP3 files, the media "format" is little more than a single codec bitstream in a file.

Container Format

A container format is the organization of objects (such as digital audio and digital video) that are located within a file or streaming media source. The location of media segments within a container format is usually not critical to the playout of the media contained within the container file. The media player is simply pointed to the area within the file and begins to sequentially read the data and convert it into video and audio formats.

Stream Format

Media streaming is a method that provides a continuous stream of information that is commonly used for the delivery of audio and video content with minimal delay (e.g. real-time). Streaming media content needs to be organized into short segments of media (video segment, audio segment). The location of media segments within a streaming format is usually critical to the playout (mixed sequence of audio and video segments) of the media contained within the container file.

Streaming signals are usually compressed and error-protected to allow the receiver to buffer, decompress, and time sequence information before it is displayed in its original format.

Figure 5.7 shows container and stream media formats. The container format has a structure of areas that contain video, audio, and other data. The stream format defines the segments of audio and video that are sent on a communication channel.

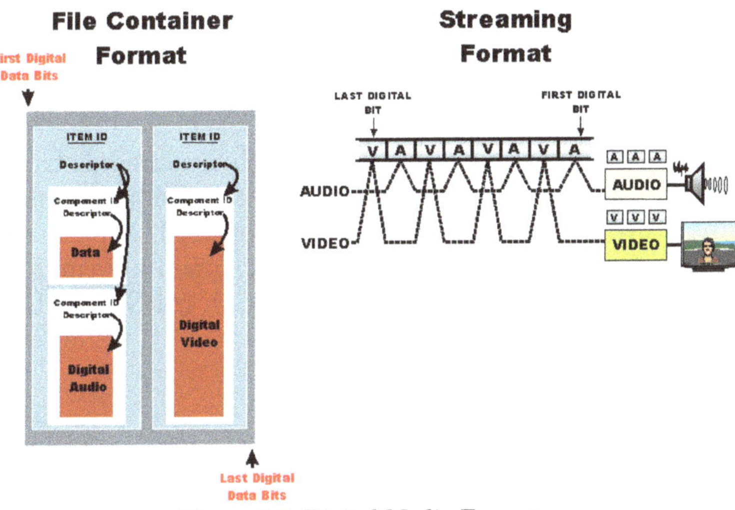

Figure 5.7, Digital Media Formats

Video Compression Formats

Common video compression formats used in Internet TV systems include MPEG-1, MPEG-2, MPEG-4, VC-1, FLV, and DivX. The video compression format defines the media elements (pixels, image blocks) and their structure within a file or media stream (data flow).

Video formats can be a raw media file that is a collection of data (bits) that represents a flow of image information or it can be a container format that is a collection of data or media segments in one data file. A file container may hold the raw data files (e.g. digital audio and digital video) along with descriptive information (meta tags).

Some of the common video formats used in Internet TV system include MPEG, Quicktime, Real media, Motion JPEG (MJPEG) and Windows Media (VC-1). Video formats that are used in the production or transfer process for video and television media include D1, D2, digital picture exchange (DPX), general exchange format (GXF), advanced authoring format (AAF) and material exchange format (MXF).

Motion picture experts group develops digital video encoding standards. The MPEG standards specify the data compression and decompression processes and how they are delivered on digital broadcast systems.

The MPEG system defines the components (such as a media stream or channel) of a multimedia signal (such as a digital television channel) and how these channels are combined, transmitted, received, separated, synchronized and converted (rendered) back into a multimedia format. MPEG has several compression standards including MPEG-1, MPEG-2, MPEG-4 (original) and MPEG-4 AVC/H.264.

MPEG-1

MPEG-1 offers less than standard television resolution. MPEG-1 was designed for slow speed stored media with moderate computer processing capabilities.

MPEG-2

MPEG-2 was designed and used for television broadcaster (radio, satellite and cable TV) of standard and high definition television.

MPEG-2 is a frame oriented multimedia transmission system that allows the combining and synchronizing of multiple media types. MPEG-2 is the current choice of video compression for digital television broadcasters as it can provide digital video quality that is similar to NTSC with a data rate of approximately 3.8 Mbps.

MPEG-4

The MPEG-4 specification was designed for allows for television transmission over packet data networks such as broadband Internet. The initial release of the MPEG-4 system has the same amount of video compression as MPEG-2. The MPEG-4 system was enhanced with a 2nd type of compression called advanced video coding (AVC)/H.264 which increased the compression amount which added significant benefit to companies installing MPEG systems (more channels in less bandwidth).

MPEG-4 is a digital multimedia transmission standard that was designed to allow for interactive digital television and it can have more efficient compression capability than MPEG-2 (more than 200:1 compression).

Figure 5.8 shows the development timeline for MPEG compression. The first standard version of MPEG-1 was introduced in 1993 and was used for CD ROMs. Layer 3 of MPEG-1 provided the audio compression (called MP3). In 1995, MPEG-2 compression was released which has been used in digital television and satellite broadcasting system. In 1999, MPEG-4 was released which efficiently provides digital video through packet data networks such as the Internet. In 2003, MPEG-4 was updated with advanced video coding (AVC) technology to provide improved video signals at higher compression rates (lower data transmission rates).

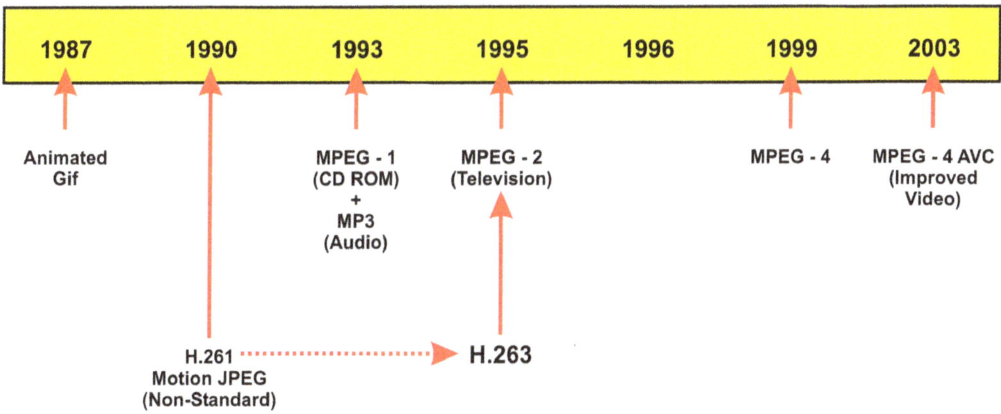

Figure 5.8, MPEG Codec Timeline

Windows Media (VC-1)

VC-1 is the designation for Microsoft's Windows Media Player codec by the SMPTE organization. VC-1 is the designation for Microsoft's Windows Media Player codec by the SMPTE organization.

Flash Video (FLV)

Flash video is a compression process that combines the Sorenson Spark codec with the Macromedia Flash Video file format. The Flash video codec has many of the same compression attributes as the H.264 MPEG compression system, which can provide up to 200:1 compression ratio.

DivX

DivX is a digital video format that evolved as an alternative to the standard MPEG digital media format to allow the use of AVI file containers. DivX uses MPEG-4 digital video compression technology and MP3 digital audio compression technology.

Motion JPEG (MJPEG)

A motion JPEG is a digital video format that is only composed of independent key frames. Because MJPEG does not use temporal compression, each video frame can be independently processed without referencing other frames. Motion JPEG may be used in content authoring or distribution of high quality content to broadcasters.

Audio Compression Formats

Common audio compression formats used in Internet TV systems include various types of MPEG audio compression including MP1, MP2, MP3, and several forms of AAC.

The type of coder that is selected can vary based on the application (such as playing music or speech) and the type of device the audio is being played through (such as a television or a battery operated portable media player). MPEG speech coders range from low complexity (layer 1) to high complexity (layer 3).

MPEG created a new type of audio coder (advanced audio codec-AAC) that offers better audio quality at lower bit rates. The AAC coder also has several variations that are used in different types of applications (e.g. broadcast radio -vs.- real time telephony).

MPEG Layer 1 (MP1)

MPEG layer 1 audio is a low complexity audio compression system. MP1 was the first digital audio and it uses the precision adaptive sub-band coding (PASC) algorithm. This process divides the digital audio signal into multiple frequency bands and only transmits the audio bands that can be heard by the listener. To obtain high fidelity quality (e.g. music) with MP1 typically requires 192 kbps per audio channel.

MPEG Layer 2 (MUSICAM - MP2)

MPEG layer 2 audio is a medium complexity audio compression system, which is also known as the MUSICAM system. The MUSICAM system achieves medium compression ratios, dividing the audio signal into sub bands, coding these sub bands and multiplexing them together. The MUSICAM system is used in the (DAB) digital audio broadcasting system. To obtain high fidelity quality (e.g. music) with MP2 typically requires 128 kbps per audio channel.

MPEG Layer 3 (MP3)

MPEG layer 3 is a lossy audio coding standard that uses a relatively high-complexity audio analysis system to characterize and highly compress audio signals. The MP3 system achieves high-compression ratios (10:1 or more) by removing redundant information and sounds that the human ear cannot detect or perceive. The removal of information components that cannot be detected (such as low level signals that occur simultaneously with high-level signals) is called psychoacoustic compression. To obtain high fidelity quality (e.g. music) with MP3 typically requires 64 kbps per audio channel.

The ISO/IEC Moving Picture Experts Group (MPEG) Committee standardized the MP3 codec in 1992. MP3 is intended for high-quality audio (like music) and expert listeners who have found some MP3-encoded audio to be indistinguishable from the original audio at bit rates around 192 kbps. The design of the Layer 3 (MP3) codec was constrained by backward compatibility with the Layer 1 and Layer 2 codecs of the same family.

MPEG Layer 3 Pro (MP3Pro)

MP3Pro is the Motion Picture Experts Group Layer 3 (MP3) system with spectral band replication (SBR) added to improve audio quality and/or lower the necessary data transmission rate.

Advanced Audio Codec (AAC™)

Advanced audio codec (AAC) is a lossy audio codec standardized by the ISO/IEC Moving Picture Experts Group (MPEG) committee in 1997 as an improved but non-backward-compatible alternative to MP3. Like MP3, AAC is intended for high-quality audio (like music) and expert listeners have found some AAC-encoded audio to be indistinguishable from the original audio at bit rates around 128 kbps, compared with 192 kbps for MP3.

Advanced Audio Codec Plus (AAC Plus™)

Advanced Audio Codec Plus is a version of the AAC coder that is used to provide enhanced audio quality at high frequencies. The AACPlus system uses spectral band replication to improve the audio quality when possible. The AACPlus system has multiple streams of audio information, which are composed of a base stream that can be combined with another stream to adjust (improve) the characteristics of the high-frequency audio signal components.

Figure 5.9 shows the different types of audio compression used in MPEG systems and the relative amount of compression that they can provide. This table uses a 2 channel stereo signal that is sampled at 44.1k samples per second, 16 bits per sample as a reference. The MPEG layer 1 coder can compress this signal to approximately 384 kbps (4:1 compression). The MPEG layer 2 coder can compress the signal to 192 kbps (8:1 compression). The MP3 coder can compress the signal to 128 kbps (12:1 compression). The AAC coder can compress the signal to 96 kbps (16:1 compression).

	MPEG Layer 1	MPEG Layer 2	MPEG Layer 3 (MP3)	AAC
Raw Data Rate (stereo @ 44.1 ksamples/sec)	1.5 Mbps	1.5 Mbps	1.5 Mbps	1.5 Mbps
Compressed Data Rate	384 kbps	192 kbps	128 kbps	96 kbps
Typical Compression	**4:1**	**8:1**	**12:1**	**16:1**

Figure 5.9, MPEG Audio Compression Comparison

Mutlimedia

To provide a television experience, video, audio, and data types of media need to be combined (multimedia). Multimedia content needs to identify and provide timing relationships (synchronizing video and audio).

MPEG

Moving picture experts group (MPEG) standards are digital video encoding processes that coordinate the transmission of multiple forms of media (multimedia). Moving picture experts group (MPEG) is a working committee that defines and develops industry standards for digital video systems. These standards specify the data compression and decompression processes and how they are delivered on digital broadcast systems. The MPEG system defines the parts of multimedia transmission that includes media streams, combined transport streams, and their timing relationships.

Elementary Streams (ES)

Elementary streams are the raw information component streams (such as audio and video) that are part of a program stream. An MPEG system divides a multimedia source component into an elementary stream (ES). Elementary streams may be video, audio or data and there may be several elementary streams for each type of media (such as multiple audio channels for surround sound).

Transport Streams (TS)

Transport Streams are the combining (multiplexing) of multiple program channels (typically digital video channels) onto a signal communication channel (such as a satellite transponder channel). These channels may be statistically combined in such a way that the bursty transmission (high video activity) of one channel is merged with the low-speed data transmission (low video activity) with other channels so more program channels can share the same limited bandwidth communication channel.

Media Synchronization

Media synchronization is the process of adjusting the relative timing of media information (such as time aligning audio and video media). Media synchronization typically involves sending timing references in each media stream that can be used to align and adjust the relative timing of multiple media signals.

Figure 5.10 shows how MPEG transmission can be used to combine video, audio, and data onto one data communication channel. This example shows that multiple types of media signals are digitized and compressed and sent to a multiplexer. The multiplexer combines these signals and their associated time reference (clock) into a single program transport stream (SPTS). When the SPTS is received, a demultiplexer separates each of the media signal streams. Each media stream is decoded, adjusted in time sequenced using the reference clock and converted back into their original media form.

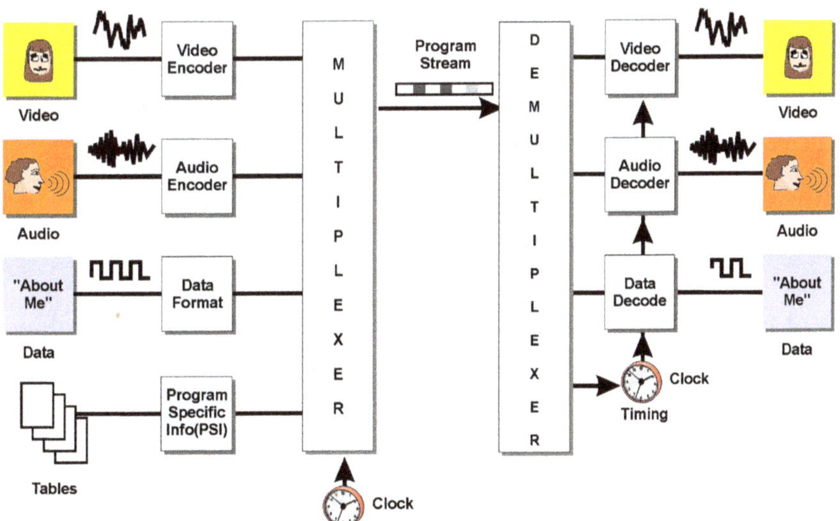

Figure 5.10, Internet TV Digital Multimedia

TV Program Metadata

Television metadata is information that describes the attributes of television media (such as program title, media format, runtime, actors, and other data. TV program metadata is used to create electronic program guides (EPGs) and for other purposes such as defining the costs of media (video on demand) and how the media may be used (usage rights).

TV program metadata is transmitted with the program as a separate data stream. Because a transmitted channel (physical transmission) may contain multiple TV channels (virtual channels), the metadata describes each virtual channel. Each TV program channel is also composed of multiple media channels (video, audio, and data) and the metadata describes each component (stream) of the program.

To obtain TV program metadata from an incoming stream, a TV capture card can be used.

TV Program Metadata

TV program metadata may include information such as the title, description, ratings (e.g. parental controls), program characteristics (run time, media formats), and other data. TV program metadata is commonly structured in flexible extensible markup language (XML) format.

Program Metadata Sources

Sources of metadata information can come from the content developer, distributor, or companies that create and distribute metadata information (such as Rovi, Gracenote, and Tribune media).

Interstitial Metadata

Additional metadata may be included that provides more details about the content contained within the program. Interstitial metadata is information (data) that describes the attributes of other data that occurs between the beginning and end of a media or data file. Interstitial metadata or meta tags can be used to describe segments of a program within a media file.

TV Metadata Standards

Television metadata standards are documents that describe how metadata may be sent (transmitted) and its structure (data format). Several broadcast systems (e.g. DVB, NTSC, ATSC) have defined metadata transmission and data structures. These standards have similar functions but can use different methods and media structures. Some of these standards include EIA-766, ETSI TS 102 818 (XML for DAB), ETSI TS 102 371 (DAB Transport for EPG), and CEA-608E.

MPEG-7 is an industry standard that describes the characteristics and related information about digital media objects. MPEG-7 system is an XML based language (flexible naming structure) that uses description definition language (DDL) to describe the characteristic objects using existing (standard) and custom created definitions. Some of the standard characteristics include shape, texture and motion.

Program Guides

A program guide is a listing or an interface (portal) that allows a customer to preview and select from possible lists of available content media. Program guides can vary from simple scrolling directory listings to interactive filters that dynamically allow the user to search through program guides by theme, time period, or other criteria. Program guides include a barker channel, electronic program guide (EPG), and an interactive program guide (IPG).

Barker Channel List

A barker channel is media source that provides information about available channels or services. Barker channels present a scrolling list of available channels. When the list reaches the end it repeats itself. Barker channels can be provided by the system without any changes to the receiving device.

Electronic Program Guides (EPG)

Electronic programming guides are an interface (portal) that allows a customer to preview and select from possible lists of available content media. EPGs can vary from simple program selection guides to interactive filters that dynamically allow the user to search through program guides by theme, time period, or other criteria. Receiving devices (STBs, PCs, or TVs) require an EPG software program (client software) to allow the user to navigate and select programs.

Interactive Program Guides (IPG)

An interactive programming guide is an interface (portal) that allows a customer to preview, search and select from possible lists of available content media. IPGs can vary from simple program selections to interactive filters that dynamically allow the user to filter through program guides by theme, time period, or other criteria. Receiving devices (STBs, PCs, or TVs) require an interactive software programs (client software) to allow the user to navigate, filter, and select programs.

Figure 5.11 shows some of the types of program guides that TV broadcasters can provide. This example shows that program metadata (descriptive information) is used to create a list of programs along with their details. A simple format of a channel listing scrolls the list of channel program times (a barker channel). The electronic program guide format allows the viewer to scroll through channel listings. An interactive program guide format allows the user to enter information to search, filter, and reorganize program listings.

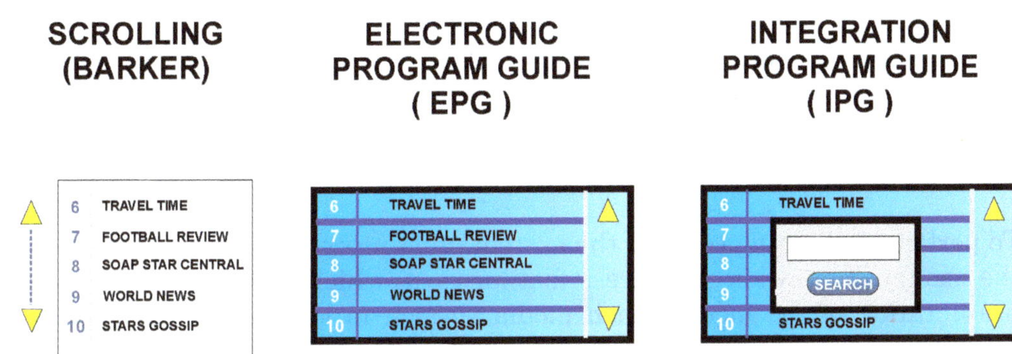

Figure 5.11, TV Program Guides

Trick Mode (Video Player Speed Control)

Trick play is the ability of a system to provide for remote control speed control operations during the streaming of a media signal. For Internet TV systems, trick mode is used to allow the viewer to change the playing mode of the program from rewind to fast forward.

Streaming Internet TV players do not store the media program so this means that changing the media playing speed requires changes from the sending device. When the user changes the playing mode (such as switching to fast forward), the system changes the source of their media to another version of the streaming program that has been stored at a different playing speed. This means that the same video program must be converted and stored in multiple bit rate versions.

Multiple Bit Rate Formats

To enable trick mode operation, the same media file must be stored in different playout formats. This means that the media file must be processed to create new files that contain more or less frames than the original program.

Timing Index

To perform streaming control, the system must process a rate request from the use (such as when they press fast forward) which includes the current presentation of the media. Each media version in the trick mode system includes a timing index that allows it to transfer to the other media programs at the associated times.

Streaming Control

Streaming control is performed by transferring the media source to the selected version (rewind, normal, fast forward) at the appropriate time reference.

Reference Key Frames

Because media programs are compressed, the process of changing modes involves more than transferring to another frame. When a user changes the mode, a new media sources must start with a key frame (a complete image frame). Some of the images in compressed media files only contain difference media (changes from previous frames). This means that a change in playout mode requires that the media server must find a previous key frame and create a new starting keyframe. This also means that many simultaneous requests for trick mode can overwhelm a system if it does not have enough capacity to start the new streams. An example of an event that can overwhelm the system is many simultaneous rewind and replay requests that can occur during a sports event.

Figure 5.12 shows how trick play can be used to provide multiple speed playback. The program digital video is stored on media players in multiple speeds (4x, 2x, standard, 1/2x, and 1/4x). When the viewer selects to fast forward (2x) or to slow down (1/2x), the trick mode system simply changes the player to the appropriate source.

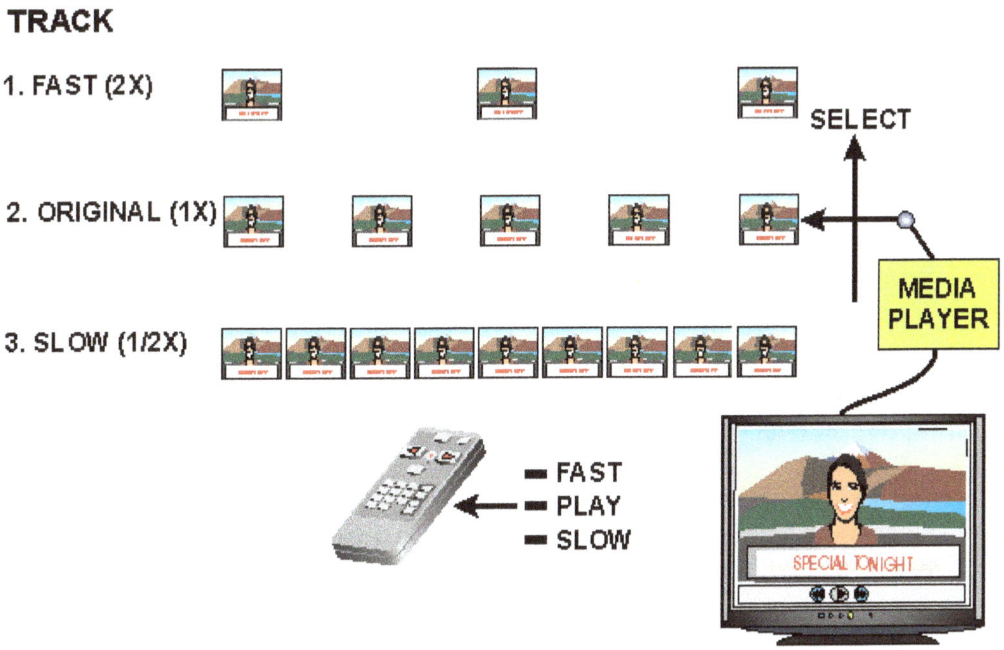

TRACK
1. FAST (2X)
2. ORIGINAL (1X)
3. SLOW (1/2X)
SELECT
MEDIA PLAYER
FAST
PLAY
SLOW
SPECIAL TONIGHT

Figure 5.12, Trick Play Operation

Geographic Targeting

Geotargeting is controlling the distribution of media based on geographic location. Internet TV systems may have the ability to control the delivery of content based on the location of the recipient. Geographic targeting may be performed by the manual updating of the location (user enters the location) or through automatic methods (such as using the geographic location of the IP address).

Location Registration

Location registration is the entry of the geographic location of a device. The user may enter their geographic location (address) when they setup the account.

IP Address Geocoding

IP address geocoding is the identification of the location of a device that is attached to the Internet by using its IP address. Each IP address that is assigned has a geographic location that is assigned to it.

Delivery Restrictions

Delivery restrictions are rules and processes that can be used to stop or limit the distribution of media or content to devices that are location in certain geographic regions (countries or states).

Internet TV systems may use location data provided by the user (subscriber information) or location data gathered automatically (such as the geographic location that is assigned to the IP address) to determine if the recipient is authorized to receive the media.

Figure 5.13 shows how Internet TV systems can identify and control distribution of media to viewers based on their location. This example shows that one viewer has selected to watch a sports game in the United States. When the request is received by the service in Australia, the location of the IP address of the United States is determined not to be authorized for viewing of the content. In another example, a viewer from Europe requests to watch the service from Australia. When the location of the IP address of that user is reviewed, it is determined that the viewer is authorized to receive the channel and a connection (video streaming session) can be setup.

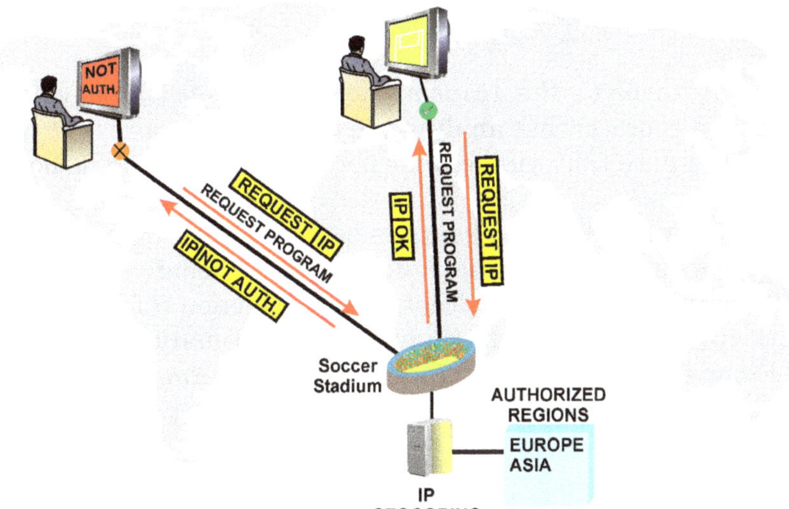

Figure 5.13, Geographic Identification

Packet Transmission

Internet TV systems transfer programs to viewers by transmitting packets through the Internet. Packet transmission is the process of addressing, transferring, and controlling packets as they pass through switching points (routers) in a packet data network. Each packet is assigned a destination address is added to the header part of each packet before it is sent into the packet data network. The packet header also contains control information (such as the maximum number of transfers or hops that may occur) is also added to the packet header.

Packet Addressing

Packet addressing is the process of assigning a destination identifier (numeric address or label) to a data block (packet) that allow it to be navigated through a data network (data routers). Each node in the network (a router) reviews the destination address and forwards the packet on to another router that will help the packet to travel towards its destination.

Packet Routing

Packet routing involves the transmission of packets through intelligent switches (called routers) that analyze the destination address of the packet and determine a path that will help the packet travel toward its destination.

Routers learn from each other about the best routes for them to select when forwarding packets toward their destination (usually paths to other routers). Routers regularly broadcast their connection information to near-by routers and they listen for connection information from connected routers. From this information, routers build information tables (called routing tables) that help them to determine the best path for them to for-ward each packet to.

Routers may forward packets towards their destination simply based on their destination address or they may look at some descriptive information about the packet. This descriptive information may include special handling instructions (called a label or tag) or priority status (such as high priority for real time voice or video signals).

Packet Control

In addition to addressing information, additional control information may be included with data packets. For example, time stamps may be included with each packet that indicates the time that the packet was created or transmitted. Priority indicators can also be included to help identify which packets (such as video or audio) should be rapidly processed and which pack-ets can take a little longer (such as a data file).

Figure 5.14 shows how blocks of data are divided into small packet sizes that can be sent through the Internet. After the data is divided into packets (envelopes shown in this example), a destination address along with some description about the contents is added to each packet (called in the packet header). As the packet enters into the Internet (routing boxes shown in this diagram), each router reviews the destination address in its routing table and determines which paths it can send the packet to so it will move further

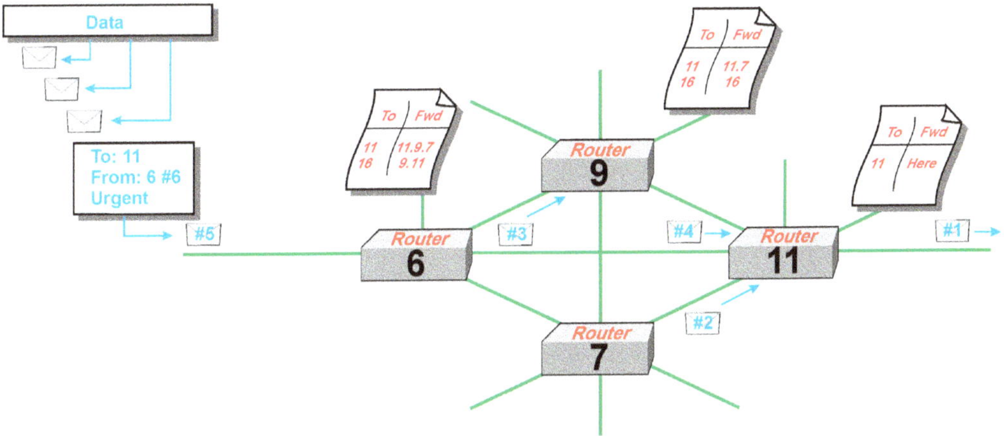

Figure 5.14, Packet Transmission

towards its destination. If a current path is busy or unavailable (such as shown for packet #3), the router can forward the packets to other routers that can forward the packet towards its destination. This example shows that because some packets will travel through different paths, packets may arrive out of sequence at their destination. When the packets arrive at their destination, they can be reassembled into proper order using the packet sequence number.

Packet Losses

Packet losses are the incomplete reception or intentional discarding of data packets as they are sent through a network. Packet data networks regularly have packet losses. If there were no packet losses, the networks would be overdesigned with excess capacity (higher network cost).

Packets may be lost due to intentional discarding due to congested switch conditions, broken line connections, or through packet corruption (such as distortion from electrical noise signal such as a lightning spike). Packet losses are usually measured by counting the number of data packets that have been lost in transmission compared to the total number of packets that have been transmitted.

Packet Congestion

Congestion is a condition that exists when the demands for service on a communications network exceed its capacity to deliver that service. To overcome network congestion, some lower priority packets may be dropped (discarded). Packet dropping is the process of discarding or not using all the packets in a transmitted through a communication processing node. When a receiving device discovers it has not received a packet (a missing sequence number), it can request that the packet be resent through the network.

Packet Corruption

Packet corruption is the changing of some of the packet data during its transmission. Packet corruption can come from a variety of sources such as poor communication line quality or momentary line loss from lightning spikes.

Figure 5.15 shows how some packets may be lost during transmission through a communications system. This example shows that several packets enter into the Internet. The packets are forwarded toward their destination as usual. Unfortunately, a lighting strike corrupts (distorts) packet 8 and it cannot be forwarded. Packet 6 is lost (discarded) when a router has exceeded its capacity to forward packets because too many were arriving at the same time. This diagram shows that the packets are serialized to allow them to be placed in correct order at the receiving end. When the receiving end determines a packet is missing in the sequence, it can request that another packet be retransmitted. If the time delivery of packets is critical (such as for packetized voice), it is common that packet retransmission requests are not performed and the lost packets simply result in distortion of the received information (such as poor audio quality).

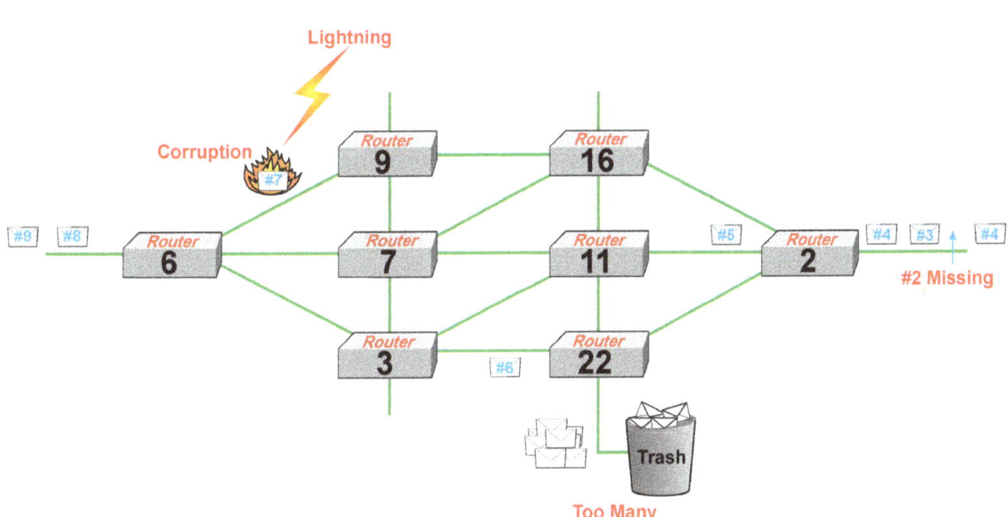

Figure 5.15, Packet Losses

Packet Timing

Packet timing is the relationship between the creation of data packets and when the information transported by the packets becomes available to use. Packet timing can very due to various delays that can occur during transmission. To overcome some of the challenges with packet timing delays, packet sequencing numbers and time stamping can be used.

Transmission Time

The time it takes for packets to be created, travel through networks, and to get decoded into its original media form can vary based on the paths the packet must travel, switching times, and packet processing times. Packets on a communication session may travel through several different connection paths on the way to their destination and the paths they take can dynamically change. Packet switching times can vary based on the type of switch (how fast it can process packets) and the amount of traffic that it receives. (congestion).

Packet Sequencing

Because packet travel times can dramatically vary, some packets may arrive out of sequence. To ensure the packets are reassembled correctly, each packet is identified with a sequence number. If the receive detects a missing sequence number (possibly a dropped packet), it may request retransmission from the sending device.

Time Stamping

To ensure media is presented to the recipient in the same relative time, time reference information, time stamps (reference time periods) are added to each packet. These time references are used to control the when the received media is presented to the user.

Packet Jitter

Another challenge for packet transmission is the random variation in packet delays (packet jitter) that can occur. If the jitter is excessive, the receiver may not be able to process the packet in enough time to present it to the user. To overcome packet jitter challenges, extra buffer time (temporary receiver storage time) may be setup.

Figure 5.16 shows how real time transmission control protocol (RTP) operates to send real time data through a packet network that may have variable transmission delays. This diagram shows that an RTP system requires that a real time signal (e.g. audio signal) be converted to digital form (digital audio) prior to transmission. This digital signal is divided into small packets. The RTP protocol is a high-level protocol and each packet of data each of the transmitted packets starts with an IP header that contains the destination address of the packet. An additional flow control protocol header is added (usually UDP protocol header) to identify the specific port the data will be routed to at it's destination. The RTP system then adds a third header (the RTP control header). The RTP system uses a precise clock to add time stamp information to each packet along with other signal recreation control information. Because the packets may have different types of compression and their recreation time can dramatically vary, the RTP protocol header uses the time stamp and other information to decode and recreate the data packet.

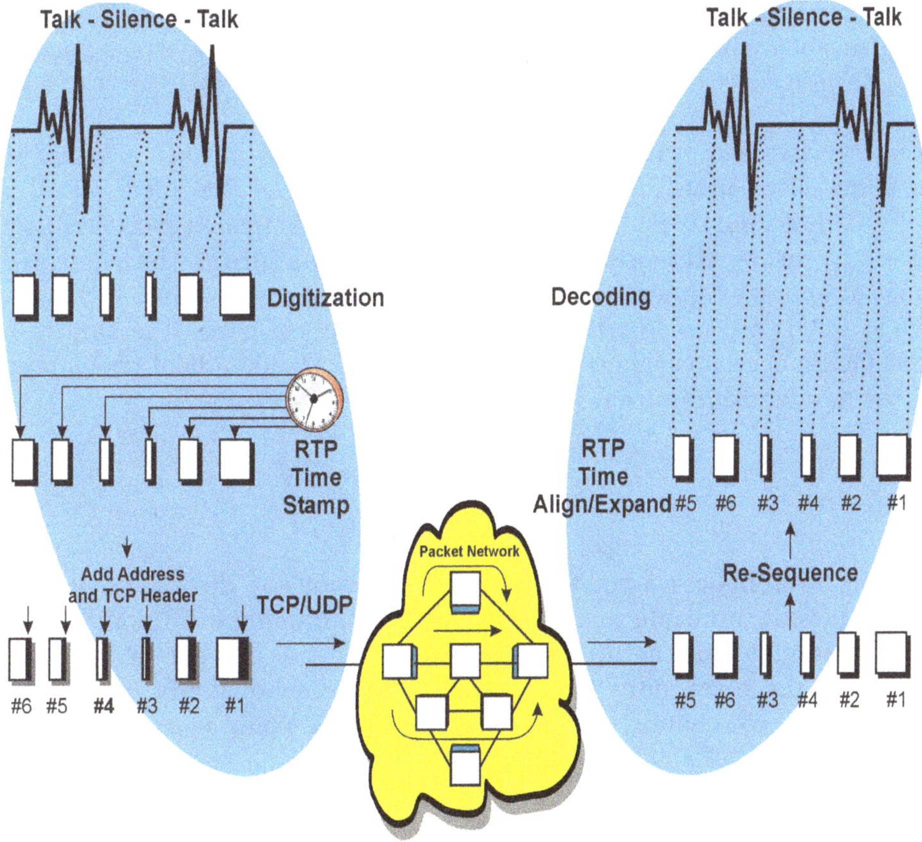

Figure 5.16, RTP

Transmission Types

Internet TV channel transmission is the process of transferring the television media from a media server or television gateway to an end customer. Internet TV channel transmission may be exclusively sent directly to specific viewer (unicast) or it may be copied and sent to multiple viewers at the same time (multicast)

Unicasting

Unicast transmission is the delivery of data to only one client within a network. Unicast transmission is typically used to describe a streaming connection from a server to a single client.

Unicast service is relatively simple to implement. Each user is given the same address to connect to when they desire to access that media (such as an IP television channel). The use of unicast transmission is not efficient when many users are receiving the same information at the same time because a separate connection for each user must be maintained. If the same media source is accessed by hundreds or thousands of users, the bandwidth to that media server will need to be hundreds or thousands of times larger than the bandwidth required for each user.

Multipoint

Multipoint systems can transfer information from one device (or point) to multiple devices (multiple receiving points). When using multipoint distribution, the sender must setup and maintain multiple unicast sessions with each user. If there are many simultaneous viewers (thousands or more), the required connection bandwidth and serving capacity can be extremely larger.

Figure 5.17 shows how Internet TV systems can deliver the same program to several users using multiple unicast (one-to-one) channels (multipoint). This example shows that each viewer is connected directly to the media server. Because each viewer is receiving 3 Mbps, the media server must have a connection that can provide 9 Mbps (3 Mbps x 3 viewers).

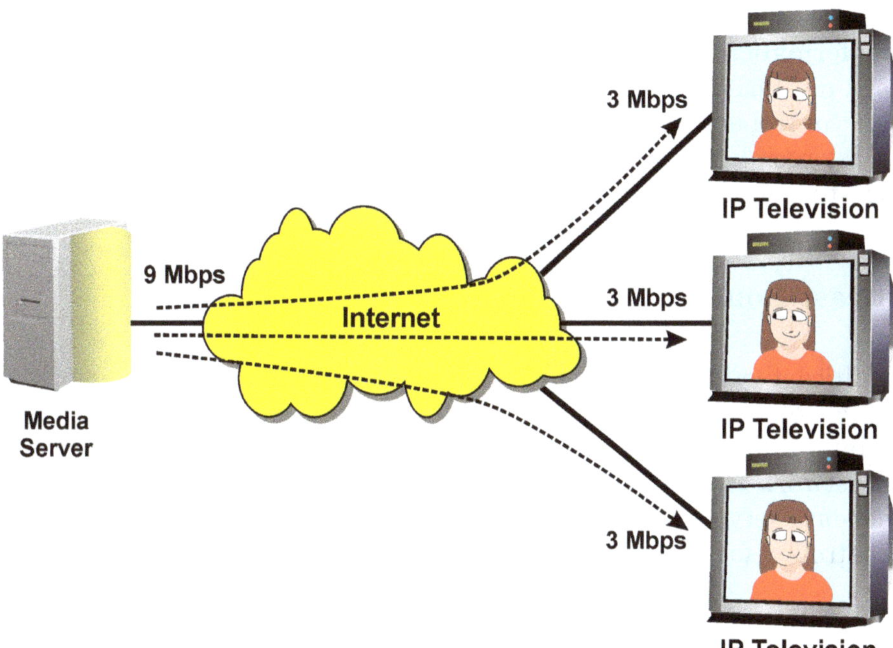

Figure 5.17, Internet TV Multipoint Transmission

Multicasting

Multicast transmission is a one-to-many media delivery process that sends a single message or information transmission that contains an address (code) that is designated to allow multiple distribution nodes in a network (e.g. routers) to receive and retransmit the same signal to multiple receivers. As a multicast signal travels through a communication network, it is copied at nodes within the network for distribution to other nodes within the network. Multicast systems form distribution trees of information. Nodes (e.g. routers) that copy the information form the branches of the tree.

Group Addressing

The use of multicast transmission can be much more efficient when the same information is sent to many users at the same time. The implementation of a multicast systems is generally more complex than unicast systems as more control is required to add and remove members of multicast groups. Multicast recipients generally submit requests to a nearby node within a multicast network to join as part of an active multicast session.

Multicast Routers

For multicast systems to operate, nodes (routers) within the network must be capable of multicast sessions. Because of the complexity and cost issues, many Internet routers do not implement multicast transmission. If the multicast network is controlled by a single company (such as a DSL or cable modem data service provider), all the nodes within the network can be setup and controlled for multicast transmission.

Mirror Sites

A mirror site is a computer server that contains duplicate data or can copy and redistribute streams of another web server. Mirror sites can be used to process communication traffic to local or regional areas as each mirror site contains the same information as the other mirror site. Because routers within the Internet cannot be setup for multicast operation, mirror sites may perform a similar function as multicast routers.

Figure 5.18 shows how an Internet TV system can distribute information through the Internet. This example shows that end users who are watching a movie that is initially supplied by central media center that is located a significant from the first user who requests the program. When the first movie watcher requests the movie, it is streamed from the central media streaming server directly to the end viewer. When another user requests to connect to the media, the central media server determines that the end users can be better served by connecting to another media streaming sever that is part of the distribution network and the end users are connected to the media server that is closer to them. As additional users request connections to the same media source, the process continues to find and distribute media to other streaming servers that are closer to the viewers.

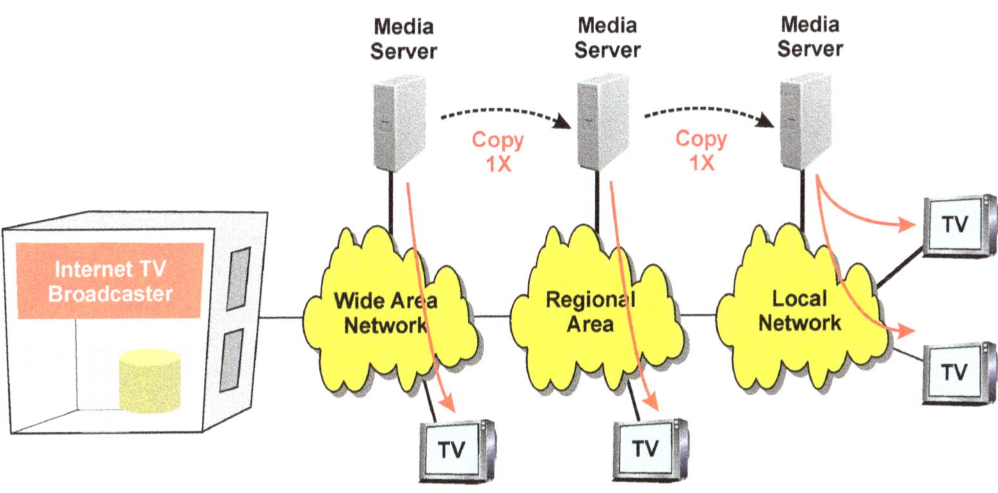

Figure 5.18, Internet TV Multicast Transmission

Peercasting (Gridcasting)

Peercasting is the process of transmitting media channels to a number of users through the use of nodes (peers) that receive and redistribute (copying media channels) as they progress through a network. The use of peercasting systems can dramatically reduce the required bandwidth for content provider as users (peers) in the network receive and forward the media streams.

Peer Relaying

Peercasting systems setup users (peers) to receive and retransmit (relay) media streams to one or more peers. Peercasting systems can be complicated to manage as peers may randomly join and leave the streaming system so new connections may need to be setup. The available bandwidth for retransmission (uplinks) may be limited and more limited than downlinks that can make relaying connections unstable.

Striping

Peercasting systems may divide a received stream into several substreams (striping). This reduces the necessary bandwidth for retransmission. Each subsstream is uniquely identified, prioritized, and coded (error protected). Multiple substreams are sent to another peer where they are combined to produce the original stream.

Peercasting Protocols

Peercasting systems use a set of protocols to identify, setup, and manage multiple peercasting streams. Intelligent peercasting systems dynamically control the sources and the media quantities (a portion of the media stream) along with the source of peer connections. Peers may connect to multiple relay sources and mange a list of alternative relay sources in the event of loss of media streams.

Figure 5.19 shows how a peercasting system can operate. This example shows that a peercasting system retransmits signals from one receiver to other receivers. In this peercasting system, end user devices receive, readdresses, and retransmit received packets towards a new destination device.

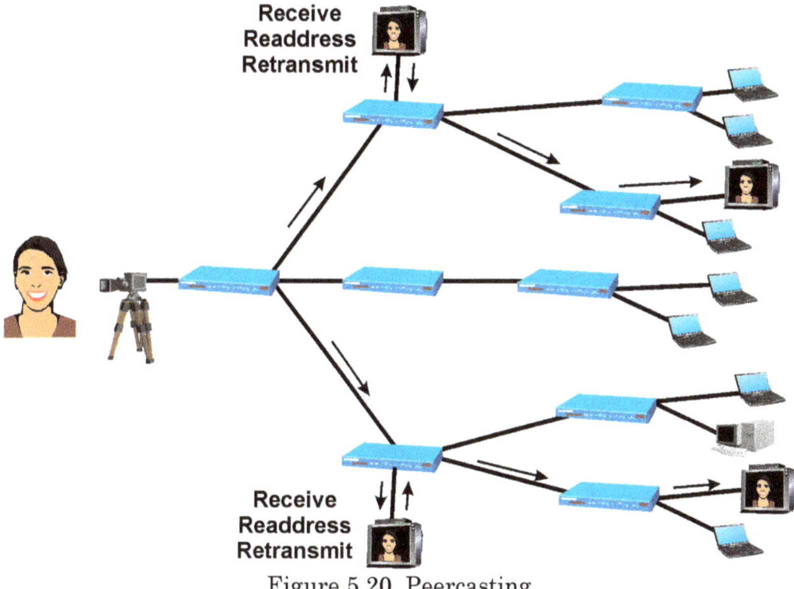

Figure 5.20, Peercasting

Packet Reception

Packet reception is the process of identifying and gathering packets with the correct destination address and routing them to the appropriate function or service within the receiving device (via the port number on the IP address).

Demultiplexing

Demultiplexing is a process that separates individual channels from a common transport or transmission channel.

Packet Buffering

Packet buffering is the process of temporarily storing (buffering) packets during the transmission of information to create a reserve of packets that can be used during packet transmission delays or retransmission requests. While a packet buffer is commonly located in the receiving device, a packet buffer may also be used in the sending device to allow the rapid selection and retransmission of packets when they are requested by the receiving device.

Packet buffering is commonly used in Internet TV television systems to overcome the transmission delays and packet losses that occur when viewing IP television signals.

A packet buffer receives and adds small amounts of delay to packets so that all the packets appear to have been received without varying delays. The amount of packet buffering for IP television systems can vary from tenths of a second to tens of seconds.

Retransmission Requests

Retransmission is a method of network error control in which hosts receiving messages acknowledge the receipt of correct messages and either do not acknowledge, or acknowledge in the negative, the receipt of incorrect messages. The lack of acknowledgment, or receipt of negative acknowledgment, is an indication to the sending host that it should transmit the failed message again.

Figure 5.20 shows how packet buffering can be used to reduce the effects of packet delays and packet loss for streaming media systems. This diagram shows that during the transmission of packets from the media server to the viewer, some of the packet transmission time varies (jitter) and some of the packets are lost during transmission. The packet buffer temporarily stores data before providing it to the media player. This provides the time necessary to time synchronize the packets and to request and replace packets that have been lost during transmission.

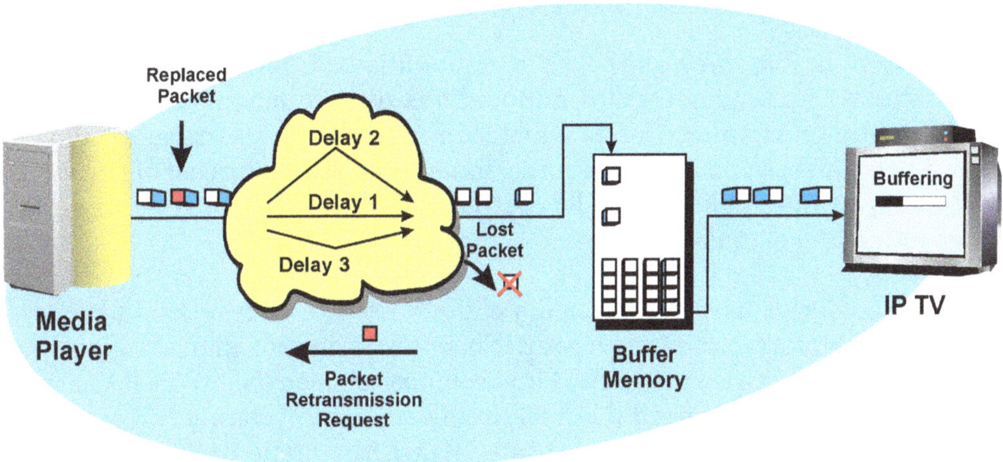

Figure 5.21, Packet Buffering

Rendering

Rendering is the process of converting media into a form that a human can view, hear or sense. An example of rendering is the conversion of a data file into an image that is displayed on a computer monitor.

Video Rendering

Video rendering is the conversion of digital media into a signal format that can be displayed on viewing devices. The signal formats may include analog composite video (NTSC or PAL), analog component video, digital video (HDMI), or other formats.

Audio Rendering

Analog rendering is the conversion of digital media into a signal format that can be played on listening devices. The signal formats may include analog audio (mono or stereo), digital audio (MP2, MP3, AAC), or other formats.

RF Output

Some adapters may process the video and audio so it is available as an RF TV channel. The rendered video and audio is used to modulate a TV channels (usually on channel 3 or 4) which can be viewed on a standard television. Each conversion of a signal tends to increase the distortion of the video and audio so the quality of an RF output may not be as good as separate video and audio signals.

Figure 5.21 shows how digital media signals need to be rendered (converted) into other forms for the viewer. This unit converts digital video into HDMI (the video portion of HDMI) and composite video (NTSC or PAL). The composite video is converted to an RF frequency for TV channels 3 or 4. The digital audio signals are converted into HDMI (the audio portion of HDMI) and to analog audio.

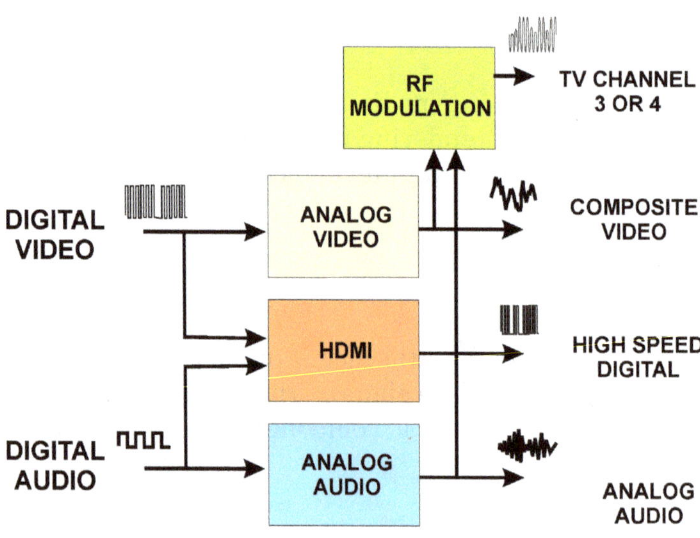

Figure 5.22, Internet TV Rendering

Internet TV Systems

Internet TV systems are the combinations of equipment, software and processes that are used to gather programs from various sources, organize them into channels and distribute them through the public Internet. Internet TV systems allow people to select and view programs on one or more types of viewing devices. The key parts of an Internet TV system include a contribution network, headend, distribution system and viewing devices.

Internet TV platforms are combinations of system parts that enable online TV and movie providers to gather, schedule, bill, and deliver programs through the Internet. While Internet TV platforms contain the system parts described in this chapter (transport, transcoding, streaming), they tend to remove the technical requirements from the production, distribution, and promotion functions of TV and movie producers.

Contribution Network

Contribution networks are composed of communication connections that allow Internet TV systems to obtain content. These connections can be a mixture of dedicated lines (satellite connections, leased lines) or shared networks (virtual connections, Internet). Content sources for Internet TV systems can include a mix of traditional television content sources and new media sources. Traditional content sources include network TV, syndicates (shared TV program sources), movies (through content aggregators), and local programming (news and sports). New media sources include independent programming (companies, organizations), community content (social media), and personal media channels.

Headend

Headends are the network components that are used to receive, mange, process and transmit (broadcast) digital media content to television network users. Headends can range from the simple devices that are used to convert analog video to digital form for transmission, to the systems used for the selection (switching), interactive control and management of digital content.

Distribution System

Internet TV systems can use a combination of connections and equipment to efficiently transfer media programs the end customers' viewing devices. Key distributions system parts can be divided into core network, access network and home media network parts. Internet TV distribution networks may contain media hubs or distribution points that rebroadcast (multicast) the same packets to people who are watching the same programs.

Viewing Devices

There are many types of devices that can be used to view Internet TV programs. These devices can have a wide variety of capabilities, use multiple types of communication protocols, have the ability to hold and process downloaded software programs (applications), and access multiple types of services. The Internet TV operator must be able to identify, configure and control the devices connected to its system.

Figure 6.1 shows a sample Internet TV system. This diagram shows that the Internet TV system gathers content from a variety of sources including network feeds, stored media, communication links and live studio sources. The headend converts the media sources into a form that can be managed and distributed. The asset management system stores, moves and sends (playout) the media at scheduled times. The distribution system simultaneously transfers multiple channels to users who are connected to the Internet TV system. Users can view Internet TV programming on multiple types of devices, including standard television (using an Internet TV set top box), gaming consoles, media players, multimedia computers, mobile phones and other types of devices that can receive and display streaming media.

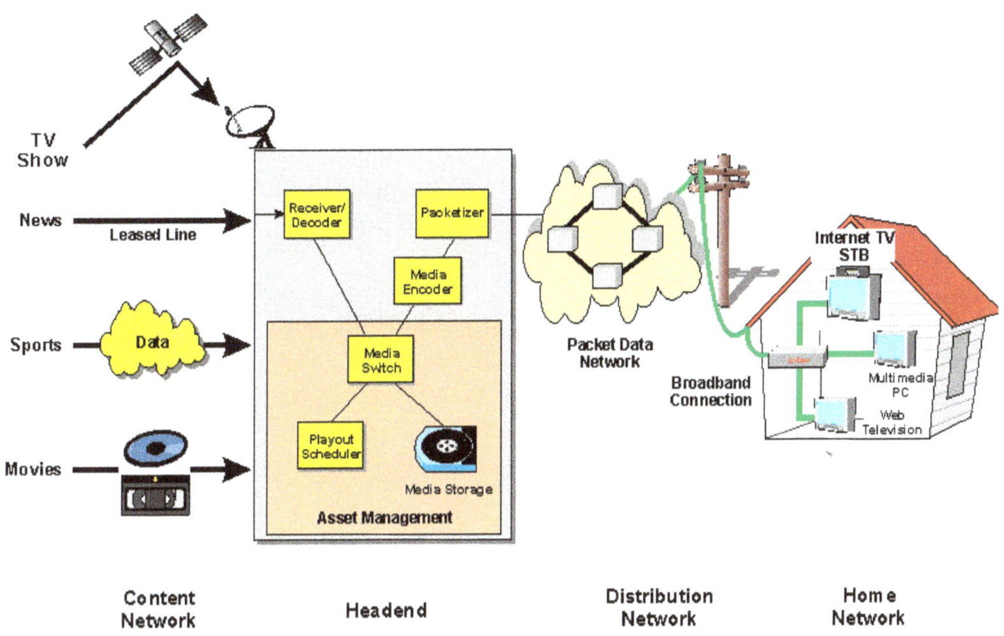

Figure 6.1, Internet TV System

Contribution Network

Internet TV systems can use various types of connections, including contribution networks, to connect contribution sources (media programs) to content management systems. Internet TV systems can receive content from multiple sources through connections that range from dedicated high-speed fiber optic connections (fast and generally high cost) to stored media delivery systems (relatively slow and low cost). Content sources include program networks, content aggregators and a variety of other government, education and public sources.

Connection Types

Internet TV content distribution network connection types include satellite connections, leased lines, virtual networks, microwave, mobile data and public data networks (the Internet).

Satellite communication systems use orbiting satellites to relay communications signals from one station to many others. The cost of launching and maintaining satellites in space can be high (over $200 million each). Because satellite systems provide signal coverage to wide geographic areas, the high cost of satellites can be shared by many broadcasting companies. This allows an Internet TV system operator to purchase the rights to receive and redistribute signals from a satellite.

Leased lines are telecommunication lines or links that have part or all of their transmission capacity reserved for the exclusive use of a single customer or company. Leased lines often come with a guaranteed level of performance for connections between two points. In general, as the length of a leased line connection increases, so does the cost.

Virtual private networks (VPNs) are private communication path(s) that transfer data or information through one or more data networks that are dedicated between two or more points. VPN connections allow data to safely and privately pass over public networks (such as the Internet) by protecting (encrypting) information that travels through the network.

A microwave link uses microwave frequencies (above 1 GHz) for line of sight radio communications (20 to 30 miles) between two directional antennas. Each microwave link transceiver usually offers a standard connection to communication networks, such as a T1/E1 or DS3 connection line. This use of microwave links eliminates the need to install cables between communication equipment. Microwave links may be licensed (filed and protected by government agencies), or unlicensed (through the use of low power within unlicensed regulatory limits). Microwave links are commonly used by TV systems to connection remote devices or locations such as a mobile news truck or a helicopter feed.

Mobile data is the transmission of digital information through a wireless network where the communication equipment can move or be located over a relatively wide geographic area. The term mobile data is typically applied to the combination of radio transmission devices and computing devices (computer electronic assemblies) that can transmit data through a mobile communication system (such as a wireless data system or cellular network).

TV systems may capture (receive) and retransmit other TV broadcasted signals such as local television channels. To do this, an off-air receiver is setup to select and convert (decode) the channel so it can be rebroadcasted.

The Internet can be cost-effectively used to privately transfer programs through the use of encryption. The programs can be transferred at the same time they are rebroadcasted (streaming), or downloaded for broadcasting at a later time.

In additional to gathering content through communication links, content may be gathered through the use of stored media. Examples of stored media include magnetic tapes (VHS or Beta), optical disks (CD or DVDs) and memory sticks.

Program Metadata

When content is delivered through a content network, its descriptive information (metadata) is sent along with it. The metadata information may be embedded within the media file(s), or it may be sent as separate data files. Some of its descriptive data may include text that is used for closed captioning compliance.

Figure 6.2 shows a contribution network that is used with an Internet TV system. This example shows that programming gathered through a contribution network can come from a variety of sources, including satellite connections, leased lines, virtual networks, microwave links, mobile data, public data networks (the Internet) and stored media (tapes and DVDs).

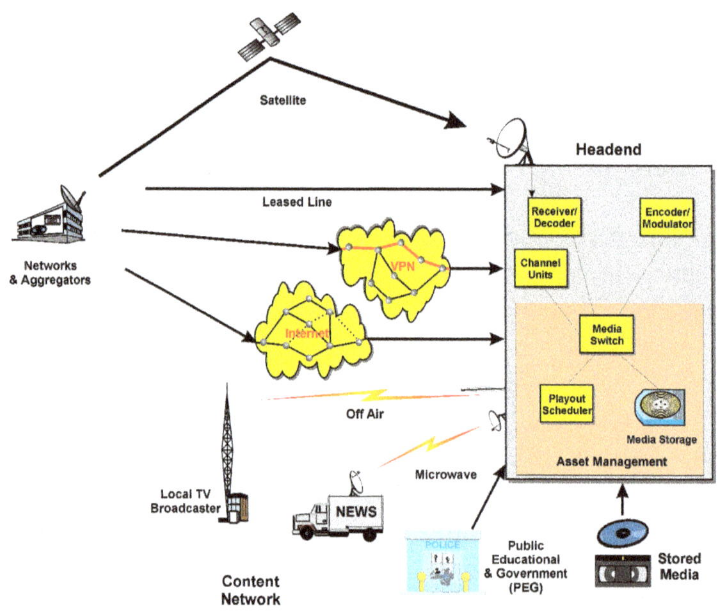

Figure 6.2, Internet TV Contribution Network

Program Transfer Scheduling

Program transfer scheduling is the set up and management of times and connection types that are used to transport media within an Internet TV system. Internet TV systems need to obtain programs before they are scheduled for broadcasting, although not too early as the systems have limited amounts of storage resources.

Storage Management

Internet TV systems have a limited amount of media storage available for television programs, so program transfer is typically scheduled a short time (possibly several days) before it scheduled broadcast within the system.

Transfer Cost

The cost of transferring content can vary based on the connection type (satellite versus Internet) and the data transfer speed. In general, as the data transfer speed increases, so does the data transfer cost. The scheduling of program transfer during low network capacity usage periods, and at lower speeds, can result in significantly reduced transfer costs.

Figure 6.3 shows how an Internet TV system may use transfer scheduling to obtain programs reliably and cost-effectively. This example shows that the IPTV system may select multiple connection types and transfer speeds depending on the program type (live versus scheduled) and transfer cost.

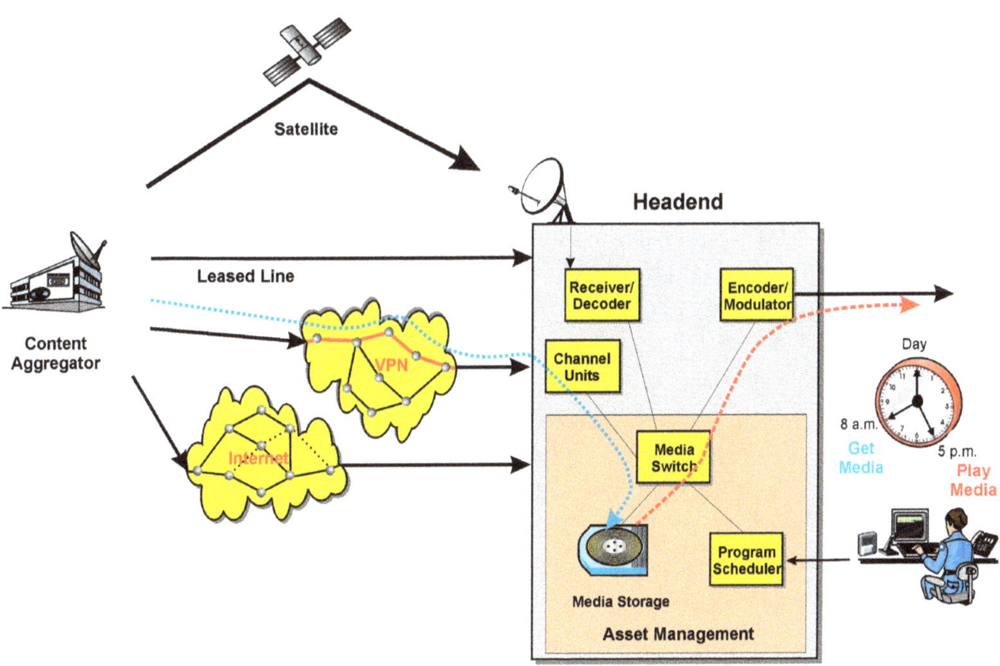

Figure 6.3, Internet TV Program Transfer Scheduling

Headend

The headend is the master distribution center of an Internet TV system where incoming television signals from video sources (off air receivers, DBS satellites, local studios and video players) are received, amplified and remodulated onto TV channels for transmission into the Internet TV distribution system.

Receivers

The incoming signals for headend systems include satellite receivers, off-air receivers and other types of transmission links. The signals are received (selected) and processed using channel decoders.

Media Decoders

Headends commonly use integrated receiver devices that combine multiple receiver, decoding and decryption functions into one assembly. After the headend receives, separates and converts incoming signals into new formats, the signals are selected and encoded so they can be retransmitted (or stored) in the IPTV network. These signals are encoded, converted into packets and sent into IPTV packet distribution systems.

Switching System

A switching system may be used to allow the Internet TV system operator to select the input source that will be connected to the broadcasting or storage systems. For example, if an Internet TV provider is receiving 24 channels from a satellite, but only wants to rebroadcast one of the channels, the switcher selects the channel and connects it to the broadcasting (streaming) system.

Media Encoders

Internet TV systems use encoders to convert media into a format that can be transmitted through the Internet. An encoder may be able to processes one or more input signals into one or more formats (multiple streams). One stream format may be used for Internet TV set top boxes, while another is used for mobile phones, and another for tablets. When media is transformed from one encoded format into another, it is called transcoding.

Figure 6.4 shows a diagram of a simple headend system. This diagram shows that the headend gathers programming sources, decodes, selects and retransmits video programming to the Internet TV distribution network. The video sources to the headend typically include satellite signals, off air receivers, microwave connections and other video feed signals. The video sources are scrambled to prevent unauthorized viewing before being sent to the cable distribution system. The headend receives, decodes and decrypts these channels. This example shows that the programs that will be broad-

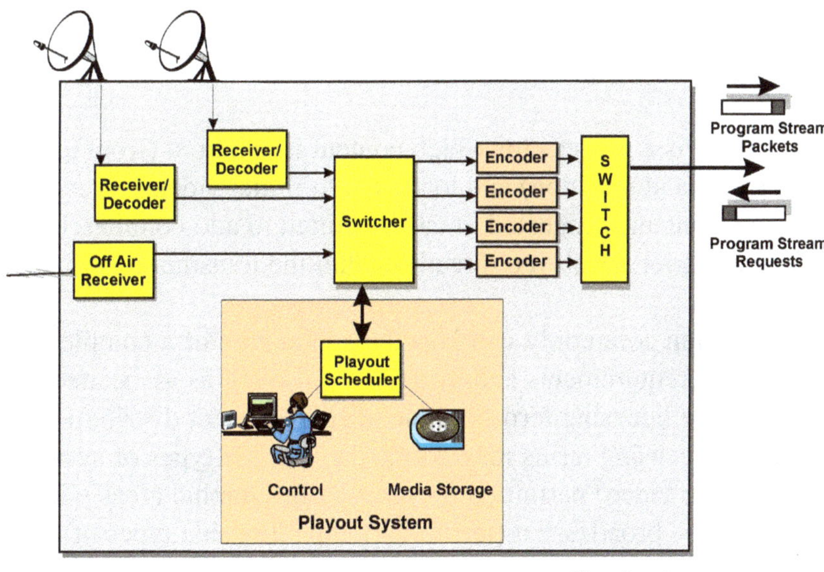

Figure 6.4, Internet TV Headend System

casted are supplied to encoders that produce Internet TV program streams. The programs are sent into the distribution network to distribution points (media servers) or directly to end user devices (Internet set top boxes).

Content Management System (CMS)

An Internet TV system uses a content management system to identify, store and organize the distributing content (media) and software programs. Content assets are managed by workflow systems. Workflow management for television systems involves content acquisition, metadata management, asset storage, playout scheduling, content processing, ad insertion and distribution control.

Content Acquisition

Content assets are acquired or created. Content acquisition involves gathering content from networks, aggregators and other sources. After content is acquired (or during the content transfer), content is ingested (adapted and stored) into the asset management system.

Ingesting content is a process for which content is acquired (from a satellite downlink or a data connection) and loaded onto initial video servers (ingest servers). Once content is ingested, it can be edited to add commercials, migrated to a playout server, or played directly within the transmission chain.

Content acquisition commonly involves the application of a complex set of content licensing requirements and restrictions, as well as associated costs, to the content. These licensing terms are included in content distribution agreements. Content licensing terms may define the specific types of systems (cable, Internet or mobile video) permitted for use, the geographic areas within which the content may be broadcasted (territories), the allowable types of viewers (residential or commercial), and specific usage limitations (such as the number of times a program can be broadcasted in a month). The content acquisition system is linked to a billing system to calculate the royalties and other costs for the media.

Metadata Management

Each asset is given an identification code, descriptive data (metadata), and the licensing usage terms and costs that are associated with the asset. Metadata management is the process of identifying, describing and applying rules to the descriptive portions (metadata) of content assets.

Metadata descriptions and formats can vary so metadata may be normalized. Metadata normalization is the adjustment of metadata elements into standard terms and formats to allow for more reliable organization, selection and presentation of program descriptive elements. For example, the category thriller can be interpreted to mean different things to different people.

Metadata may be used to create or supplement an electronic programming guide (EPG). An EPG is an interface (portal) that allows a customer to preview and select from a possible list of available content media. EPG features can vary, and may include simple program selection to interactive filters that dynamically allow the user to filter through program guides by theme, time period or other criteria.

Content Storage

Assets are transferred into short-term or long-term storage systems that allow for program retrieval as needed. Asset management systems commonly use several types of storage devices that have varying access types, storage and transfer capabilities. Analog television storage systems may include tape cartridge (magnetic tape) storage. Digital storage systems may include magnetic tape, removable and fixed disks and electronic memory. Some of the different types of storage systems include cache storage (high speed immediate access), online storage, nearline storage and offline storage.

Online storage is a device or system that stores data that is directly and immediately accessible by other devices or systems. Online storage types can vary from disk drives to electronic memory modules. Media may be moved from one type of online storage system to another type of online storage system (such as a disk drive), to yet another type of online storage (such as electronic memory) that would allow for rapid access and caching. Caching is the process by which information is moved to a temporary storage area to assist in the processing or future transfer of information to other parts of a processor or system.

Nearline storage is a device or system that stores data or information that is accessible with some connection set up processes and/or delays. The requirement to find and/or set up a connection to media or information on a nearline storage system is relatively small. Data or media that is scheduled to be transmitted (broadcasted) may be moved to nearline storage before it is moved to an online storage system.

Offline storage is a device or system that stores data or information that is not immediately accessible. Media in offline storage systems must be located and set up in order for connection or transfer to be obtained. Examples of offline storage systems include storage tapes and removable disks.

Media Encoding

Media encoding is the conversion (encoding) of media into forms that are suitable for transmission (via radio broadcast channels or mobile telephones). Media encoding is commonly performed before the media is broadcasted.

Content encoding may include media compression (reducing bandwidth), transmission coding (adapting for the transmission channel), and channel coding (adding control commands for specific channels).

When media is converted from one format to another, it is called transcoding. An example of transcoding is the conversion of MPEG-2 compressed signals into MPEG-4 AVC coded signals.

Figure 6.5 shows a content management system. This diagrams shows that the basic functions for a digital asset management system include ingestion, cataloging and distribution. This example shows that content may be ingested from a variety of sources, including live feeds, and analog and digital stored media formats. New content may also be created through the editing and production of existing assets. The asset manager coordinates the storage and retrieval of media into online (cache), nearline and offline repositories, and coordinates the conversion (transcoding) of media into other formats (such as MPEG). This example shows that the asset manager creates and uses catalog information to allow the system and users to find, organize and obtain media. The distribution portion is responsible for transferring the assets to broadcast channels (real time), other storage systems (time delayed) and/or to Internet streams.

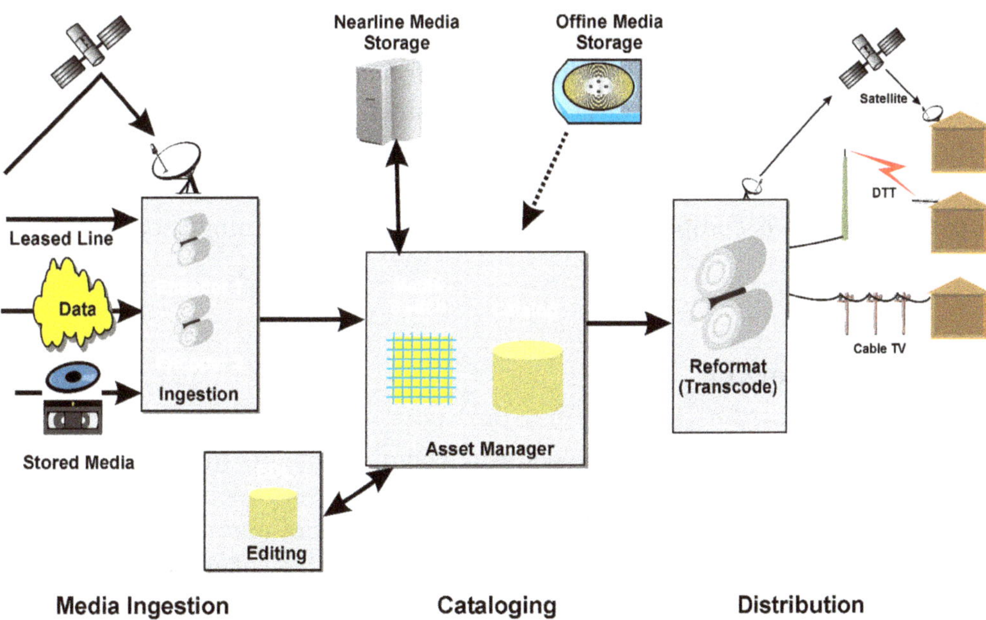

Figure 6.5, Content Management System

Playout System

A playout system is a combination of devices and software that can initiate, manage and terminate the streaming or transferring of media to users or distributors at predetermined time schedules (such as time slots on linear television channels). Playout systems may also setup schedules (program bookings) that can be used to retrieve the assets from storage shortly before they are to be broadcasted to viewers.

Playout systems may be capable of selecting primary and secondary events. Primary events are the programs that will be broadcasted, and secondary events are media items that will be combined or used with primary events. Examples of secondary events include logo insertion, text crawls (scrolling text), voice over (narrative audio clips) and special effects (such as a squeeze back).

Because the number of channels and programs is increasing, broadcasters may use playout automation to reduce the effort (workload) required to set up playout schedules. Playout automation is the process of using a system that has established rules or procedures, which allows for the streaming or transferring of media to a user or distributor at a predetermined time, or when specific criteria have been met (such as user registration and payment).

A playout system is composed of a scheduling server, streaming servers and media gateways.

Scheduling Server

A scheduling server is used to select and assign programs (digital assets) to time slots on linear television channels. Scheduling servers create and manage playlists that can initiate the automatic playout of media during scheduled broadcast times, or alert operators to manually setup and start the playout of media programs (taps or DVDs).

Playlist

The scheduling server stores the event time (when the program is scheduled to start playing) and the queuing time (a time that allows the media server to find and setup the media that will be broadcasted or played).

Streaming Servers

Streaming servers are storage devices that hold files or programs that will be transferred (broadcasted) to viewers. The playout system identifies which program files are ready for transfer, and the methods and devices that will be used to stream the media. Media servers may store the same program in multiple formats (QVGA for mobile and SD for standard televisions).

Media Gateways

Media gateways are devices that receive media from one source (such as a live broadcast feed) and adapt the media to one or more formats that can be distributed through the broadcast system. The playout system identifies the media gateway, as well as which streams will be selected and which formats the gateway should provide to the broadcast system.

Figure 6.6 shows a functional diagram of an Internet TV playout system. This system includes a scheduling server, a media gateway and a streaming server. The scheduling server coordinates the selection and connection of media to viewers from either the media gateway or the streaming server (the playout list). When programs are scheduled to be broadcasted from the media gateway, the scheduling server identifies the receiving source (satellite channel), the streaming parameters (media formats), and the streaming server configuration. The media may originate from a media server (stored media) or from a streaming source (such as a live feed).

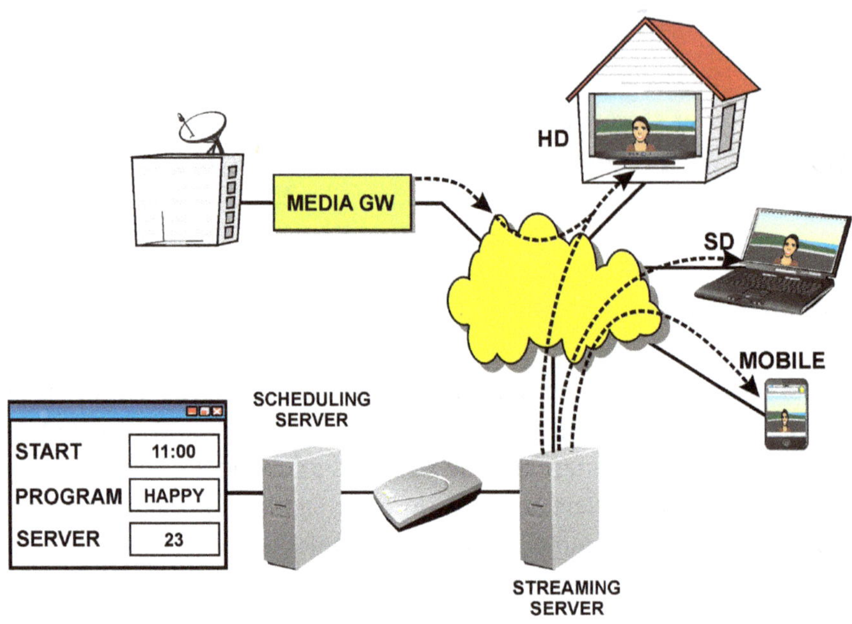

Figure 6.6, Television Playout System

Ad Insertion

Ad insertion is the process of splicing or replacing a portion of the media that appears within a program with promotional messages (commercials). For broadcasting systems, commercials are typically inserted on a national or geographic basis as determined by the distribution network. For IP television systems, ad inserts can be directed to specific users based on the viewer's profile.

Insertion Opportunities (Avails)

An 'avail' is the time slot within which an advertisement is placed. Avail time periods usually are available in standard lengths of 10, 20, 30 or 40 seconds. Through the use of addressable advertising, which may provide access to hundreds of thousands of ads with different time lengths, it is possible for numerous different advertisements to be displayed to different audiences using a single avail.

Cue Tones

Cue tones are signals that are embedded within or sent along with media as an indication that an action or event is about to happen. Cue tones can be simple event signals, or they can contain additional information about the event that is about to occur. An example of a cue tone is a signal in a television program that indicates that a time period for a commercial will occur and how long the time period will last.

An analog cue tone is an audio sequence (such as DTMF tones) that indicates a time period that will be available ('avail') for the insertion of another media program (a commercial).

Ad Splicer

An advertising splicer is a device that selects from two or more media program inputs to produce one media output. Ad splicers receive cueing messages (get ready) and splice commands (switch now) to identify when and which media programs will be spliced.

Insertion Channels

Television commercials are transferred by an insertion channel (a secondary channel) that will replace (switch with) a primary channel (the broadcast TV channel).

Analog Splicing

Analog splicing is the process of transferring the analog video signal from one channel to another channel.

Digital Splicing

Digital program insertion is the process of splicing media segments or programs together. Digital media is typically composed of key frames and difference pictures that compose a group of pictures (GOP). The splicing of digital media is more complex than the splicing of analog media that has picture information in each frame, which allows direct frame to frame splicing.

Figure 6.7 shows how an ad insertion system works in an Internet TV network. This diagram shows that the program media is received and a cue tone indicates the beginning of an advertising spot. When the incoming media is received by the splicer/remultiplexer, it informs the ad server that an advertising media clip is required. The ad server provides this media to the splicer which splices (attaches) each ad to the appropriate media stream. The resulting media stream with the new ad is sent to the viewers in the distribution system.

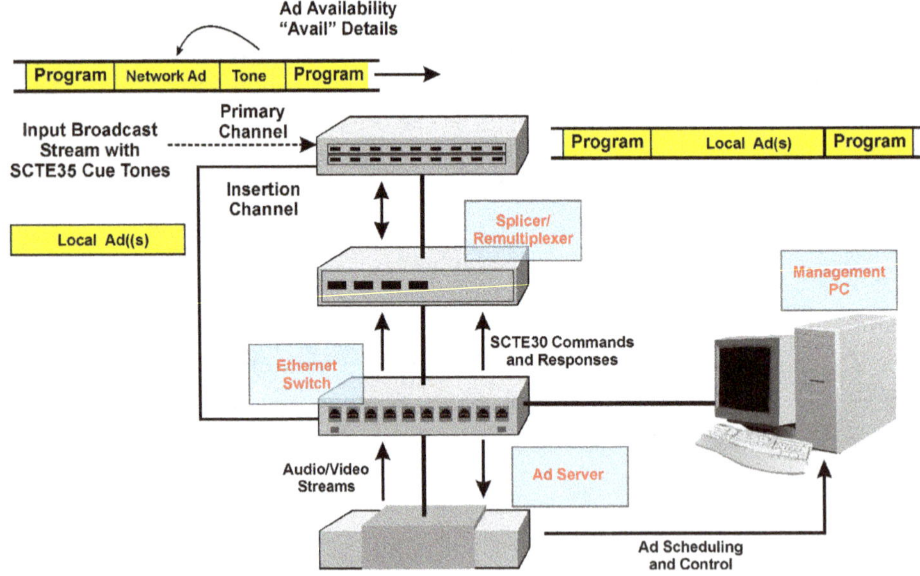

Figure 6.7, Television Ad Splicer

Distribution Network

The distribution network is the part of an Internet TV system that connects the headend of the system (video and media sources) to the customer's location. Internet TV signals are transmitted over an Internet broadband connection to the subscriber's home. Internet TV distribution systems may use a combination of media sources (gateways, media servers) and core distribution networks with caching servers. Internet TV distribution systems may transfer through multiple types of access networks and be distributed within a home media network.

Content Sources

The content sources that feed distribution systems include media servers, streaming servers and streaming gateways. Media sources may distribute their content using a combination of multipoint (many connections), distributed caching and multicast methods (media copied and redistributed in routers).

Core Network

The core network primarily provides interconnection and transfer between the media sources and the access networks. Core networks in Internet systems are commonly set up as ring networks that have automatic recovery. A ring network topology is used to enable the creation of a backup distribution path in the event of a connection loss.

Internet TV distribution systems commonly locate caching servers and media servers throughout the distribution network to temporarily store popular television content. This allows for the supply of popular content (such as sports programs) during and shortly after the program has been broadcasted from local media servers.

Access Networks

An access network is a portion of a communication network (such as the public switched telephone network) that allows individual subscribers or devices to connect to the core network. Common access network types that are used for Internet include DSL, cable television, optical networks and broadband wireless.

The quality and performance of Internet TV services can be affected by the available bandwidth and delays on access networks. While the Internet TV provider may not be able to control the access network, monitoring (available bandwidth) and understanding the effects of access network transmission can help to solve trouble reports.

Home Media Servers (HMS)

A home media server is a storage device that is located in a building or near-by area that may allow devices within the home to obtain and store media content. Home media servers may be accessible by an Internet TV provider for the storage of popular content. This content may be pre-loaded (pushed) to the HMS before the viewer is aware that the programs are available (such as popular movies or TV programs). The implementation of a home media server can allow for much higher quality of service rates, as there are no access bandwidth challenges when the viewer obtains programs directly from the HMS instead of the Internet TV system.

Figure 6.8 shows how an Internet TV distribution system can be divided into core network, access network and home network parts. The content may originate from a streaming server, streaming gateway, or media server (download) at the Internet TV headend. The TV channel content passes through the core network, and then transfers through an access network and a home network, where it can be received by various types of viewing devices. The Internet TV system may locate mirror sites or caching servers which may temporarily store media that may be accessed often to reduce the need for viewers to always directly connect to the Internet TV headend. This example shows a caching server that is located near an access network connection. A home media server may also be used for the temporary storage of content.

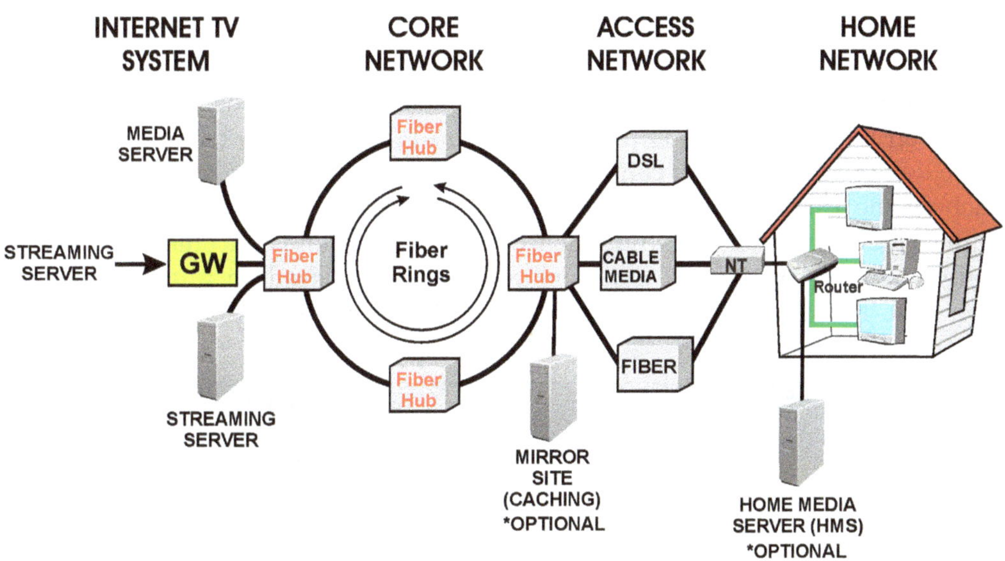

Figure 6.8, Internet TV Distribution Systems

Home Media Network

Home multimedia networks (HMNs) are the combination of equipment and software used to transfer data and other media within a customer's facility, home or personal area. A home multimedia network is used for media devices such as digital televisions, computers and audio visual equipment to transfer media to one another, and to other networks, through the use of wide area network connections. HMN systems may use wired Ethernet, wireless LAN, electrical power lines, telephone lines, coaxial cables or optical connections.

Home Multimedia Service Needs

The communication requirements for multimedia networks in the home are based on the types and amounts of applications used, as well as the times during which the usage occurs. The typical types of applications used in the home include telephone, Internet access, television, interactive video and media streaming.

Figure 6.9 shows some of the types of communication devices used in a home and their estimated data transmission requirements. This table shows that some devices may require connections through a gateway to other networks, such as the Internet or a television system. This table also shows that the highest consumption of bandwidth occurs from television channels, especially when simultaneous HDTV channels are accessed on multiple television sets. This figure suggests that a total home media capacity of 70 Mbps

Service	Bandwidth	Number of Devices	Bandwidth Residential Gateway
TV	2 to 20 Mbps	3	2 to 54 Mbps
Digital Video Recorder (DVR)	2 to 20 Mbps	1	0
Home Theater	1 to 6 Mbps * Audio	1 System	0
Internet Browsing	1 to 2 Mbps	1 to 5	1 to 10 Mbps
Printer	0.5 to 1 Mbps	1 to 5	0
Digital Imaging	1 to 20 Mbps	1 to 3	0
Digital Telephone	0.2 Mbps	1 to 5	0.2 to 1 Mbps
Online Gaming	0.2 to 1 Mbps	1-3	0.2 to 3 Mbps
Video Capturing	0.1 to 1 Mbps	1-10 * Security Cameras	0
Portable Audio	0.1 to 20 Mbps	1 to 3	0
Total	70 Mbps to 100 Mbps		2 to 60 Mbps+

Figure 6.9, Home Media Services Bandwidth Requirements

to 100 Mbps is required to simultaneously provide for all devices within a home, and a residential gateway must have broadband capability of 50+ Mbps.

Home Media Network System Types

Home network systems have transitioned from low speed data, simple command and control systems to high-speed multimedia networks along with the ability to transfer a variety of media types that have different transmission and management requirements. Each of the applications that operate through a home media network can have different communication requirements that typically include a maximum data transmission rate, continuous or bursty transmission, packet delay and jitter and error tolerance. The HMN system may manage these connections using a mix of protocols that can define and manage quality of service (QoS). Transmission medium types for home distribution include wired Ethernet (data cable), wireless, powerline, phoneline. Coaxial and optical cables.

Wired LAN

Wired LAN systems use cables to connect routers and communication devices. These cables can be composed of twisted pairs of wires or optical fibers. Wired LAN data transmission rates vary from 10 Mbps to more than 1 Gbps. While wired Ethernet systems offer high data throughput and reliability, many homes do not have dedicated wiring installed for Ethernet LAN networks and, for the homes that do have data networks, the outlets are often located near computers rather than near televisions.

Wireless LAN

Multimedia signals (such as television and music) can be converted into wireless local area network (WLAN) packet data format and distributed through the home or business by wireless signals. Wi-Fi distribution is important because it's an easy and efficient way to get digital multimedia information where it is needed without the addition of new wires.

WLAN networks were not initially designed specifically for multimedia. In the mid 2000s, several new WLAN standards were created to enable and ensure different types of quality of service (QoS) over WLAN. Some versions of the 802.11 (such as 802.11n) include the ability to apply a quality of service (QoS) to the distributed signals, giving priority to time sensitive information (such as video and audio), to ensure that it can get through before non-time sensitive information (such as web browsing).

Electrical Power Line Carrier

Electrical power line carrier systems allow signals to be simultaneously transmitted on electrical power lines. A power line carrier signal is transmitted above the standard 60 Hz power line power frequency (50 Hz in Europe). Power line premises distribution for television is important because televisions, set-top boxes, digital media adapters (DMAs) and other media devices are already connected to power outlets installed in homes and small businesses.

Older (legacy) power line communication systems had challenges with wiring systems that used two or more phases of electrical power. Today, with the benefit of modern signal processing techniques and algorithms, most of these impairments are no longer an impediment to performance and some powerline data systems have data transmission rates of over 500 Mbps.

Coaxial Cable

Coax (television cable) systems are set up as simple tree distribution systems. The root of the tree is usually at the entrance point to the home or building and the tree may divide several times as it progresses from the root to each television outlet through the use of signal splitters. When coaxial systems are set up as data networks (distribution of Internet TV signals), the data signals are transferred using high frequencies (above 860 MHz), which are combined with cable TV broadcast signals over the same coaxial lines.

Because the coax cable is shielded and RF channels are virtually free from the effects of interfering signals, coaxial cable provides a large information pipe that is capable of distributing multiple wide radio frequency channels. Coaxial cable data transmission rates vary from 1 Mbps to over 1 Gbps. Many homes have existing cable television networks and outlets which are located near video accessory and television viewing points.

Telephone Line

Home media networks may transfer user information over existing telephone lines in a home or building. Telephone lines to and from the telephone company may contain analog or digital telephone signals. Telephone line data networks use frequencies above 1 MHz so they do not interfere with existing telephone signals. Home media networks that use telephone lines can have data transmission rates that range from 1 Mbps to over 300 Mbps. Telephone line outlets may be located near television viewing points, making it easy to connect adapters or viewing devices that have telephone line home media network connections.

Optical Cable

Some home networks, or portions of them, may transfer data over fibers in optical cables. The transmission rates in some optical cables can vary dramatically, based on the type of fiber and the type of optical signal source such as laser (very high) or LED (moderately high). The choices of fiber and optical transmitter can also determine the types of connectors and installation that may be required for optical systems. Typical data transmission rates for home optical networks range from 25 Mbps to 250 Mbps.

Figure 6.10 shows the common types of premises distribution systems that can be used for IP television systems. This diagram shows that an IP television signal arrives at the premises at a broadband modem. The broadband

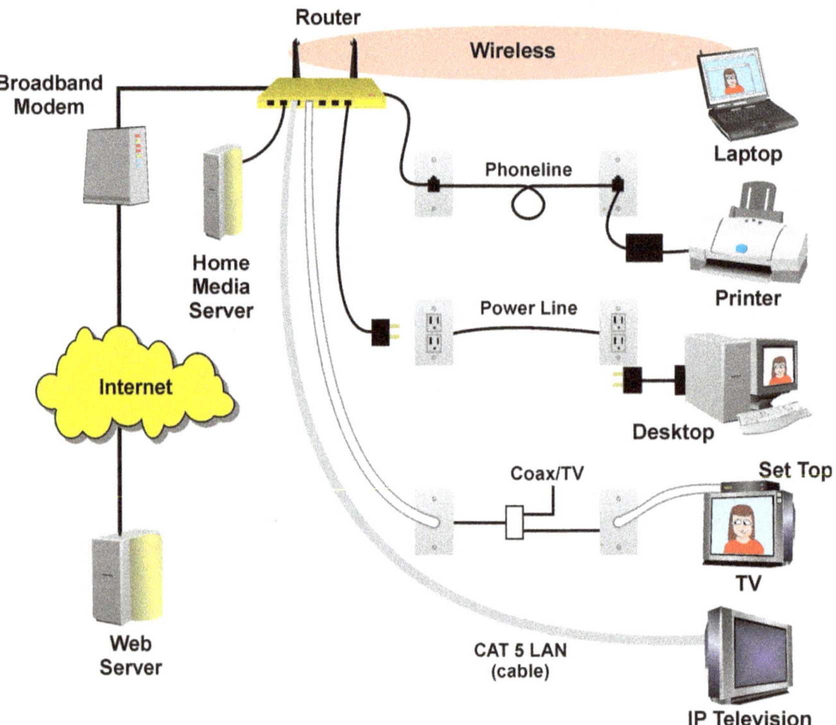

Figure 6.10, Internet TV Home Distribution

modem is connected to a router that can distribute the media signals to forward data packets to different devices within the home, such as IP televisions. This example shows that routers may be able to forward packets through power lines, telephone lines, coaxial lines, data cables or even via wireless signals to adapters that receive the packets and recreate them into a form that can be used by the IP television.

Device Management

Device management is the process of identifying, adding and configuring devices that are part of a system. Device management may be a manual process or it may be automatically performed through the use of protocols that can discover and configure equipment that is added to a network, and remove registrations from devices that are removed from a network.

Device Capabilities

Device capability is the set of features, functions and options that are available within a device. Device capabilities can include display, processing, control and other options. Internet TV viewing devices can have a mix of display, audio, control and application processing capabilities. The Internet TV system should be able to discover the capabilities of the device so it can adjust what it sends to the device.

Communication Protocols

Communication protocols are sets of rules and processes that manage how transmissions are initiated and maintained between communication points. Internet TV devices can have a mixture of protocols and the Internet TV system must be able to identify which protocols the device can use to communicate.

Software Versions

There are many software programs that exist within an Internet TV system and the devices with which it communicates. Over time, software programs tend to evolve to include new capabilities and features. To determine which features a device or system is capable of processing, the Internet TV system should be able to identify and classify devices that use certain versions of software.

Configuration

Devices that operate within a system need to store and use certain types of information. This can include access addresses, service lists, protocol types and other information. The Internet TV system may communicate and provide the necessary configuration settings to the devices. In some cases, the user may need to setup and configure devices before they can work with the Internet TV system.

Figure 6.11 shows how Internet TV systems manage multiple types of devices with different decoding capabilities, display formats and software versions. The Internet set top box has MPEG-4 decoding capability, a display resolution of 1080p (HD), and a middleware software version 6. The multimedia computer has MPEG-2 decoding capability, a display resolution of 640x480, and middleware software version 3. The mobile smartphone can process 3G video format, has QVGA resolution (320 x 240), and has middleware software version 2 capabilities. The Internet TV system device management server keeps track of these devices and their capabilities.

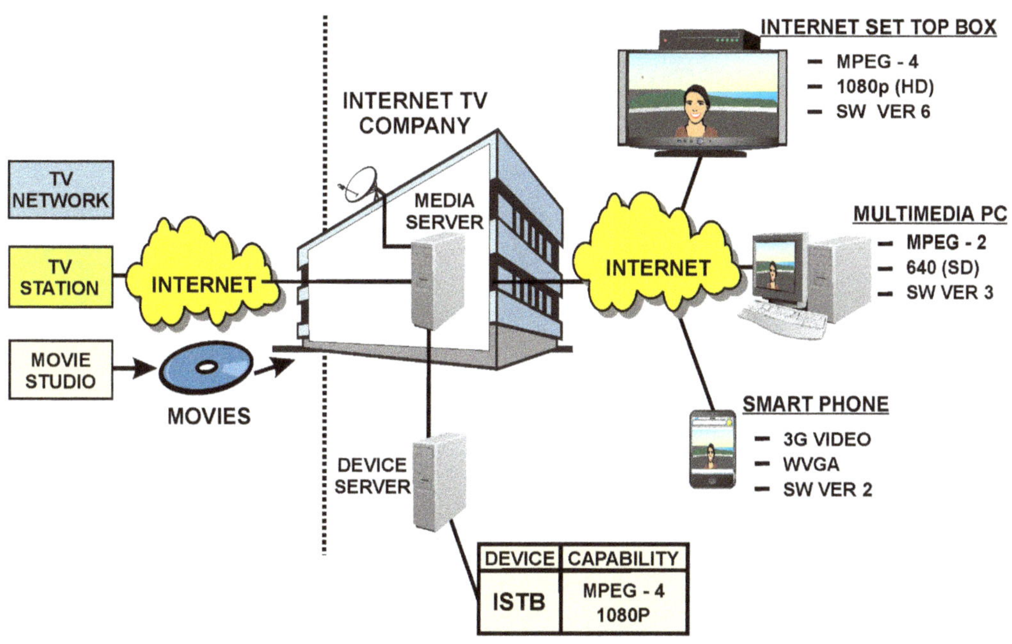

Figure 6.11, Device Management

Internet TV System Operation

Operating an Internet TV is similar in most ways to operating a broadcast or cable television network. The primary distinction is the technical architecture that is used to deliver the content to viewers. Otherwise, the Internet TV operator is required to manage the same functions; content generation, programming, distribution, subscriber management, advertising and order processing.

Content Acquisition Strategy

A core axiom in the video entertainment industry is “content is king.” There are endless sources of video content; each competing for the attention of the viewing audience. In order to establish a viable Internet TV, the operator must create a content strategy that viewers will want and value.

Single Channel Services

For operators that offer a single channel of content, the individual programming that populates the channel must be compelling to the viewer. It must provide content that the viewer feels they cannot get elsewhere for the same value. Content that meets these criteria is often considered specialized or “niche.” It appeals to a specific demographic that shares the same unique interests. Ethnic, religious and hobby-related content often meet these criteria. The downside is that the majority of the population may not find the content interesting; however, the target demographic may value the content above all other. This generates a loyal subscriber base that can power the Internet TV operator. Remember, with an Internet TV, viewers can be reached all over the world using a single delivery architecture. So, the operator only needs a small percentage of the world’s viewers to finance his/her station.

Multiple Channel Services

Internet TV operators that offer multiple channels, such as cable operators, Telcos and satellite operators, need to assemble a bouquet of channels that viewers will value. If the operator wishes to compete with cable, telco and satellite operators to provide a service selected by the viewer as their primary source of television programming (a "cord cutter" service), then the Internet TV operator must provide programming that viewers value as much as incumbent operators' programming. This remains a significant challenge for Internet TV operators as the major networks are hesitant to license their content for distribution over the Internet. However, this hesitation is steadily fading.

Many operators elect to offer programming that will supplement the content viewers get through traditional programming sources. Such services are offered without the intention of becoming a sole source of content for viewers, but they do intend to provide specialized content that is desired by viewers, but inaccessible from a better source; that is, a source that offers a combination of availability, quality, ease of use and price. As with single channel services, these operators typically offer niche content such as ethnic, religious and special interest programming. For example, viewers of Russian decent who value Russian programming, would also value an Internet TV service that provides a bundle of desirable Russian language content. Such viewers might maintain a subscription with a local cable operator, but also supplement it with Russian programming from an Internet TV provider.

Likewise, if an operator's target audience is made up of outdoor enthusiasts, that operator will want to assemble and offer a selection of content that appeals to that audience. The appeal may be because of the subject matter presented, the people featured in the programming or even the social and political attitudes represented by the content. The key is to ensure that the resulting bundle of content appeals to the target audience and offers them something they cannot get elsewhere for a better value.

Ingestion

Ingestion refers to the process of taking content from its source and bringing it into the distribution architecture of the Internet TV. This applies to both individual programming (VOD/Pay-Per-View content) and entire channels (24/7 programming).

Individual programming is typically ingested by simply uploading the content to the OTT system via a web interface. In this way, content producers can deliver the programming to the operator from any location. This process is similar to uploading a file for any other application. The OTT system will receive the file, store it and identify it so that it can be retrieved and delivered to the viewer. Alternatively, the content can be delivered on other forms of storage media (tapes, DVDs, hard drives) and uploaded directly into the system.

A linear channel is most often ingested by either down-linking the channel from a satellite broadcast and playing it into an encoder for streaming to the CDN, or by installing an encoder at the source and delivering the stream to the CDN via a broadband connection.

Workflow Management

Workflow is the tasks and processes that are necessary to perform projects or assignments. Workflow is used to produce segments that will be broadcasted or made available to viewers. Workflow system software may be used to plan, track and coordinate the overall production process. Some of the workflow tasks may be assigned (outsourced) to vendors and contractors. These companies may be provided access to the workflow management software via the Internet, so they can see and update their tasks.

Projects

The workflow process begins with the creation of a project. Projects are groups of tasks or processes that are planned to be performed to achieve an objective for the creation of a media program, service or product. An example of an Internet TV project is the creation of a 30 minute cooking show.

Production Tasks

Production tasks are jobs or assignments that are associated with a content creation project. Examples of production tasks include scripting, shooting and editing. Task information may include data pertaining to time and status, which may be used to provide a visual graph of the when assignments are to be performed, and if they have been completed.

Resources

Resources are elements that are required to complete a task, which may include equipment, staff, contractors and other items. For each task, a resource list is typically created, consisting of the resource category, name (company, person or other entity), cost and any other related information (such as acceptable form of payment).

Workflow Systems

Workflow systems organize and track project tasks, resources, and people. Workflow systems are connected to production and broadcast equipment. Internet TV systems use workflow systems to produce programs, publish media, and schedule broadcasts. Distributed workflow systems allow for non-staff people (contractors and other companies) to access parts of the workflow system.

Workflow Automation

Workflow automation is the process of using a system that has established rules or procedures that allows for the acquisition, creation, scheduling or transmission of content assets. Internet TV providers may have many repeated tasks in their production processes such as adding pre-roll clips, subtitle slides, interview editing. Tasks and resources for these projects can be pre-defined to speed up the production process.

Figure 7.1 shows a TV workflow management process. This software shows a program project list view of Kitchen Remodel, Gourmet Cooking 3, and Travel Tips 7. The tasks window shows that this project includes the scripting, casting, shooting and editing. The resources window shows that the project requires a writer for $650 (B Quick), studio rental for $800 (Studio Rent

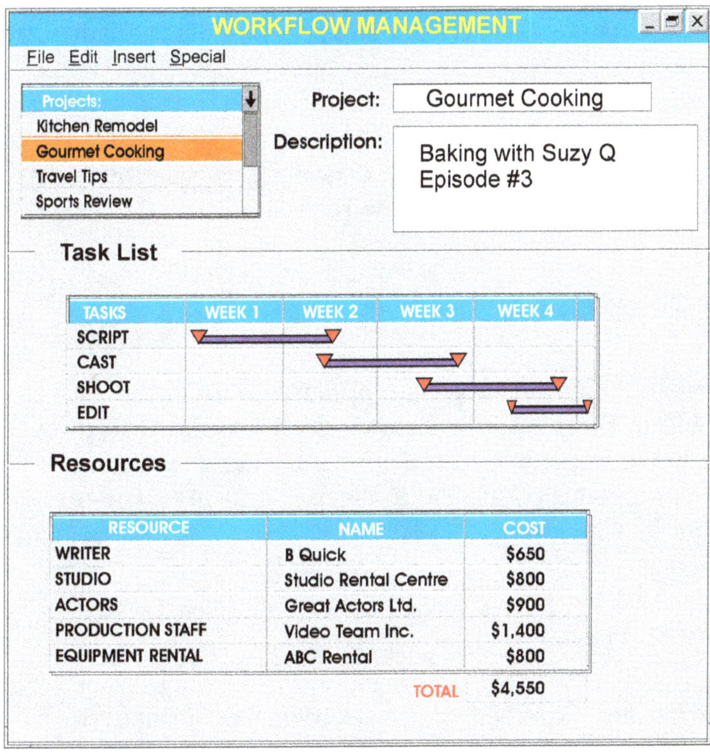

Figure 7.1, TV Workflow Management Process

Center), actors which cost $900 (Great Actors Ltd), a production staff costing $1,300 (Video Team, Inc), and equipment rental fees of $800 (ABC Rental). The total cost for this program is $4550.

Content Management

An Internet TV will store all of its content, both programming and advertisements, until it determines that the files are no longer of use. The method used for content storage depends on the anticipated use of the content.

Online (Real Time)

Content that is expected to be used in the immediate future is stored in a matter that makes it accessible to the operator at any time. This usually includes storing the content on a media server so that it can be ingested into a play list and streamed out as part of a linear channel. It also includes pushing the content to the CDN's co-location servers where it is stored and then streamed to local viewers as it is requested.

Nearline (Short Time)

Content that is not currently being made available to the viewer, but will be made available to the viewer sometime soon, can be stored on other media servers, which are accessible to the operator's system (on line). The operator can pull the content off of the media server and ingest it into the distribution system as it is needed.

Offline (Long Term)

Content that is not expected to be used in the immediate future can be stored inexpensively and kept so that it is accessible by the operator only if needed. Such content is often stored on physical media such as tapes, DVDs and hard drives. Should the operator wish to distribute such content, it can easily be loaded onto a media server and made available for real time viewing.

Program Scheduling

Program scheduling is the assignment of times during which programs will be broadcasted or made available for viewing on channels.

Channel Lineup Schedules

Internet TV can provide the same user experiences as traditional television services, such as cable and satellite. The viewer is provided a channel guide that can display not only the channels available for viewing, but also the individual programs available on each channel with corresponding broadcast dates and times. The program guide is regularly updated to show available future programming for a period of time; usually the upcoming two weeks. It is presented in an easy-to-use graphic user interface which can be accessed and controlled through a remote that is sent along with the Set Top Box.

On Demand Programming

Some Internet TV will also provide Virtual DVRs, which allow the viewer to watch programs that have already been broadcast. The viewer simply selects from previous time slots on the channel guide and chooses the desired program. The content is then streamed to their viewing device as though it was a VOD file request.

For VOD/Pay-Per-View content, the programming is usually presented in categories such as drama, comedy, romance, etc. or by subject matter such as news, sports, weather, etc. The viewer simply selects a category of content and toggles through the listed content to find the desired program. The content is requested and streamed to the viewer.

Automatic Scheduling

The distribution of content is carefully choreographed to ensure that programs are delivered to viewers at appropriate times of day; a typical schedule might consist of children's programming in the morning, news in the afternoon and most popular programming in the evening. Programs are broadcast on a reliable schedule, such as a popular drama being broadcasted on Mondays at 8:00 PM.

Advertisers will pay for the number of times their advertisement is broadcast and may pay more for certain broadcast time periods. An advertisement that is broadcast during prime viewing hours will have more value than an ad that is broadcast at an hour when few people are watching. It is therefore important that the operators' systems have the capability to schedule and distribute both entertainment content and advertisement content on a predetermined schedule.

Content Delivery Network

A major component of any Internet TV is the content delivery network (CDN). CDNs are usually third party service providers that own co-location servers, which are strategically positioned around the world, as well as large pipes (bandwidth) that are capable of delivering content to and from those servers. Most content delivered by an Internet TV will be primarily distributed by CDNs to each individual subscriber's local Internet service provider (ISP). The ISP then delivers the content over the "last mile" to the subscriber's Set Top Box.

The Internet TV will deliver the content into the cloud where it is accessed by the CDN and then distributed as instructed by the content management system.

CDNs often constitute the largest single operating expense of an Internet TV, so a keen understanding of how CDNs operate and charge for their services is imperative.

Monitoring and Maintenance

An Internet TV must have facilities and personnel in place to ensure that content is delivered to the subscribers as contracted. This includes monitoring systems designed to identify issues, as well as systems to fall back on should an issue arise.

Monitoring

Any complete Internet TV should be able to monitor all content, including that which is coming into the system as well as that which is distributed by the system. Diagnostic equipment can be installed to actively monitor the content streams and send alarms should an undesirable variation in the service occur. Support technicians must be available to analyze any variation, determine its origin and take whatever action is necessary to remedy the problem.

Back-up Systems

An Internet TV is, in essence, a data server and, like any data server, the operator should anticipate failures in the system and establish secondary service plans should a failure occur. This means building redundancy into the system. Redundancy may come from having hot swappable spares available such as extra encoders, or it might come from having entire backup systems available, in addition to the primary systems. For example, UPS (uninterruptable power supplies) and emergency generators should be made available to power the station should the primary source of power be lost. Backup broadband connectivity should be in place should the primary connection go down. This might be provided by a microwave link or a satellite uplink system. Since the costs to provide these systems can prove to be high, operators will typically weigh the system costs against the potential damages incurred should programming become suspended.

Subscriber Management

A subscriber management system identifies each viewer and determines the types of content they are authorized to receive. A key to any content delivery system is the ability to control who receives access to content. The operator needs to ensure that only authorized customers receive the content. These may be paying subscribers or members that have signed up to receive free content. Additionally, the operator must ensure that each viewer receives only the content that he has signed up to receive.

A subscriber management system also maintains individual subscriber records to ensure that the correct equipment and services are received, and that the appropriate fees for those services are paid.

New Subscribers

The name, address, billing information and services purchased of each new subscriber or viewer is entered into the subscriber management system. Entry can be done manually from information taken over the telephone or it can be done electronically through a web interface.

Billing can be managed and affected through the subscriber management system through credit card payments made immediately or the issuance of invoices to be paid via checks. Automated payments directly from bank accounts can also be effectuated.

Customer Profiles

The subscriber management system, in coordination with the billing system, maintains a complete record of each individual subscriber's history. This includes any hardware sent to the subscriber, any services ordered, the individual Pay-Per-View content purchased, and all payments made by the subscriber.

Service Plans

The subscriber management system can also function as a customer resource management system. As all pertinent information about each individual subscriber is stored and made readily available, the subscriber management system is a valuable tool for assisting subscribers with any customer service-related needs. Most systems will allow the customer support technician to enter notes about service requests and complaints directly into the system to create a history and to prompt future corrective action, such as the sending out of new equipment or the prompting of a support call from another technician.

Each operator must determine the level of support they wish to provide their customers. Some operators may make support available only during normal business hours, while others may opt to provide 24/7 customer support. At a minimum, the operator must ensure that the customers' issues are understood and addressed.

Customer Care History

The cumulative data generated from a complete subscriber management system provides a valuable archive of information on each individual viewer. Any questions regarding billing or services provided can be quickly researched and addressed.

Additionally, information regarding each individual subscriber can be aggregated and analyzed to develop valuable data regarding the performance of the system, technical and customer support issues and customer satisfaction.

Advertising Sales

Advertising sales for TV broadcasters involves the identification, negotiation and generation of orders from people or companies for the insertion of promotional materials. Advertising sales processes include prospecting, advertising offer presentation, advertising contracts and advertising sales reports.

Sales Prospecting

Sales prospecting for advertisers involves identify people or companies which are likely qualified to purchase advertising services. Advertising sales may be performed by in-house staff, sales representatives or sales agencies. Different types of customers may be assigned to different types of sales representatives. For example, in-house sales staff may handle promotions for large corporations, while independent sales representatives may sell to small businesses.

A key part of the prospecting process is an understanding of the available advertising sales opportunities. The sales representatives must know how many ad insertion opportunities remain available to sell (ad inventory).

Some key challenges for TV advertising include identifying new contacts (possibly from phone books or chamber of commerce directories), determining which sales representative or agency is responsible for selling (inside or outside sales), and tracking the sales process, perhaps through the use of a sales management system such as www.salesforce.com.

Advertising Proposals

TV broadcaster sales representatives may provide one or more advertising proposals to companies. An advertising proposal contains the set of advertising terms, such as available networks and the number of ads, as well as the related costs. The advertising proposal may include a package of advertising options and a price that decreases based on increased advertising commitments. Part of the payment for advertising services may be provided in goods or services rather than cash payments (free hotel rooms, credit at local restaurants).

Advertising Contracts

Advertising proposals become contracts when they have been approved by both the advertiser and the TV broadcaster. The broadcaster may have a person on staff who is responsible for overseeing the advertising program, who must ultimately approve the advertising offer. This ensures that sales representatives are not overselling advertising services, or pricing them too low.

The advertising contract is used to determine which networks, channels and programs are authorized for advertising insertions. The contract may include the desired broadcast time periods, such as advertisements for food before or during meal times, as well as the desired costs (per number of viewers) and limits (maximum cost or insertions).

Insertion Reporting

Ad insertion reports provide the results of advertising campaigns. The reports may identify which ads were inserted, networks and programs they were inserted into, the date and time of insertion, the number of viewers and the cost of the insertion.

Figure 7.2 shows a TV ad sales system. Companies that may potentially advertise are identified and assigned to a sales person or agent. Available ad insertion opportunities (ad inventory) are regularly identified and provided to the sales representatives, helping to ensure that they know which ads insertion opportunities are available and which are already sold. Using information gathered from the potential advertiser and available inventory, the sales representative creates advertising proposals. When the advertising proposal is accepted by both the advertising company and the TV broadcast advertising manager, an advertising contract is created. After the ads are inserted, performance reports (identifying the ads, dates and times) are crated which can be provided to the advertiser so they can track their progress.

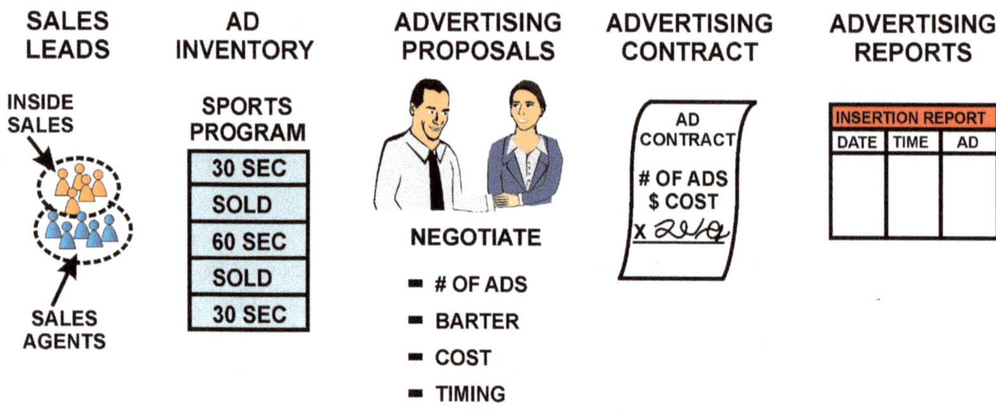

Figure 7.2, Internet TV Advertising Sales Process

Order Processing

An Internet TV must have an efficient process for registering new subscribers with the system and making changes to subscriber accounts. This can be accomplished simply, by taking calls from subscribers and entering their billing information into the subscriber management system, or it can be accomplished more elaborately, through a web-based user interface.

Services

The order processing system must enable the customer or customer support technician to register all pertinent information with the operator's data base. This will include name, billing address, address where hardware is to be delivered, billing preference (credit card, check, automatic debit) and, of course, the services that the subscriber is purchasing. Most operators will offer multiple packages, or bouquets of content, from which subscribers may choose. Some operators also offer optional subscription periods to chose from (monthly, quarterly, annually) with a discount associated for longer periods purchased.

The order processing system must also enable the subscriber's information to be amended should they desire a change in their services, or should their information change (address, credit card number, etc.).

Products

Many operators will offer their subscribers options for paying for hardware. For example, Set Top Boxes may be purchased out right, or they might be leased for a monthly fee. Operators may offer Set Top Boxes at discounted prices to subscribers who are willing to purchase programming for an entire year in advance. Regardless of how the operator elects to sell the hardware to the subscriber, the order processing system must have the capability of handling all potential transactions.

Third Party Sales

In some Internet TV models, hardware, and even content, can be obtained from third parties. An example of this architecture is the system offered by Roku. A content owner can distribute its unique content to its own subscribers for viewing by anyone with a Roku Set Top Box. To do this, the content owner must establish his/her own Internet TV, very much like the ones discussed in this book; however, subscribers purchase the Set Top Box from Roku instead of the content owner.

The process for registering a subscriber on a platform such as Roku's is:
1. A Roku Set Top Box is purchased (or turned on if already owned).
2. On the Roku Set Top Box, the viewer uses the Roku remote to select the icon identifying the channel they wish to subscribe to.
3. The content owner's web address is displayed, along with a code identifying the viewer's specific Roku Set Top Box.
4. The viewer goes to the content owner's website, registers as a subscriber (as discussed above), and then enters the code identifying the viewer's specific Roku Set Top Box.
5. The content owner's system will then activate the subscriber's account, process the charge, and authorize the Roku Set Top Box to receive the content purchased.

Thereafter, the delivery of content to the Roku Set Top Box functions very similarly to any other Internet TV, except that the content is being played on a device sold by the third party Roku.

Internet TV System Options

Internet TV system options include using the system of a contracted company to host Internet TV content and services, using an integrated system (Internet TV in a box), and using an Internet TV system built from functional components (custom system).

Internet TV Hosting

A hosted Internet TV system is storage and transmission equipment that is owned by one company, which can be used by other companies to manage and broadcast its content through the Internet (a virtual TV system). Using other companies to provide TV storage and transmission services can enable companies to have very low startup costs and a quick operation setup time. The common challenge of using hosted Internet TV systems is limited customization options.

Integrated Internet TV System

An integrated Internet TV system is a group of functional components that are designed with the ability to work together to provide TV broadcasting services. Broadcasting companies may choose Internet TV in a box solutions to ensure that their system works reliably upon setup, and to get access to support services.

Custom Internet TV System

A custom Internet TV system is a group of equipment that is selected and combined to provide TV broadcasting services through the Internet. Custom Internet TV systems can use a mixture of functional components, software applications and services from different vendors. Developing a custom Internet TV system allows for a choice of devices that can have more features and, potentially, the lowest system and operational costs, provided the number of customers is sufficient. A key challenge with custom Internet TV systems is the delivery of support service solutions in situations that involve multiple vendors, as vendors have a tendency to blame others for any issues or problems.

Figure 8.1 shows some of the options for Internet TV systems. The hosting option allows an Internet TV station to setup and run the system from an administrative terminal. All the equipment that is necessary to manage media, perform billing and playout media is owned and maintained by the Internet TV system host company. The integrated Internet TV station option uses a complete hardware system (usually several pieces of equipment in a rack) that includes media management, billing and playout functions. The custom option allows the Internet TV station to use separate equipment for media management, billing and playout scheduling.

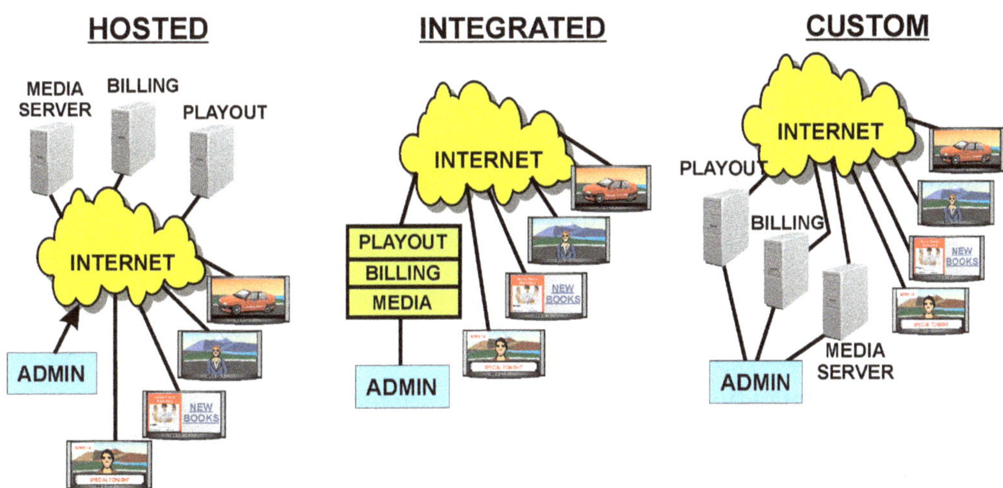

Figure 8.1, Internet TV System Options

Hosted Internet TV System

A hosted Internet TV system is a video streaming platform that provides all the storage and streaming services that are necessary to allow viewers to watch Internet TV programming. It is possible to setup and operate a hosted Internet TV station through the use of a computer with a web browser that is connected to the Internet.

Hosting Internet TV service provider systems include a media ingestion, a playout system and subscriber management. Hosted Internet TV systems may also include advertising and billing services. The equipment used by the hosting system may be directly managed by an Internet TV station or by another company (shared hosting).

Hosted Internet TV systems may be setup for customization and branding (white label). To control the hosted system, Internet TV providers use web portals with specific functions, including media ingestion (content uploading), content management, playout systems, subscriber management and system administration.

White Label Platforms

White label platforms are systems that can be customized, branded and operated by other entities. White label platforms are designed to allow a company to customize the appearance and functions offered to customers. Because white label platforms are already setup, the creation of an Internet TV station may be accomplished in a very short amount of time.

Hosted Media Ingestion

Hosted media ingestion is the process of transferring media into a storage or content management system. These systems may be designed to automatically identify specific types of media formats and convert them into other formats that can be processed and broadcasted by the Internet TV system. Uploading content to the hosted system may be performed by using Internet file transfer protocol (FTP), which either uploads files from a local computer (such as from a DVD) or from another source (online content distributor).

Content Management

Content management processes provided by Internet TV hosting systems include online editing systems that allow Internet TV providers to label, select and create media segments to produce programs.

Playout System

Hosted playout systems allow providers to select, schedule and control how media programs are transmitted. Programs may be selected according to program ID, title or other identifying information. Hosted playout systems may also allow for the selection of media format and resolution as this influences the amount of bandwidth used, which the Internet TV provider usually pays for. Choosing a lower resolution format reduces the transmission cost.

Subscriber Management

A subscriber management portal allows the Internet TV provider to add, setup and remove subscribers who are provided access to the Internet TV system. Some subscriber management functions may be performed directly by the subscribers, such as account setup. The subscriber management system may be connected to a billing system, which allows customers to be charged for their access to Internet TV programs or services.

Broadcaster Service Packages

Hosted Internet TV system service packages control the types and amounts of broadcasting offered by an Internet TV service provider. Broadcaster service packages may be offered in tiers (levels). Lower cost levels may require the Internet TV broadcaster to allow for the insertion of advertising, while higher level packages may allow for the broadcasting of high resolution content.

Figure 8.2 shows the key parts of a hosted Internet TV system. This example shows that the hosting company owns almost all of the necessary equipment for an Internet TV system. The Internet TV provider accesses the system through web portals (web browser portals on computers that are connected to the Internet). The media ingestion portal system allows for the transfer of media (such as DVDs and files) through the Internet to media storage servers. The host system identifies the media uploaded format and uses encoders to convert the media into formats that can be stored and broadcasted through the Internet. The content management portal provides an online editing system that allows for the selection and combination of media segments to produce TV programs. The playout system portal allows the Internet TV provider to setup times and access criteria for the broadcasting of TV programs. The subscriber management portal allows the service provider to add, setup and remove customers. The administration portal can be used to setup the overall settings (such as bandwidth allocation) for the manage portion of the system.

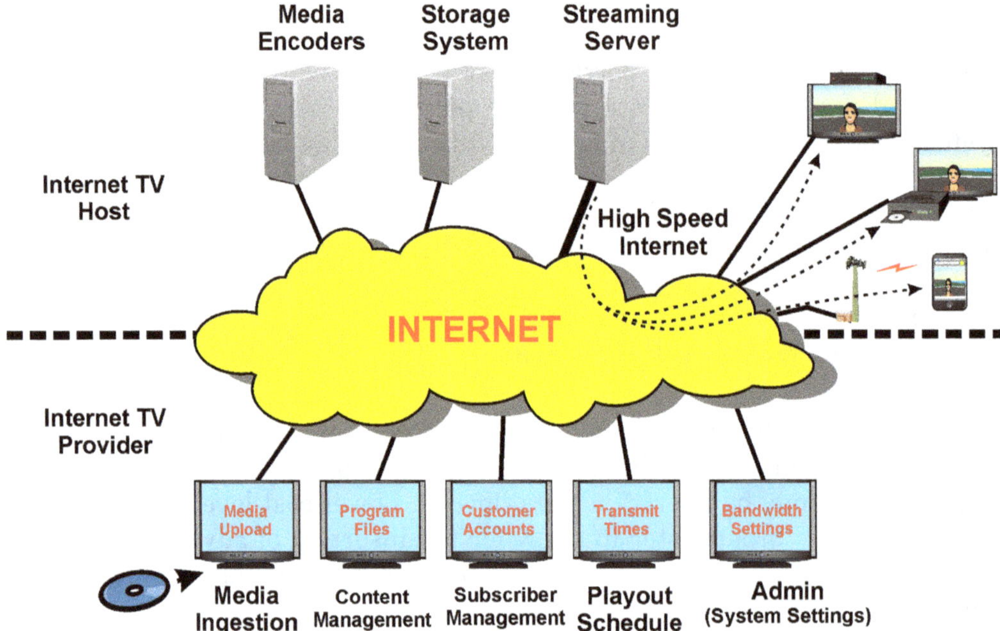

Figure 8.2, Hosted Internet TV System

Integrated Internet TV System

An integrated Internet TV system is a combination of equipment that has been setup to work together. This includes equipment that has been pre-configured to work, software programs that are ready for use and support services that enable Internet TV providers to customize and use the system.

Integrated Turn-Key System

An integrated turn-key system is a set of equipment that is selected and setup in a ready-to-use (customized) condition. An integrated Internet TV system may be a single rack of equipment with all the cables necessary for interconnection.

Pre-Configured Equipment

An integrated Internet TV system utilizes multiple pieces of equipment that are tested and validated to ensure they will operate with one another. The system may be setup at the vendor's facility to be ready for operation. Some settings, such as the Internet address, network names and specific service settings, may need to be configured on location.

Broadcast Software Package

Integrated systems come with a set of software programs (as software package) that is used to setup services and control all of the devices. The software package contains all the necessary programs to transfer, product, and schedule broadcasts. While the software programs may be produced by separate companies, they have been tested and setup to interoperate with each other.

Support Services

The ready-to-use system may include support services such as configuration, training and updating. Training and operational procedures may be provided to ensure the Internet TV provider's staff can develop the skills necessary to operate the system. Maintenance and update services may be provided such as equipment repairs, software patches and new service upgrades.

Figure 8.3 shows an integrated turn-key, ready-to-use Internet TV system. This system includes an equipment rack that contains most of the equipment that is needed for the Internet TV system; encoders, a storage system and media server. The system comes with a software package that includes multiple applications, including media management, a playout system and subscriber management. The equipment and software programs are preconfigured and tested to ensure they work with each other by the integrated system vendor. The Internet TV system is connected by a high speed connection to the Internet.

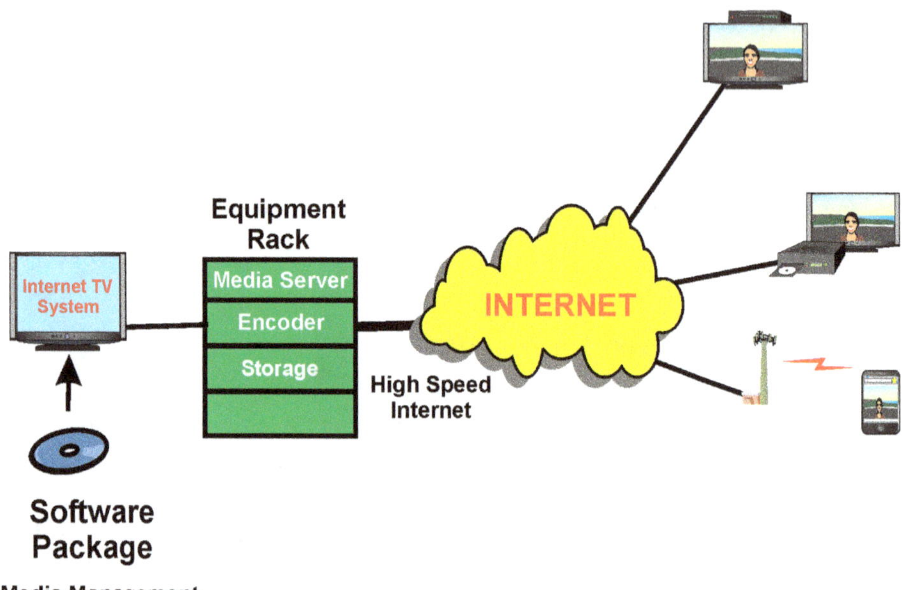

Figure 8.3, Integrated Internet TV System

Custom Internet TV System

A custom Internet TV system is a combination of equipments that may be independently selected by the Internet TV system operator. Some of the key components of a custom Internet TV system include media encoders, play-out system, production system, billing system and software programs. To help setup and configure the system, a systems integration company may be used.

Media Encoders

Media encoders are devices that can convert (encode) the format of media into another format (typically digital). Media encoders may be used to ingest content (from video tape, DVD or files) and convert it into one or more formats (SD, HD, mobile video).

While the input and output formats for media encoders may be standardized, the actual encoding process can dramatically vary, producing video with different quality levels. Media encoders analyze input media and create coded versions of it. Encoders with more processing capability (analyze more) the use more advanced coding algorithms can produce much higher video quality.

In addition to the processing capabilities of media encoders, the optional settings can affect quality levels. More advanced (and expensive) media encoders tend to produce higher quality video.

Playout System

A playout system consists of computer servers that can select and transfer media to viewers. Media servers may be designed and setup to simply transfer files, or they may be created to provide continuous (streaming) services. A standard media server must transfer a significant amount of media before viewers can see the program, while a streaming server can broadcast media to viewers upon request. This means that playout systems may be created by using a combination of file servers and streaming media servers.

Media Production System

Media production systems allow for the creation of content that may be broadcasted or made available to viewers. This content may be produced over a period of time (such as a TV program) or it may be produced immediately as it occurs (live media).

Content production involves the use of recording equipment, studios, actors, production staff, switching and effects generators, and a mixture of other resources. Live media production requires additional types of equipment and processes to ensure that the broadcast can be reliably transmitted (backup connections), that it contains desired content and that any undesired media (restricted content) has been eliminated.

Billing System

A billing system is the combination of equipment and software that can gather billing related information, apply a value to it (rating), and collect fees (invoicing). TV billing systems combine traditional accounting systems with additional billing functions. This includes the use of monitoring equipment and mediation devices that can identify, gather and create billing event records, advertising rating systems and tax processing. Billing systems must also link (integrate) to other systems, such as sales and customer care.

Software Programs

Some of the software programs that are used in Internet TV systems include content management, media production (editing), databases (subscribers, equipment), operations (sales and customer relationship management), and middleware that can link the customer equipment to the Internet TV system.

Systems Integrators

Developing a custom Internet TV system allows for the choice of the best equipment and software options for each function. It also requires that these devices and software programs are setup to work with one another. The skills and experience that is required can be substantial so Internet TV providers may use a systems integrator. A systems integrator is a company or person that assists with the definition, selection, combination and configuration of multiple types of systems to operate together to perform specific functions and/or services.

Systems integrators commonly setup and test multiple types of equipment and software programs. They are typically experienced, and know which devices work well together. Systems integrators may also represent equipment vendors, allowing them to purchase equipment at lower cost. The reduced cost of equipment may offset the cost of hiring a system integration company.

Figure 8.4 shows a diagram of a custom Internet TV system. Media is transferred into the system through media encoders that ingest (convert) the media into formats that can be used by the system. A playout system consists of media servers and streaming servers that can select, transfer and broadcast content based on schedules and access methods setup by the Internet TV provider. The billing system consists of network monitoring devices and mediation devices that can gather and combine service and usage event information. Several software programs are used by this system, including content management, databases, media production and middleware.

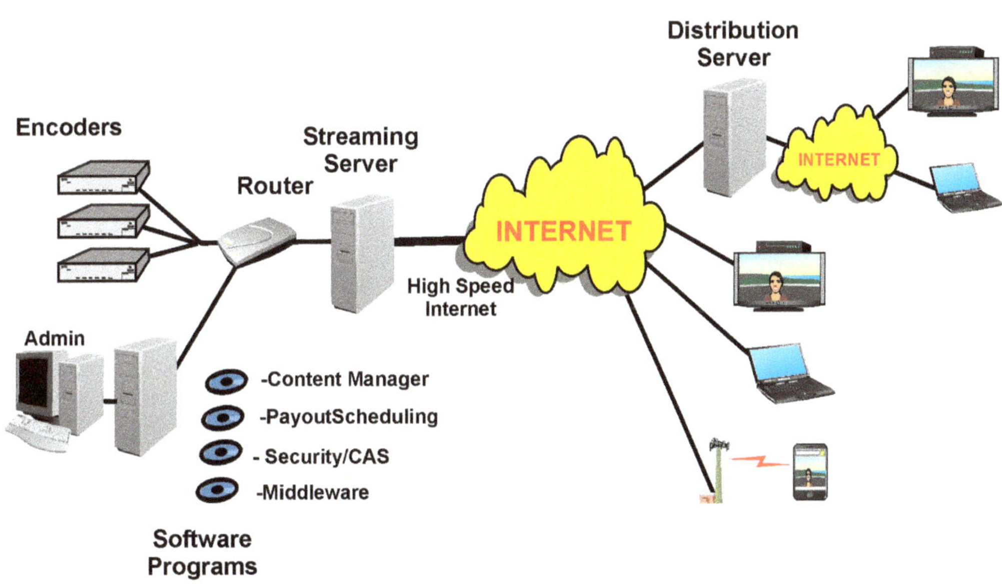

Figure 8.4, Custom Internet TV System

Content Production

Content production is the systems and steps that are used to capture, organize and process media content to produce new programs or media segments. Content production for Internet TV systems includes program development processes, storyboarding, workflow management, finding and using existing media (stock media), studio production and editing systems.

Program Development

Program development is the processes that are used for the identification and coordination of content development activities. A program development system can be divided into phases, which may include concept (program idea), feasibility, pre-production planning, production shooting, post-production editing and media packaging.

Program Concept (Topic Idea)

Program conception is the definition of the initial scope and characteristics of a media segment that may be developed. A program concept phase may involve the interaction of multiple people (TV station staff, experts and viewers) to establish the program definition and the key characteristics that the program may or should include.

Feasibility

A feasibility analysis is a review of information to determine the potential success of a product, project or business. Information used in a feasibility analysis may include the definition and scope of anticipated products or services, and target markets (and their sizes) that have a need or want for those products or services. This may also include the resources, such as skills, equipment and capital, that will be required to develop and provide these products or services.

Preproduction Plan

Preproduction includes the necessary media creation tasks performed prior to the creation of media. A preproduction plan includes creating lists of necessary people, and identifying and scheduling the use of equipment and other resources.

Shooting (Recording)

Shooting is the capturing of image information onto a medium such as film or digital media files. Once each recorded segment is identified, segment reviews (screenings) are performed to identify segments that will be included and segments that will not be used (helpful in the final editing process).

Post Production

Post production is the tasks necessary for the creation of media programs that are performed after a service or process (recording) has finished. Post production includes creating special effects, creating an edit list, adding transitions, mixing audio and any other processes used to create the final media program.

Program Packaging (for Distribution)

Program packaging is the storing of media programs and supporting materials into a file or storage device that can be transferred for distribution. In addition to the storing of the media program in multiple formats (SD, HD), the program package may contain associated metadata (for program guides) and promotional materials, such as brochures and trailers.

Figure 9.1 shows a basic video production process. This example shows a product development process that evolves through a series of phases. The process starts with a program idea (concept), which is described along with any specific talent or specific content rights that would be required. In the feasibility phase, the marketing objectives are reviewed, along with the required resources and skills that will be required for the production. In the planning stage, the steps, tasks and people are identified and scheduled. In the shooting phase, crews and sets are created so filming can be performed. During the filming phase, the director and other staff may screen content to determine if the media should be included in the final production. The post production phase includes selecting, organizing and adding effects to film

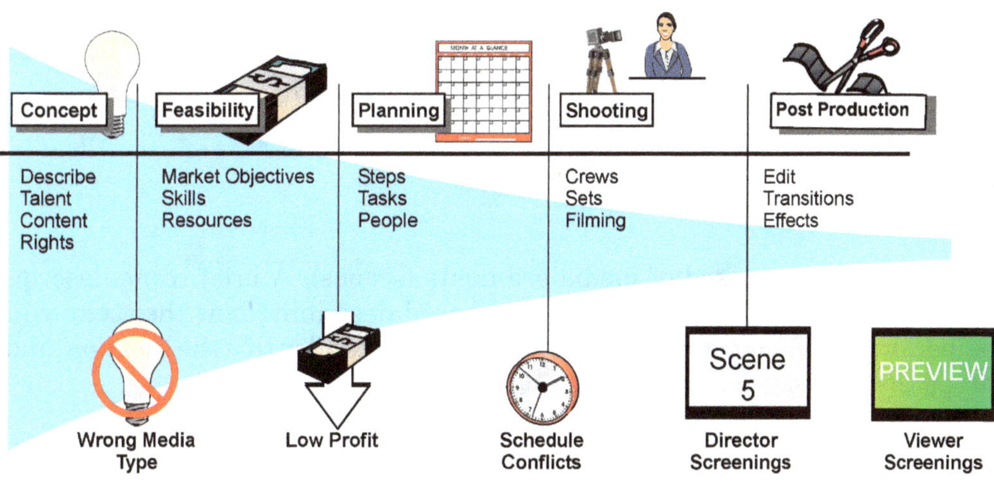

Figure 9.1, Video Program Development Process

segments (editing). In the packaging phase, the final program is made available for distribution in disk or file format, along with any promotional materials.

Storyboarding

A storyboard is a group of images or media segments that describe the key elements of a media ad, campaign or program. Storyboard images may contain rough sketches of proposed images along with some captions or descriptions. Storyboards identify the theme and key scenes, and may be used as the basis for creating scripts and direction recommendations.

Program Theme

A program theme is the combination of visual elements, style, story and structure of the program. Multiple themes may be considered when creating a program, such as a history of a town or the biography of a person. The theme may be chosen to match the type of existing or desired audience, as well as the creative expertise and available budgets for production.

Scenes

Programs are composed of media segments (scenes). A brief scene description is typically included within a storyboard describing how the scene will be performed. A scene description can be used to identify the location and props that are needed for the scene.

Scripting

Script writing is a process of creating or preparing text that will be used for dialog in media programs. In addition to narration text (name and text), supplemental details may be included in the script, such as props and actors' facial expressions. Occasionally, scripts can contain recommendations for shooting the scenes. There are software programs that can simplify the scripting process, which keep track of actors' names and other items.

Figure 9.2 shows a TV ad storyboard for logo animation. This storyboard shows how the Althos logo (a question mark combined with a light bulb) will hop across the screen (1) until it finds a book (2). The book opens and the pages begin to turn (3) and each page that turns causes the logo to get bigger (4). After several page turns, the logo lights up (5) and the company tag line "Simplifying Knowledge" is added below the logo (6).

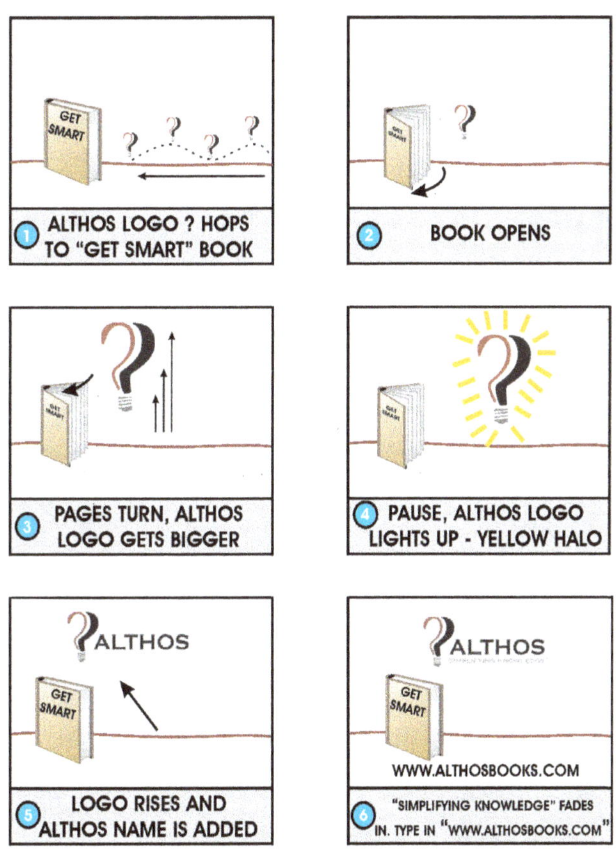

Figure 9.2, TV Storyboard Production Process

Content Sources

The content that is used to produce television programs can come from multiple sources that include original production (recording), stock media and program archives.

Original Content

Original content is the creation of new media. Original content can be produced in studios, on location or at events. When producing original content, some of the key considerations include obtaining the appropriate licenses and permissions, which can include performance rights, location releases, personal releases, music releases and other authorization for the use of the media.

Stock Media

Stock media is comprised of existing sets of media items, such as images, audio and video segments, which can be used or inserted into media materials. Stock media items are often categorized to help producers find and select appropriate media items for their content production needs. Stock media may be owned by people or companies who sell or license the images for use, may be offered for free use by their owners in return for promotional mention (citations), or may be publicly available at no cost (such as government media items).

Stock media may be licensed on an exclusive (single user) or non-exclusive (multiple users) basis. Some stock media companies will display the number of licenses that have been issued and allow companies to purchase the remaining rights to license the content. Stock media providers that identify their content as royalty free usually charge a fixed fee for the use of the content.

Program Archives

Existing media may be available from previously created movies, shows or other programs (archives). TV networks and movie studios have departments that are setup to catalog and license segments of movies and television programs. Content that has become part of the public domain, such as NASA space program military footage, may be cataloged and made available for use.

Figure 9.3 shows some of the sources of content that may be used to produce media programs. Original content can come from studio production, on location production or coverage of events. Stock media may be exclusive or non-exclusive content that is provided by other companies. Archives can include media segments from movies, TV programs or other media sources.

Content Source	Description	Notes
Original Content	Created by the System Operator	Studio Content On Location Content
Stock Media	Content Produced by Companies for other Companies to Use	Exclusive, Non-Exclusive
Archives	Content that was Previously Produced	Movies, TV Shows
Public Content	Content that is available for Anyone to Use	Government Video, Expired Copyrights
Content Aggregators	Content that is Available for Licensing	Aggregators tend to Specialize in Content Types

Figure 9.3, TV Program Production Content Sources

Talent

Some of the types of people (talent) that may be used to produce TV programs include directors, actors, and production staff. A production company may be used to find and manage the talent for the production of programs.

Directors

A director is a person who is responsible for coordinating the activities of actors and the production of media (television, film) programs. The director's role is to convert the script into a media program. The director decides how scenes should be staged, where the cameras will be located, and how the actors should perform (coaching). Directors may specialize in certain types of media such as documentaries, commercials or dramas. The director may be the first person hired, and may play a key part of the selection of actors and production staff.

Actors

Actors are people who are willing to perform actions based on scripts and direction from other people. Actors may be professional actors, amateur actors or volunteers (extras).

Professional actors may be represented by agencies which catalog and promote them (images, descriptions and videos). Professional actors may belong to unions that restrict their ability to perform in programs that are produced by companies that do not belong to a union. Amateur actors may come from staff or from other sources such as schools or groups. Amateur actors may be willing to perform as actors in return for the publicity the content will create. Volunteers (extras) are people who may be willing to participate without roles or compensation.

Production Staff

Production staff is the people that build, setup and operate the equipment at the shooting locations. Production staff roles include many job functions, including videographers (camera operators), labor for set construction and setup, electricians and other technical trades that setup power and communication for equipments.

Figure 9.4 shows some of the talent that may be used to create media programs. Directors define scene staging and camera locations, and coach actors. Actors may be professional performers, amateur actors or volunteers (extras). Production staff includes videographers, technical workers and labor for set construction and setup.

Studio Production

A studio is a room or facility that is designed for the recording of audio, video or other forms of media. Internet TV broadcasters may have their own studio, lease studio space, use virtual studios (simulated sets), or perform remote recording (such as remote interviews).

Talent	Description	Notes
Director	Define screen staging, camera locations, and coach actors	Directors may focus on specific types of media such as documentaries or commercials.
Actors	People who perform using scripts and direction.	May be professional (paid) or amateur people (volunteers).
Production Staff	Videographer, technical workers, laborers	There are many specific roles for production. Small productions require the same people to be used for multiple types of jobs.

Figure 9.4, TV Program Talent

Television Studios

A television studio is composed of one or more rooms that are designed or setup for the recording of video and audio. Television studios usually have a production control room that allows for the selection, processing and mixing of media signals to produce a television program.

Television studios may be located near loading docks to provide easy access to receive and move props. They may include a mixture of mounting stands and rigs that can be used to mount cameras and lighting equipment. Television studios may also be located near other rooms such as green rooms (guest preparation rooms), control rooms and dressing rooms.

Studio Rental

Television recording studios may be rented from TV stations or from media production companies. Rented studios may come equipped with production equipment. Some studio rental companies may also be able to provide skilled production staff that can be hired to assist in the production. This can be extremely helpful to Internet TV broadcasters that are relatively new to media production and have limited knowledge and experience.

Virtual Studios

A virtual studio is a media production area or facility that uses video processing equipment to replace parts of a traditional studio facility. A virtual studio may be an open area with a single color background that can be replaced by a graphic image. For example, a TV broadcaster can set up a table for interviews and insert a background image from another location such as in front of the White House or Eiffel Tower.

Remote Sites

Remote sites are locations where a reporter or another person can be recorded. Remote sites can be setup using relatively inexpensive web cameras and directional microphones that can be connected through the Internet. With a bit of experience, it is possible to do remote interviews with people that look professional with little cost to the producer.

Figure 9.5 shows some of the types of studios and locations that can be used to produce content. Television studios have a controlled environment (visual and sound), contain lighting and recording equipment, and are located close to a door so that props and other items can be easily moved in and out. Studios may be rented and the companies that own them may also be able to provide experienced staff to assist in the production. Virtual studios replace the background with computer generated graphics. It is also possible to record from remote locations (such as within a building) using relatively low cost cameras and microphones, which are linked to the production studio via Internet connections.

Production Location	Description	Notes
Studios	Controlled environment that contains lighting and recording equipment.	TV Studios may be rented from production companies or other TV stations
Virtual Studios	An area that contains a single color backdrop that allows the insertion of another background image.	Almost any location can be converted into a virtual studio
Remote Sites	A location that is not directly controlled by the producing company	Requires coordinating with site owner and getting permission to use video (release forms)

Figure 9.5, TV Production Locations

Video Editing Systems

Video editing systems are used to create a media program from one or more segments or content sources. Editing systems can utilize online editing (select and modify the high resolution media) or offline editing (selecting segments and identifying splice in and splice out points). Some of the key features for video editing systems include media formats, timelines, effects and remote editing capabilities.

Video editing systems can be set up on standard personal computers (Windows, MAC, Linux). However, it is helpful to have additional memory and media processing equipment (accelerator cards) to speed up the editing process. Video editing systems may be available through trial downloads (typically 30 days).

Media Components Formats

Video editing systems identify and organize video and audio media segments. There are many types of video and audio formats and not all video editing systems can recognize and use all types. For example, older video editing systems will not be able to edit newer media formats such as MPEG-4.

Timeline Editing

Video editing systems manage timelines for video and audio. These timelines may be presented in graphic user interface form, allowing editors to simply drag entry and exit points for each media segment.

Effects

Video editing systems can include many types of enhancements (effects), which can provide visual elements and transition effects. Video elements can include text titles, graphics and logos that may be added to the media. Video editing systems may offer many types of transition effects between segments such as fades and wipes. These visual effects are merged with the original media to produce the final media programs.

Remote Editing

Remote editing is the ability of a person or device to select, manage and organize media or data via communication links (such as an Internet connection). Remote editing can be important if there are several people who are making edits to a media program.

It is usually not practical to allow remote editing sessions to control the actual media (uncrompessed media), as the bandwidth and processing requirements would be too much for standard computers and Internet connections. To overcome this, remote editing systems provide low resolution previews of media.

Figure 9.6 shows some of the key features that may be included in video editing systems. Video editing systems may be able to use many types of video and audio formats. Editing may be performed in graphic user interface (GUI) form allowing the editor to drag entry and exit points. Video effects can include graphic overlays and transitions between media segments. Remote editing is the ability to allow one or more editors to connect from other locations (such as through the Internet) providing low res version of the media for display.

Feature	Description	Notes
Supported Media Formats	The structure of video and audio media.	Should support multiple compressed and uncompressed formats and profiles such as MPEG-2 and AVI.
Graphic User Interface (GUI)	The ability to modify content by selecting and dragging images.	More simple GUIs allow semi-skilled workers to edit and produce content.
Video and Audio Effects	The ability to modify media.	A good set of video and audio effects can dramatically improve the media content.
Remote Editing	Allows viewing and editing in lower resolution format at remote locations. Creates an edit decision list that is used to produce the final content.	Automatically provided using a hosted video editing platform.

Figure 9.6, Key Video Editing System Features

Live Internet TV

Live Internet TV broadcasting (real time streaming) is the capturing and immediate retransmitting of media through the public Internet. Live Internet TV involves media acquisition, content selection and mixing, and formatting of information so that it can be transmitted through the Internet.

Production systems have been evolving from simple video switching systems to smart automated workflow systems that can switch, record, and live stream media through the Internet. Manufacturers of smart live TV production and streaming switchers include NewTek (Tricaster), Telestream (Wirecast), and Livestream.

Location Preparation

Location preparation involves a review of the site, talking with staff and getting permissions, identification of lighting and sound requirements, and selection and installation of equipment.

Live Content Acquisition

Live content acquisition is the capturing of video and audio content immediately when it happens. Live acquisition may include the use of multiple cameras and microphones that are connected by multiple types of communication links.

Real Time Production

Real time production is the gathering, editing, and distributing of content as it occurs or within a short time period after it occurs. Real time production may involve the use of specialized editing tools such as instant replay or on display editing.

Live Broadcasting

Live broadcasting may involve the transfer of real time media to streaming servers that repackage and redistribute the media to multiple recipients. The live broadcasting system may control the access that viewers have to the broadcasted media (paid or subscribed services).

Figure 10.1 shows how live TV production includes acquisition, real time production and live broadcasting transmission. Live acquisition requires the use of a switching system and effects software to select and modify content. The live feed signal is connected to a broadcast system by a broadband connection. Live broadcasting is performed by receiving media and rapidly formatting and retransmitting the information to multiple viewers.

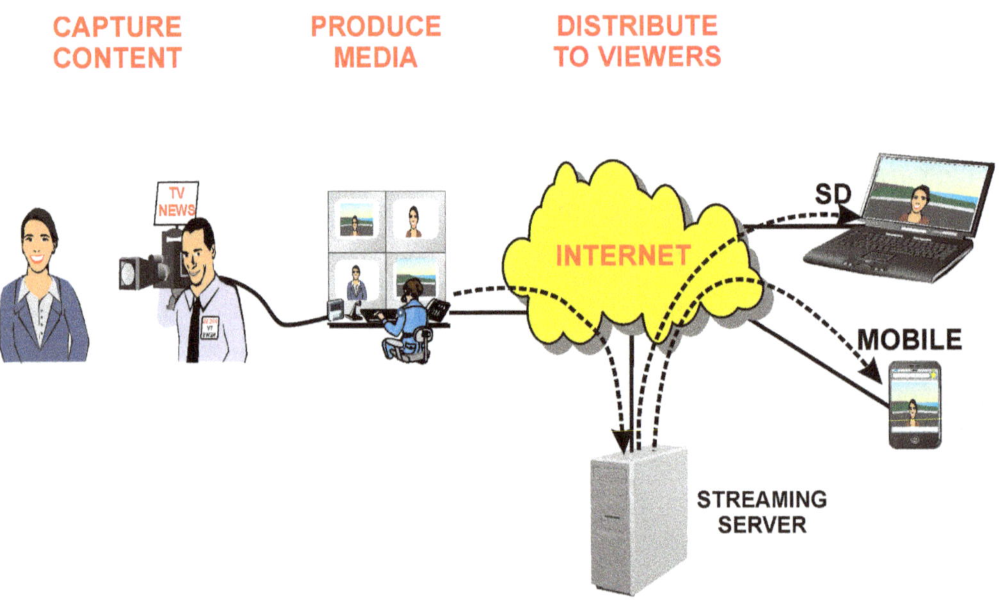

Figure 10.1, Live Video Production

Live Event Preparation

Live event preparation requires the producer to think about what is necessary in order to have a successful live broadcast. For live production, it's necessary to review the location for production options, meet the staff and acquire authorization to use the facilities, assess lighting and acoustic conditions, and identify the equipment choices and decide where they will be located.

Shoot Plan

A shoot plan should be created for a live event. The plan identifies shots, equipments, crew, and a schedule of tasks to complete them.

Site Review

The location of the event should be reviewed to determine how to setup video and audio recording and how the production will be run. Determine the locations at which equipment can be carried in and stored. Identify where the production crew can be located and how they can move around. Find power sources and determine how cables can be run between different equipment such that those in attendance will not be able to trip over or interfere with them.

Staff Introductions and Permissions

Talk with the staff at the location and note the names of the owner, manager, and key staff members at the location. Make sure that workers at the location know who you and your production crew are. This will help to prevent interference with production if a crew member cannot get into a restricted area, such as one permissible to employees only.

Get release forms signed by the manager of the facility (location release) and people who are participating in the event. Identify logos and brand names in the background that may require release forms for inclusion in the video.

Lighting Requirements

Lighting is the combination of natural and artificial lights that ensure the important elements of the event can be captured on video. Be careful when pointing light toward or directly at the person being recorded as this can create unwanted shadows. You can diffuse (spread) light over a wider area by using paper sheets or umbrellas, or by reflecting the light off ceilings, which can reduce the effects of shadows. You can use multiple lights to fill in background areas.

One method used to set up a lighting system is three point lighting. The three point lighting system helps eliminate unwanted shadows from direct light sources. In this arrangement, the problems with shading and shadows are eliminated through the use of three different angles of lighting including key lighting, backlighting and fill lighting.

Identify other sources of artificial lighting, such as lamps or candles, which can influence the lighting of the event. Identify the controls for these lights and ensure that people do not control these at unwanted times.

Acoustics

Review the acoustics of the location such as noise sources and background noise levels. Turn off noisy equipment if possible and identify other potential noise sources that are likely to occur (such as fans or compressors).

Equipment Positioning

Equipment positioning involves the selection and placement of video cameras, microphones, lighting, production switching systems, and anything else vital to set the stage for the recording of the event. Positioning options can include multiple camera and microphone locations. Multiple camera shoots can avoid the recording of talking heads (boring video).

In addition to the creative aspects of camera locations, the placements should be selected with the anticipation of what will be likely to occur. This can include where groups of people may be located (camera above their heads) or activities that may occur.

Live Media Acquisition

Live media acquisition involves the setup and use of video cameras, microphones and other equipment that can capture media. A production crew and assistants should understand and have experience with their tasks.

Daily Call Sheet

A daily call sheet contains a list of crew and cast who are expected to be at a shoot with the times they are expected to arrive along with other useful information such as contacts, location, parking, safety notes, and other logistical information.

Live Video Cameras

Video cameras that are used for live media recording may have features that enable quick setup and operation in difficult-to-control conditions. Cameras should be mounted on tripods or attached to stable objects whenever possible.

Some of the key features that can be helpful for video cameras that are used in live production include solid state digital storage, low light level sensitivity, automatic focus, and image stabilization, and power zoom.

Cameras that use solid state digital media storage (memory cards) can be setup in a shorter amount of time. It is recommended to use memory cards that can store more than enough video, without requiring the changing of the memory card during an event. Have storage containers available for the memory cards with labels that make them easy to identify (not just 1, 2, 3).

Cameras that can operate in low light conditions are helpful. While these cameras may be more expensive and have larger lenses than consumer grade cameras, it can be very helpful in situations when additional lighting cannot be setup or provided.

Automatic focus can be extremely helpful in time limited situations. Be careful of automatic focus because it is possible that the camera will adjust to focus in on the wrong object. Some cameras have face identification which allows them to focus on the subject rather than an object in the background.

Image stabilization can be an essential feature for cameras that must be handheld. This feature keeps the image as a steady shot even though the camera is moving. Be careful when using image stabilization as the frame area is reduced to compensate for the movement.

While zoom can enhance the impact of an event, it is better to get closer and avoid the use of zoom. Be careful with rapid transitions as they can disorient the viewer. A power zoom feature can provide a gradual transition. Zoom increases sensitivity to movement. When zooming in, remember that even small changes in camera position can result in big shifts in the viewing frame.

Microphones

Try to get microphones on or close to the people being recorded. Consider mounting a microphone on a mechanical arm (a boom) that places it near the people. Use digital wireless microphones that are not susceptible to radio interference and bring backup batteries for wireless microphones.

Use external microphones, not the microphone in the camera. Avoid mounting the microphone on devices with motors as this can create a hum. Continuously monitoring audio levels using headphones will allow you to hear what is actually being recorded.

Mount station logos on the microphones for an added branding opportunity and use foam wind guards when the microphones will be used outside.

Production Crew

A production crew is a group of people who assist in the capturing and production of media programs or services. It is helpful to have procedures and check lists for the tasks that the production crew should perform. Each production crew member should understand what they are expected to d and when they are expected to do it. It may be helpful to practice routines before the event occurs. This can include operating cameras, adjusting lighting and other tasks.

Live Media Production Console

Live media production consoles enable the input of multiple media sources, switching controls and the addition of effects in real time.

Console Inputs

Console inputs can include multiple video, audio and media inputs. These may be in multiple formats ranging from composite analog video to digital media. Using digital inputs can dramatically reduce the distortion of the media signals.

Switching

A production console enables a producer to select the input sources that will be used. The production console allows for the selection of multiple media sources, the grouping of video and audio channels, and level controls.

The console allows for the selection of which video and audio sources will be used. To simplify the production process, the console may be able to group inputs together (ganging). This allows the producer to select different cameras and have the audio sources (microphones near the cameras) automatically selected. The console buttons may allow for the display of labels which can be helpful when there are multiple camera feeds.

The console typically allows for the control of audio levels. Automatic audio leveling can be helpful. However, the ability to use manual controls can be essential to setting the right audio levels.

When using a software based production console that is used on a computer (such as a laptop), it is recommended to remove background processes. Unfortunately, this can include turning off virus scanning and firewalls.

Effects

Real time effects are changes to live media content such as visual overlays, playbacks and transitional effects (between scenes).

Overlay is the process of adding additional media items such as images (logos) or text on top of a media source (such as a video program). Overlays may be used to add graphics (visual objects) or live text. Live text allows for the manual insertion of text such as names, sports scores and comments. Overlays may be setup using templates that are quick and easy to use which can be critical during live production.

Some production consoles have direct digital recording (DDR) capability which allows for instant playback. It is helpful if the console has a simple to use content management process that allows for the identification of stored media segments, which allow for easy identification, selection and insertion (drag and play).

Production consoles may be able to provide hundreds of transition effects including wipes, peels, fades and others. It is helpful to select and use a limited number of transition effects throughout much of the production. Continuously changing the transition effects can confuse the viewer.

Figure 10.2 shows some of the key parts of a live production system. This includes multiple video and audio inputs, switching controls and effects generators. Input connections include video, audio and media (graphics and text). Switching controls enable the splicing of media sources (digital splicing), the associating (ganging) of video and audio sources together, and the mixing of audio channels. The effects generator can modify the video with text overlays, instant playback and transition effects (such as wipes, fades).

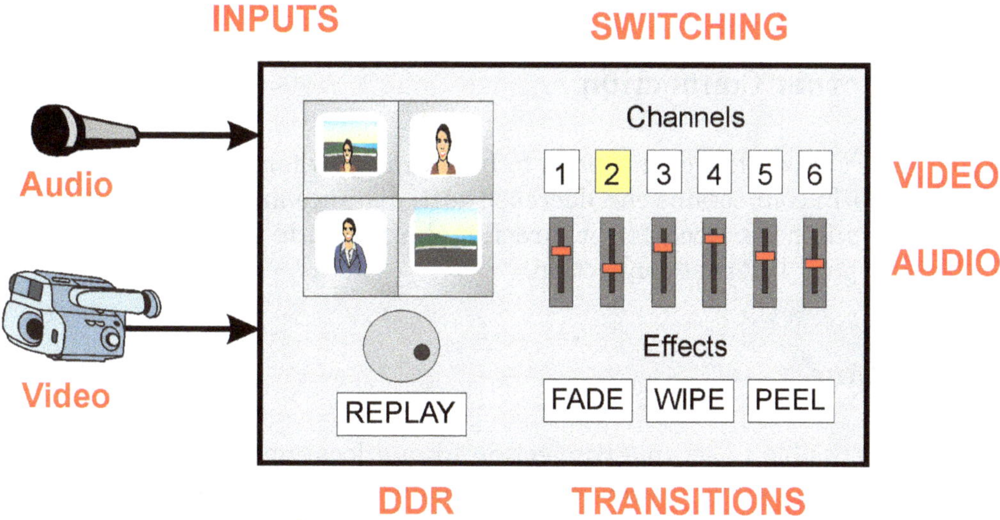

Figure 10.2, Live Video Production Console

Live Broadcast Communication Links

Communication links that are used for live broadcasting can include a broadband fee, video links, audio links and intercom communication lines. Live communication links need to be reliable and have backup connections, and it is helpful if they are easy to setup and use. The broadband connection should be reliable. Broadband feed connection options include fixed data connections, wireless links (Wi-Fi), wireless broadband, satellite expensive and mobile telephones.

Wired Internet Connection

A wired Internet connection can provide a fairly reliable connection to the Internet. Bring a long cord and a data hub in case there is no available plug in the data router. Test your connection early to ensure that it operates correctly. The maximum distance at which an Ethernet data cable can operate reliably is several hundred feet.

Wi-Fi Internet Connection

While Wi-Fi may allow connections to be setup anywhere, the data transfer rates on Wi-Fi connections can decrease with distance and fluctuate. It may be wise to purchase a booster or directional antenna to ensure a more reliable high-speed Internet connection.

Leased Line

It may be possible to setup a connection from a location through a dedicated communication line (leased line). This may be an excellent option for extremely critical live events. However, it can take some time to setup a leased line connection and the cost can be hundreds of dollars, even for a single day.

Mobile Data

Wireless broadband systems (WiMAX, 3G/4G mobile) may offer a low cost way to provide a broadband connection in remote locations. Some of the risks of using wireless broadband data connections include varying data rates. This can happen at any time if many people decide to simultaneously use the Internet in the same location. It is recommended to have at least two mobile data devices from different service providers (such as Verizon and T-Mobile). Some companies specialize in providing mobile data communication systems that can combine mobile data connections (clustering) from multiple service providers.

Satellite Links

Satellite links offer the ability to connect virtually anywhere through the use of a relatively small dish antenna. Using satellite link connections for video (high bandwidth) can be costly (over $10 per minute). However, in situations where no other broadband connections are available, it may be the only choice.

Intercoms

Intercoms are private communication systems that can be used by a production crew to coordinate the broadcast operation. Intercoms may share the bandwidth of connection lines or they may be separate connections. Intercoms can be wired or wireless systems and they commonly use headsets to allow staff to complete their jobs without having to carry a communication device.

There may be several intercom connections. The director may talk to camera operators while the stage manager talks with stage hands and lighting operators.

Figure 10.3 shows some of the available communication link options for live broadcast feeds. A broadband data connection is used to carry both digital video and digital audio links. This broadband data connection can be sent over satellite, over wireless links (such as Wi-Fi), or through a wired data connection (Internet or leased data line). Backup video and audio links (mobile phone and telephone line) are setup on other communication systems to be used in the event that the primary broadband communication link becomes disabled. Intercoms are communication links that allow production staff to coordinate their actions.

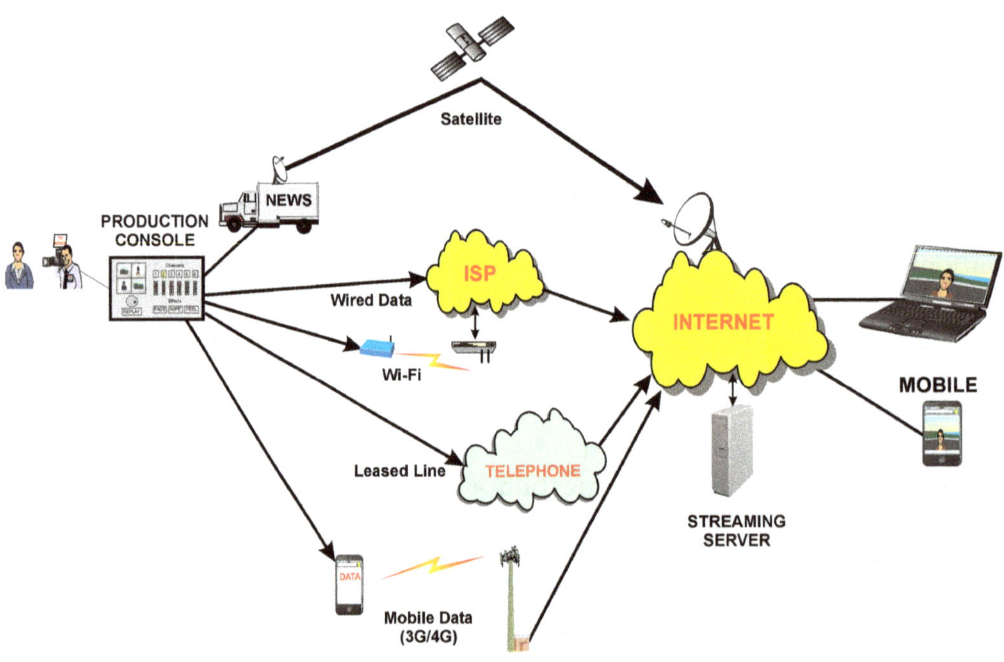

Figure 10.3, Live Broadcasting Communication Links

Live IP Broadcasting

Live IP broadcasting is the transmission of the same media stream to many recipients that are connected to the Internet. Live IP broadcasting involves connecting the event media feed to a media encoding system and managing the streams to multiple viewing devices. Live IP broadcasting can be provided through the use of a content distribution network (CDN) service.

Media Uplink

A key part of IP broadcasting is the connecting (linking) of the event media feed to the content distribution system. The connection to the IP media broadcasting system requires the stream to be in a defined media format (such as MPEG-2).

Media Encoding

Live media encoders must be capable of receiving and converting the incoming media into multiple formats that can be sent to viewers. Real time media encoding has very limited compression analysis time and, in general, benefits from the use of more expensive hardware based media encoders.

The media encoding system must also create different wrappers (stream formats) for different types of devices such as Apple iPads and Android mobile telephones.

Streaming Sessions

IP broadcast systems control access to streams and manage the streaming sessions. When broadcasters use content distribution network services, they typically pay fees that are based on the number of viewers (sessions) and the data rates that the viewers receive.

Some of the options for streaming services include supported media format types (TV, PC, mobile phone), data rates (quality levels), number of viewers, authorized geographic locations and other options.

Figure 10.4 shows how an IP streaming system can operate. The broadcaster performs the media capturing using a camera and microphone that is connected to a laptop computer. The laptop computer is connected to an IP streaming service provider, which converts (encodes) the incoming media into a format that is transmitted to a streaming service. The streaming service converts the stream into multiple formats that can be provided to different types of viewing devices (mobile phones, computers, TV set top boxes). The streaming service also manages how viewers can access (connect to) the streaming channels.

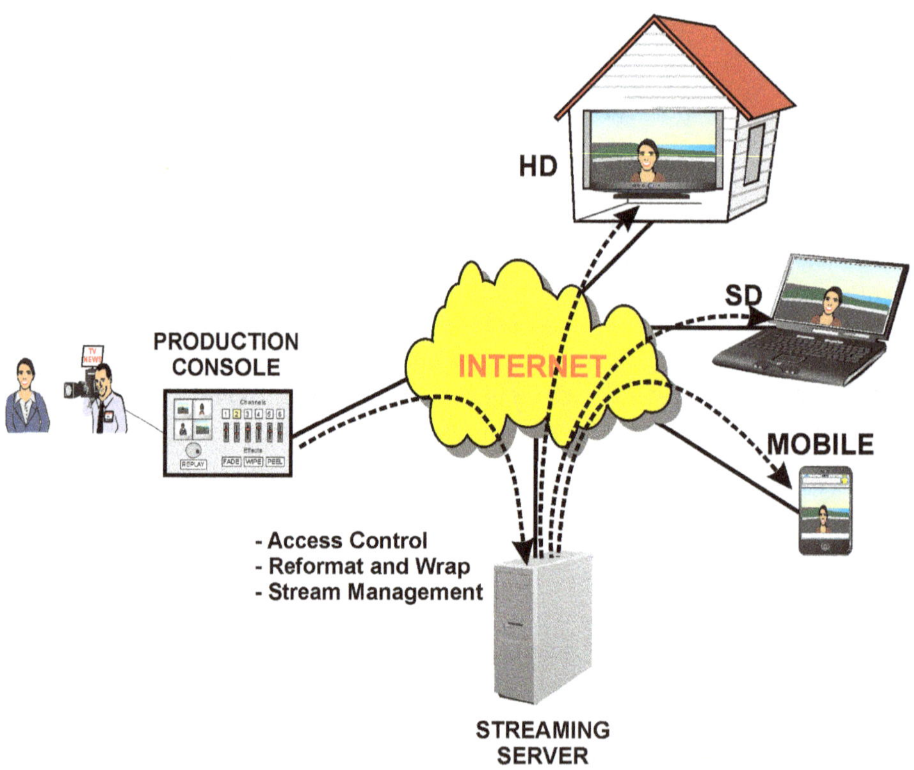

Figure 10.4, Internet TV Live Broadcasting

Backup Plans

Another important part of production is understanding the challenges that can possibly arise during an interview. A broadband connection could possibly fail in the middle of the interview, or one of the microphones could malfunction. It is not only important to understand how to find and use the right equipment, but how to recover by having a backup plan, should something fail during the broadcast.

Connection Loss

In the case of a broadcast that takes place between two separate locations, several technical difficulties can potentially arise. To avoid the chance of any of these occurring, make sure transmission and communication links are checked before broadcasting live. Also, run a complete technical check. All technical requirements should be evaluated, even if both the interviewer and interviewee are at the same location.

Backup Image

A backup image is a media item that can be displayed in the event of a connection loss or technical difficulty. An example of a backup image is a photo of a previous event or a person that is part of the current event.

Alternate Sources

Even if you check all technical aspects of the interview before broadcasting live, it is still possible to have technical failures during the stream. Consider having some prerecorded audio clips for the remote TV broadcast just in case, as well as visual to replace video content, such as a split screen picture or photo of the speaker that could be used while technical difficulties are being solved.

Figure 10.5 shows a sample backup image. A still image may be a good substitution to upload should problems arise with video quality, eliminating occurrences where viewers are forced to look at a blank screen. The backup image may also be used to introduce the speaker.

Figure 10.5 Remote TV Interview Backup Image

Internet TV Billing

Internet TV billing systems are composed of computers, software programs and databases of information, along with system interfaces (Network, Marketing, Customer Care, Finance, etc.) that can gather, organize, rate and combine billing-related events. TV billing systems need to have unique features and services compared to other types of billing systems, such as the ability to process many types of transaction and subscription services, dynamic advertising ratings, and web-based billing interfaces.

The key functional parts of a billing system include event recording, usage records creation, events rating, bill calculation, customer care, bill rendering, payment processing and management reporting. In addition to the basic billing system functions, billing systems share information with many other business functions such as sales, marketing, customer care, finance and operations.

A typical billing process involves collecting usage information from network equipment (such as media servers, access devices and set top boxes), translating and formatting the usage information into records that can be understood by a billing system, transferring these records to the billing system, assigning charge fees to each event, creating invoices, and receiving and recording payments from the customers.

Subscriber Database

A subscriber database is an informational and relational database which includes subscriber information, including usage patterns, billing records, personal information and other related data. This base is often "mined" for information, which helps identify potential new service buyers, churn candidates and provide useful marketing information.

Services List

A services list identifies each service that may be provided by the system. The services list contains unique identifiers, descriptions and service requirements.

Rate Plans

A rate plan is the structure of service fees that a user will pay for the use of services. Rate plans are typically divided into monthly fees and usage fees.

Advertising Campaigns

Advertising campaigns are marketing activities designed to send specific advertising messages to customers about products, services and options offered by a company.

Sales Transactions

Sales transactions are actions or completed events, such as product orders or subscription registrations, which are managed or controlled by a company or person that sells products or services.

Revenue Sharing Agreements

Revenue sharing is the process of transferring revenues generated by one or more companies to one or more other companies for the exchange of products or services. The products or services that are provided by the recipient(s) of revenue sharing may or may not be related to the creation of the revenues that are shared.

Rating System

Rating is a function within the billing system that assigns a rate (cost parameter) to a usage record. Rating typically involves the use of the originating number or network address, the terminating number or destination network address, the date the service was used, the amount and type of usage, and the tax jurisdiction to determine the initial charge assigned to the usage record. The actual cost of the usage record may be adjusted based on volume discounts or other rate plan considerations.

Invoicing

Invoicing is the process of gathering (aggregating) and totaling all billing records associated with a specific account during a billing cycle in a bill pool. Invoicing also includes the application of recurring charges (monthly charges) and the totaling of all charges.

Payment Processing

Payment processing is the tasks and functions that are used to collect payments from a buyer of products or services. Payment systems may involve the use of money instruments, credit memos, coupons or other forms of compensation used to pay for one or more order invoices.

Customer Support

Customer support is the processes and communications that occur between customers and companies, enabling customers to resolve problems and successfully obtain products and services from the company.

Figure 11.1 shows an overview of a billing and customer care system that can be used for Internet TV communication services. First, the network records events that contain usage information. This example shows that billing information usually includes a user identification code, service request date and time, destination address, source address, media type, and usage duration or amount of service provision. Next, these events are combined and reformatted into a single usage detail record (UDR). Because these events only contain network usage information, the identity of the user must be matched (guided) to the event detail record, and the service rate must be determined. After the total charge for the service is calculated using the service rate for that particular user, the billing record is updated and sent to a bill pool (list of ready-to-bill usage records). Periodically, a bill is produced for the customer and, as payments are received, they are recorded (posted) to the customer's account. The charge is then "journalized"; it is assigned a financial account.

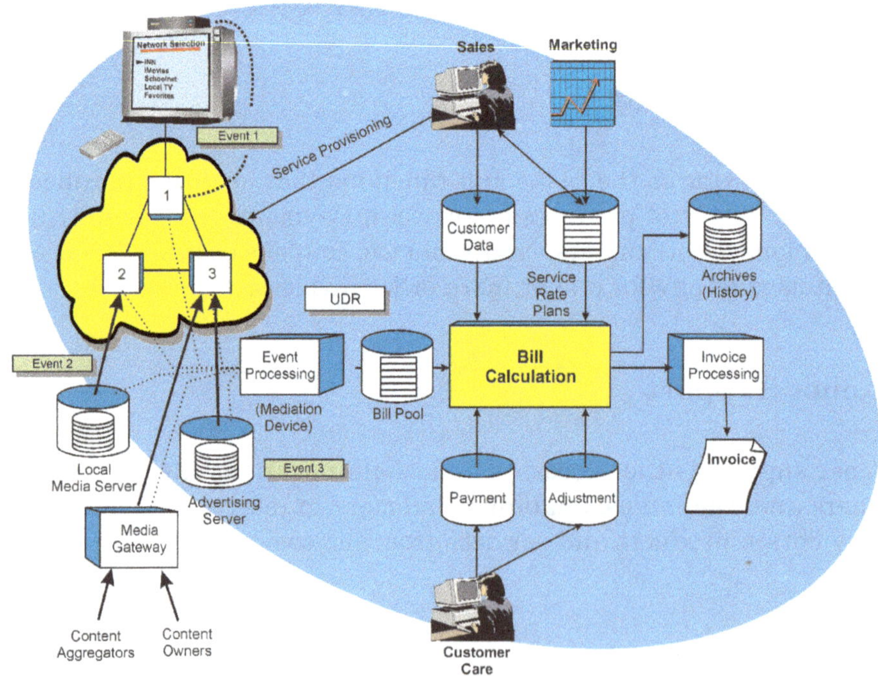

Figure 11.1, Internet TV Billing and Customer Care System

Subscriber Database

A subscriber database is an informational and relational database which includes subscriber information, including usage patterns, billing records, personal information and other related data. A subscriber database may be linked to other information databases, including customer care, maintenance history and marketing.

Subscriber Account

A subscriber account is a unique identifier that designates a customer or company that is used to associate billing charges for products and services. A single customer may have multiple billing accounts which may be linked to a single master account.

Subscriber Profile

A subscriber profile is the characteristics that are associated with a person or device that has been registered or setup to receive a service, such as a news program, over a period of time. Several details may be used to define a subscriber profile for each subscriber account.

Subscriber Services

Subscriber services are the list of items that the subscriber has agreed to obtain on a continuous (subscription) basis. Customers may purchase multiple services, which may influence how other services are billed and provided.

Subscriber Communication History

Account communication history is the set of records or event information used to identify or provide information on customer communication, transaction events or other data associated with an account.

Figure 11.2 shows that a subscriber database can contain several parts (tables and relationships). The subscriber table contains a customer identification code (subscriber_ID), which is the unique key that is used by other tables. A subscriber_details table contains the details and preferences associated with the customer such as the billing and shipping address. A subscriber_services table identifies the subscription items the customer has purchased or authorized. A subscriber_communication table contains communication event records such as email communication (CE_4721) and telephone communication (CT_1619).

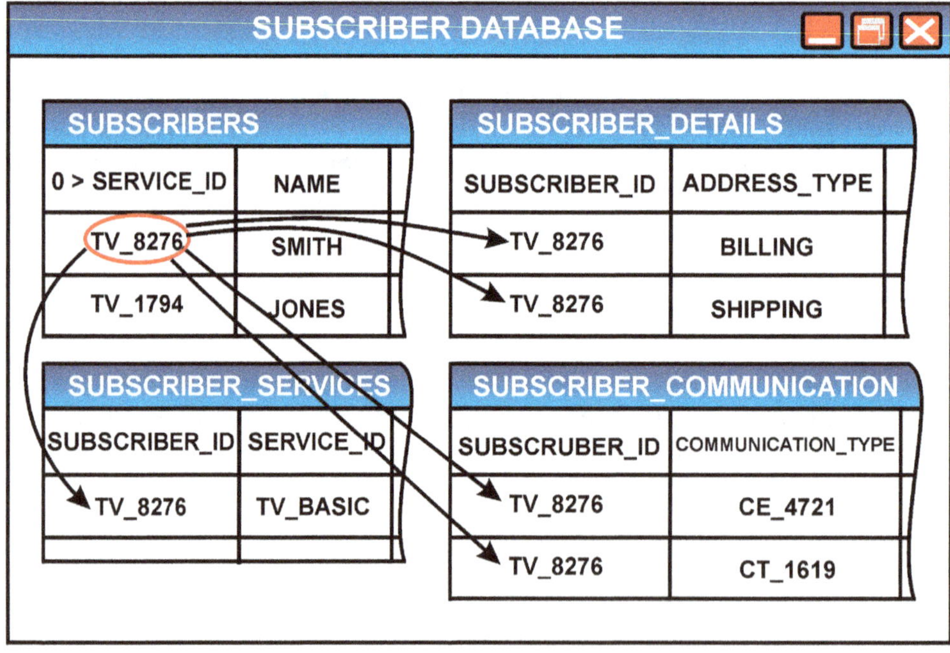

Figure 11.2, Internet TV Subscriber Database

Services Database

A services database contains a list of content access functions and items available for purchase, and the parameters needed to use or interact with them. Internet TV systems typically combine several different types of services, such as subscription, on demand, advertising and applications. Some services may be dependent on the availability of equipment and the subscription of other services.

Service Items

A service item is a resource assignment, such as access to a channel or media program. A service item record may contain details of the service or product, which may include the service identifier code, name, assigned cost and other details associated with the service.

Service Descriptions

Service descriptions are written statements that provide information that can identify available services, and possibly motivate people to purchase those services. A service record may contain multiple text descriptions of varying lengths. Shorter descriptions may be used for invoice item service descriptions while longer descriptions (more marketing focused) may be used on product description web pages.

Service Types

Service types are the classifications of items so they can be identified with group characteristics such as subscription, event (on demand), advertising, software application, or other service categories. The use of service classification allows billing systems to use different types of processing, such as single transaction rating or repetitive billing, when certain services or items are provided.

Subscription Services

Subscription services are access authorizations that are provided over a period of time. These authorizations may include allowing access to channels (ability to view channels), distribution of media, or processing of data (information services).

On Demand

On demand services are the authorizations to access media or programs on an event or time limited basis. On demand services include the identification of a media source (such as a file or program) and a designation of where and how the media can be accessed by a user (possibly stored on a marketing partner's content management system).

Advertising Services

Advertising services charge companies for the insertion or availability of advertising messages. Internet TV systems may provide many types of advertising such as ad insertion, overlays or interactive promotional services. Billing for advertising services may involve direct rating systems (cost per thousand measured impressions) or estimated rating systems (estimated number of viewers of a shared broadcast channel).

Advertising services may be sold by other companies, such as advertising agencies, requiring commissions (agency fees) to be paid.

Applications

Internet TV users may purchase or use application programs (such as games, information processing, news services). The identification and rating of applications can involve tracking application functions such as the application ID, start time, end time, usage amounts (bandwidth and/or storage) and other measurable items.

Service Provisioning

When users purchase services, the system must be configured to allow for service usage, tracking and billing.

Service Requirements

Service requirements are the combination of equipment and configurations that are necessary to enable users or devices to obtain desired media or operations. Service requirements can include minimum bandwidth levels, media formats and types of compatible devices. Service requirements may identify the tasks and scripts (sequences of commands) used to setup and configure equipment, along with the network addresses and access codes required for use.

Figure 11.3 shows how a services database holds service items, descriptions and provisioning requirements. A service_items table holds the unique service_ID (key). A service_type table identifies the classification and characteristics of the service (standard definition video, high definition video). A service_requirements table holds the necessary services or values (such as minimum bandwidth). A service_provisioning table identifies the tasks or scripts that need to be performed in order to activate a service.

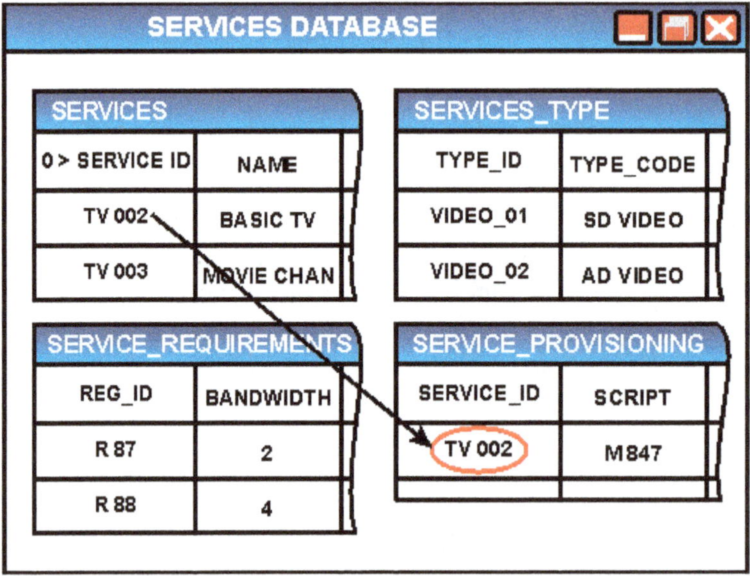

Figure 11.3, Internet TV Services Database

Rate Plans

A rate plan is the structure of service fees that a user will pay to obtain access to content or features. Rate plans are typically divided into periodic charges (monthly subscription costs) and transaction charges (usage fees). Multiple service rate plans may also be grouped into packages (bundles), which provide a discount to the customer.

Periodic Charges

Periodic charges are fees that are associated with a product or service that is assessed on a regular interval (monthly, quarterly, annually).

Transaction Rates

A transaction rate is a value that is assessed for each event (transaction) that occurs. There may be multiple types of transactions such as single view transactions or daily rental rates. Transaction rates may also vary based on the type of content. Newer movies may have much higher viewing costs compared to older movies.

Packages (Bundles)

Packages are combinations of services and products. Billing systems may use package item numbers to identify the discount rates or they may use the full value of the service item rates and apply discounts based on the combination of services.

Figure 11.4 shows how rate plans may include a combination of periodic and transaction fees. The rate plan for a specific customer is determined by the selection of a mixture of subscription services (recurring fees). This example shows that a customer has combined a basic subscription service with a pre-

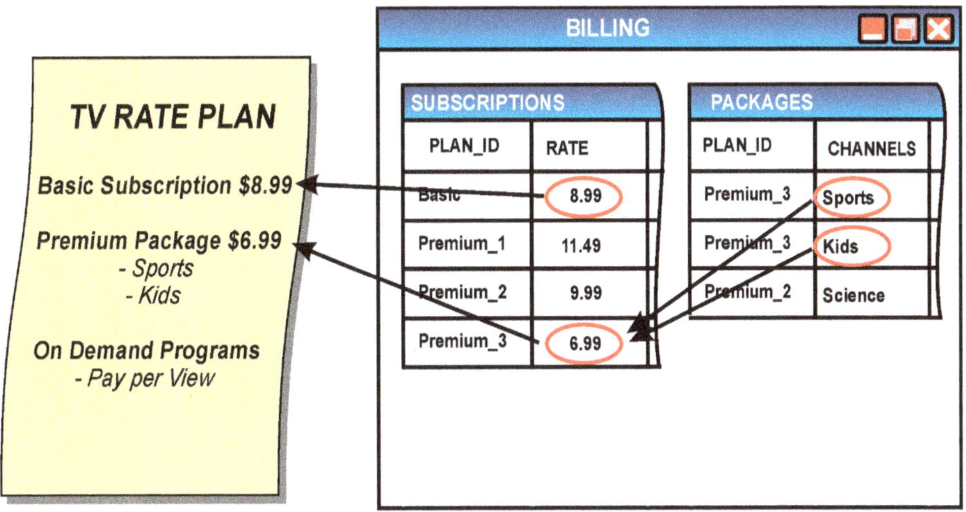

Figure 11.4, Internet TV Rate Plans

mium subscription service (sports and kids channel). This user's rate plan also allows the customer to purchase on demand content on a pay per view basis.

Advertising Sales

Billing for Internet TV advertising involves identifying the terms in the advertising contract, creating insertion orders, tracking insertion events, rating the cost of each insertion, and determining commissions that should be paid to agencies or sales representatives.

Advertising Contract Terms

Advertising contract terms include the advertising rates, authorized insertions and controls (limits) placed on the advertising campaign. The advertising contract is used to create the insertion orders and determine the values that are used for calculating (rating) the ad insertion amounts. The rates charged for insertions can vary by region, time of day, channel and program type.

Insertion Orders

An ad insertion order is an authorization to place advertising messages within TV programs or other types of media. Ad insertion orders usually contain specifications regarding media types, dates and times, and may assign other restrictions that control the placement of the ads.

Insertion Events

Insertion events are the actual placements of ads within programs. Insertion orders may not be processed for several reasons, which may include being pre-empted by an ad with a higher priority (higher paid ad), unavailability of the ad time slot (program pre-empted by a news alert) or other reasons. Insertion events are stored in an ad insertion log. The insertion log contains ad identification information, network and program identification, date and time of the insertion event, and the results of the insertion (full insertion, partial insertion).

Insertion Rating

Insertion rating is the process that assigns a cost to the insertion of an advertising message. Different programs and time periods may require the use of different rating amounts (different cpms). The cost of the insertion may be calculated using the number of viewers, which may be directly measured or estimated by rating services (such as Nielsen ratings).

Sales Commissions

Sales commissions may be paid on advertising sales to direct staff or sales agents. Advertising agencies receive a commission (typically 15% to 20%) of the negotiated broadcast rate. The advertiser may pay the advertising agency, which then pays the Internet TV provider the agreed rate less the commission amount.

Figure 11.5 shows how a TV billing system can track, rate and invoice for advertising services. The process starts with an advertising agreement that contains the terms, such as advertising rates (per thousand), authorized networks, budget limits and other criteria. The TV system uses these rules to create ad insertion orders. Actual ad insertions are recorded (logged) which can be used by the billing system for tracking. The billing system can use insertion log reports to determine which ads were inserted into specific networks, channels and programs. The rating for the ad insertion can vary based on the number of viewers, network and program type. The rated ad insertions are combined to produce invoices, which may be used to determine sales commissions for agencies and sales representatives.

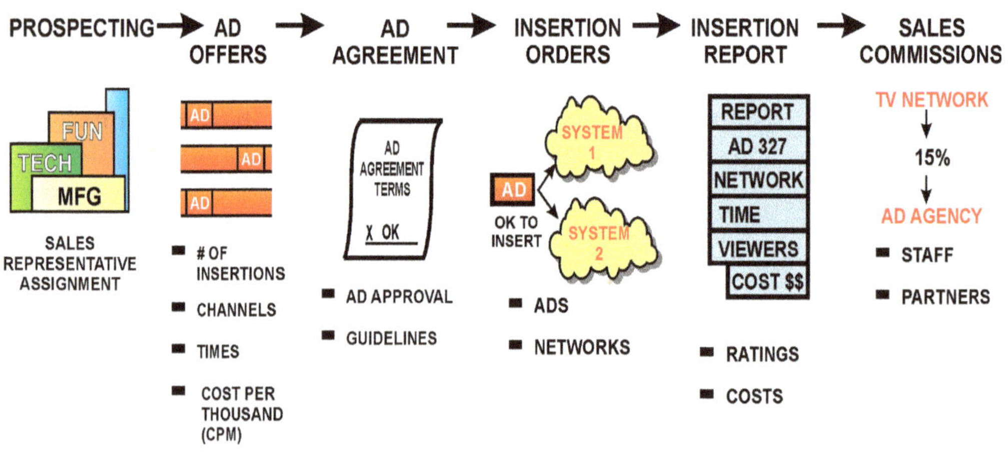

Figure 11.5, Internet TV Advertising Billing

Equipment Billing

Equipment billing is the association of costs and revenues to devices. These can include product costs, leasing revenues, activation fees and service contracts.

Product Cost

The Internet TV viewing device, such as a digital media adapter or media player, may be purchased by the consumer from a retailer, or it may be available from the Internet TV provider. The Internet TV provider may sell the product below its retail cost (subsidized) by requiring the customer to sign a service contract.

Leasing Rates

Some Internet TV service providers lease Internet TV devices to their customers. The leasing costs that the Internet TV provider must pay include the initial product cost, repair costs, and the costs of refurbishing the leased equipment.

Activation Fees

An activation fee is a one-time charge for the initial setup of communication services. Activation fees may be not be charged (waived) when certain conditions occur, such as when the customer purchases a product directly from the Internet TV provider.

Service Contracts

Service contracts are documents or recordings that define the terms for the provision of services by a person or company to a person or company that will use or have the rights to use the services. Service contracts may define how an equipment subsidy may be provided and the penalties for breaking the agreement (early termination).

Figure 11.6 shows some of the billing processes that are related to equipment purchase and usage. The example shows that the user may purchase a product from a retailer (own the product), purchase the product from the Internet TV company, or lease the product from the Internet TV company.

User 1 purchased an Internet TV device from a retail store for $80 (a Blu-ray player), was charged a product activation fee of $15, and has a monthly contract of $7.99. User 2 leases an Internet TV device from the Internet TV provider for $7.99 per month, has no activation fee (waived), and pays a monthly fee of $7.99. User 3 purchased their device from the Internet TV provider for $39.99 (subsidy of $60), has no activation fee (waived), and pays a monthly fee of $6.99 (lower rate for a 1 year service contract).

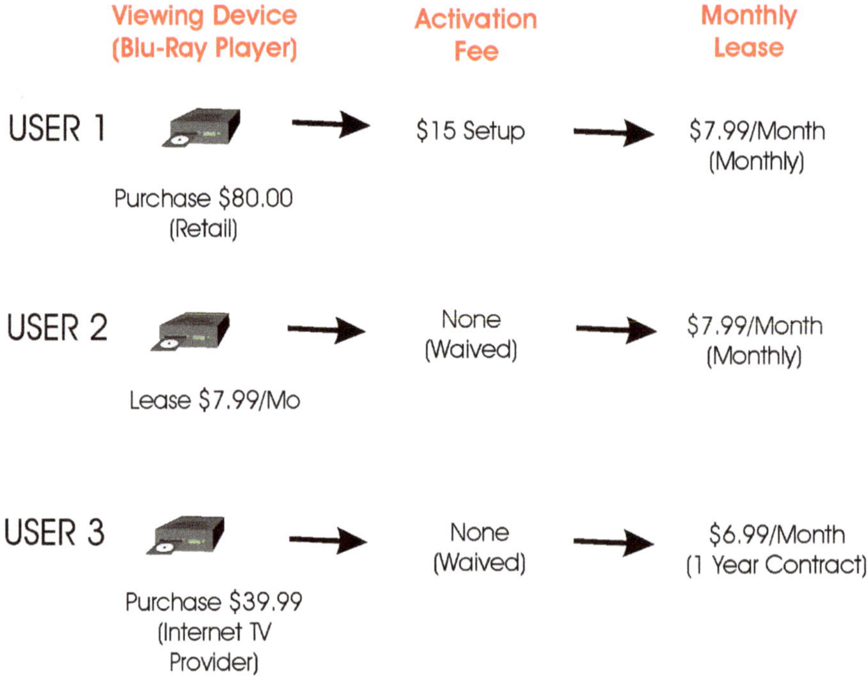

Figure 11.6, Internet TV Equipment Billing

Online Billing

Online billing is the process of grouping service cost or product usage information for specific accounts or customers with usage records, invoices and payments that may be viewed, and possibly controlled, via an Internet web portal.

Online Account Presentation

Online account presentation is the conversion (rendering) of billing information into a form that can be displayed to a viewer that is connected to the Internet. The presentation of billing information can vary based on the type of device, such as presentation on computers with large screens or mobile devices that have Internet browsing capability. The online presentation system should be able to detect the type of device and adapt the presentation format so the device can use it.

To present information to a customer's web browser, a web server may be used. The web server formats the information that it obtains from a billing system through an application program interface (API).

Pending Transactions

Some of the billing information that has not been processed may need to be estimated (temporarily rated) and shown as pending transactions. Traditional billing systems perform invoicing in batch format (one time at the end of a billing period). Online invoicing may require the billing system to gather and rate services that have not been billed yet. This means that customers may see and create transactions before they are processed or approved. These transactions are shown as pending transactions (they may change).

Online Invoicing

Online invoicing is the process of providing customers with access to their invoices (current and previous) so they can view, select and pay for them. Invoicing is the process of gathering (aggregating) and adding up all billing records associated with a specific account during a billing cycle in a bill pool (collection of billing records to be paid), applying recurring charges (monthly charges) and totaling all the charges. Invoices may be presented to the viewer in HTML (web) or PDF (exact image).

Payment Gateway

When customers enter payment information, it is sent to a merchant processor via a payment gateway. The merchant processor's payment gateway receives the payment details from the merchant and adapts the information into a format that can be submitted to the bank for payment collection.

Figure 11.7 shows how an online billing system allows users to view and interact with their account billing information. A web server communicates with a billing system through an application program interface (API). The billing system can retrieve billing records (such as previous invoices). The billing system may be setup to provide pending charges (temporary rating). The web server identifies the type of viewing device (such as a personal computer or a mobile device) and adapts its billing information into a format that can be displayed on device's web browser (bill presentation). When users provide payment information, the billing system can receive the information and send it to a payment processor (via an API). The payment processor then obtains the money from the bank and informs the billing system of successful payment, and the user's account billing records can be updated with the successful payment.

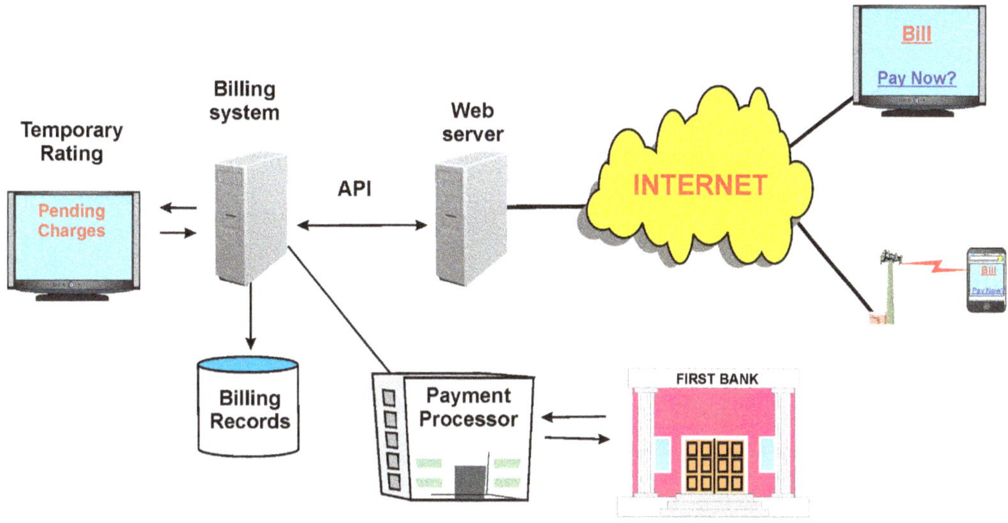

Figure 11.7, TV Online Billing

Recurring Billing

Recurring billing is the processing of a predetermined cost associated with a product or service that is assessed on a regular interval (monthly, quarterly, annually). Recurring billing obtains pre-authorization from the user (such as a monthly subscriber), stores the payment information (credit card or bank information) and processes the transactions.

Billing Pre-Authorization

Pre-authorization for recurring billing may occur when a customer purchases subscription (continuous) services. This authorization may define limits to a maximum amount that may be charged. This can become important when the purchase amounts vary, such as when people purchase additional services (movie rentals).

Payment Information

Payment information such as credit card data or bank account numbers must be stored to enable repetitive billing. There can be significant penalties for the unprotected storage of payment information (customer privacy and financial security). Some merchant processors (credit card companies) provide recurring billing services and do not allow the payment information to be stored or seen by the merchant.

Payment Processing

Payment processing is the submission of a charge to a company that obtains the funds from the account (merchant processor). After the payment processor has confirmed a successful payment transaction, the billing system may send a confirmation message (via email) to the customer that payment has been processed.

Figure 11.8 shows a repeated billing process. The process starts when the customer provides a billing pre-authorization. The customer enters the payment information (credit card data) which is stored by the vendor or by the merchant processor (merchant processor in this example). Each month, the invoice amount is submitted to the payment processor and, when the payment transaction is complete, a confirmation message is sent to the customer.

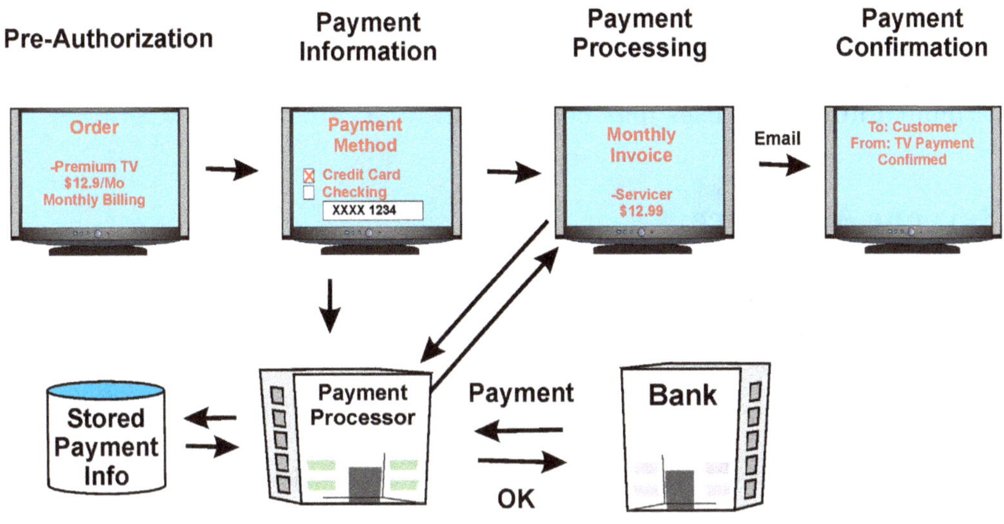

Figure 11.8, Internet TV Recurring Billing

Royalty Management

Royalties are fees that are paid for the use of content or resources that are owned by other companies.

Content License Types

There are many types of content that may be used and distributed by Internet TV providers. These include TV programs, audio (music) and performances. Internet TV stations need to acquire authorization or licenses to distribute and use content for the production and distribution of media.

License Fees

The license fees that may be paid for the use of content can include fixed fees, usage fees or a combination of both. To simplify the licensing process and reduce the complexity of billing, fixed license fees that are based on an estimated number of uses may be utilized.

Revenue Assurance

Owners of content want to ensure that they will be correctly paid for content usage. To do this, revenue assurance systems or processes are used. Revenue assurance can be performed by processing test orders or allowing content owners to review and audit systems to verify correct operation.

Figure 11.9 shows the types of royalties and how they may be paid by Internet TV systems. Royalties may be assessed for the distribution of TV programs, audio or performances. License fees may be paid in fixed

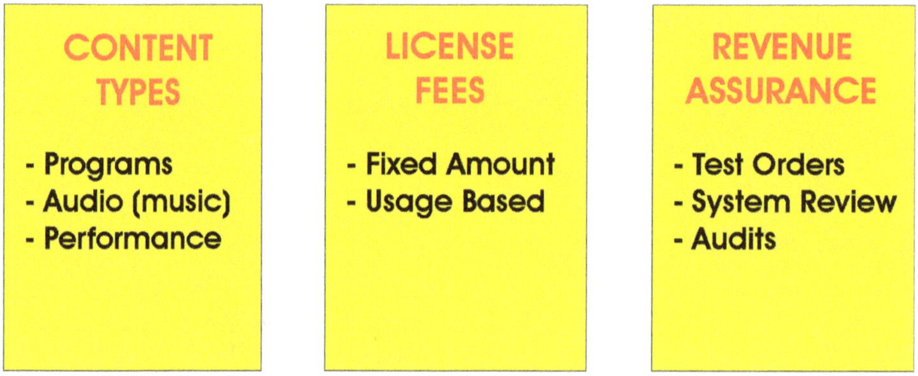

Figure 11.9, Royalty Management

amounts, usage based amounts or a combination of fixed and usage royalties. Tests may be performed to ensure revenues are correctly tracked and applied (revenue assurance).

Billing Service Bureau

A billing service bureau is a company that provides billing services to other companies. The services provided can range from billing consolidation to complete billing operations that include gathering billing records, processing invoices, mailing or issuing invoices and posting payments.

Hosted Billing

Hosted billing is the use of a contracted company to gather and process billing functions. Billing information is transferred to the hosted billing so they can perform some or all of the billing processes.

Mediation Devices

To convert billing event information, such as program requests or data consumption amounts, mediation devices may be used. Billing mediation devices receive, process and reformat data or information (billing events) into formats that can be used by other systems or devices (billing records).

Billing Interfaces

To transfer billing information to billing service bureaus, secure billing application program interface (API) links are used. These links need to be setup using account identification codes and passwords.

Figure 11.10 shows how a billing service bureau can be used to process billing information. The hosted billing system is owned and operated by another company. Mediation devices gather and process billing event information (channel viewing and downloads) into a form that can be sent to the billing system (billing records). Billing interfaces transport the information from the service provider to hosted billing systems through application program interfaces (APIs). This billing service provider performs online presentation, invoicing and payment processing services.

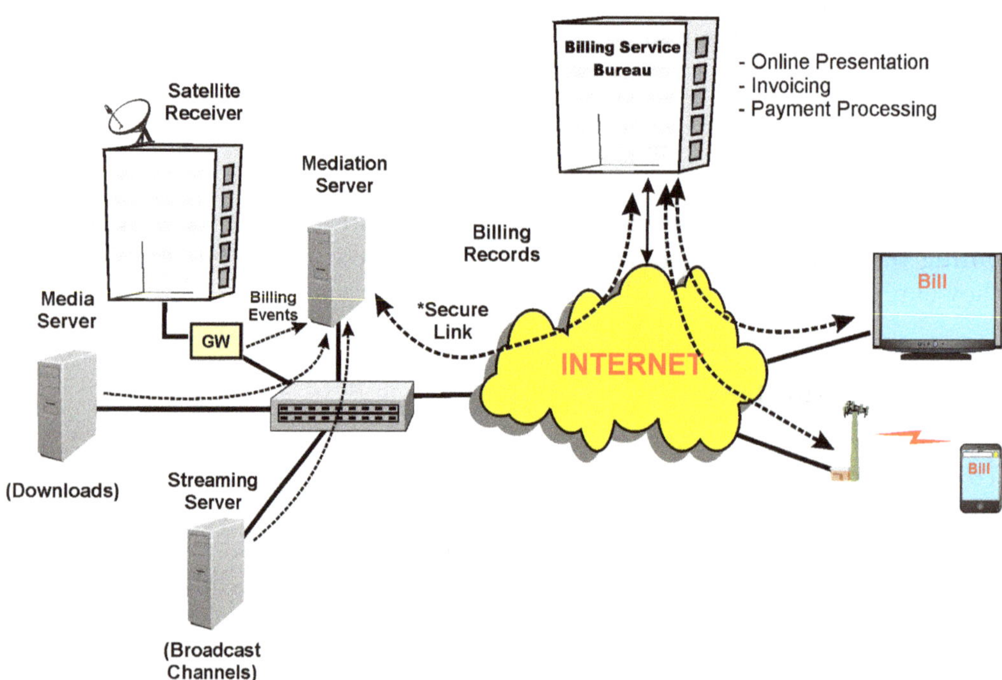

Figure 11.10, Billing Service Bureau

Internet TV Marketing

Internet TV marketing is the sending or presentation of media messages that inform and motivate people to view Internet TV shows or movies. Even small amounts of good marketing publicity can result in a big increase in the number of viewers for Internet TV programs.

Internet TV marketing may be a mixture of paid advertising and free publicity (unpaid media channels). Paid content is more controllable, while unpaid content (free publicity) tends to be a bit harder to manage.

All media promotion requires some type of investment or cost (financial, time, resources). The key objectives for Internet TV marketing include increasing viewers and obtaining advertisers.

Internet TV Marketing Objectives

Internet TV marketing objectives include the number and quality of viewers, revenue, and advertisers.

Viewership

Viewer marketing is the communication of messages that obtain or increase the amount of viewing of Internet TV shows or movies.

While the main objective might be to increase the numbers of viewers (viewership), the types of viewers are also very important. Viewer marketing may be targeted to specific types of audience profiles such as an age range, economic status, and specific types of interests. The more focused viewer profiles are to certain types of interests, the more valuable the audience is to advertisers.

Viewer marketing programs may focus on helping people in certain groups to become aware of the Internet TV channel and its programs. The programs help the potential viewers to understand how the programs will help them or become of interest to them.

Sales Revenue

Sales revenue objectives can include sales subscription and pay per view revenue generated by the TV shows and movies. Sales revenue marketing goals can include increasing the number of paid subscriptions, the number of paid programming views, and the average revenue generated per viewer.

Advertisers

Advertiser marketing is the communication of messages that obtain or increase the number of advertisers and/or the amounts that advertisers will pay to be included in or with the media that is broadcasted by the Internet TV.

Advertiser marketing programs identify the types of companies that are likely to reach the audience of the TV station, the options available to advertisers (advertising opportunities), and the advantages that they have by advertising on Internet TV systems (such as detailed viewing reports).

Figure 12.1 shows some of the key marketing objectives for Internet TVs. Viewership objectives include increasing the number of viewers, profile types of viewers, and location of viewers. Advertiser marketing objectives include getting new advertisers and increasing the amount of advertising ordered by each advertiser.

Objective	Description
Viewership	Attracting more viewers to watch or subscribe to Internet TV programs.
Sales Revenues	The revenue generated by subscriptions, paid content viewing, and average revenue per viewer.
Advertisers	The number of advertisers and how much each advertiser spends.

Figure 12.1, Internet TV Station Marketing Objectives

Internet TV Promotion

Internet TV promotion is the communication of a message or media content to one or more potential customers or advertisers. Advertising objectives are statements that identify targets that should be achieved through paid promotional communication efforts, including such items as product awareness, brand recognition and response rates to promotional programs.

Network Advertising

Network advertising is the promotion of the overall image or concept of the meaning or value of a media broadcaster (such as its values and content types). A content owner may have multiple programs under one network brand.

Channel Advertising

Channel advertising is the promotion of scheduled source of media content (such as a TV channel). Channel advertising may include promotions for the theme of the channel (such as a family channel) or promote groups of programs that are provided through the channel (television series).

Program Advertising

Program advertising is the promotion of a specific media segment or a related series of media. An example of program advertising is the announcement of a new television show.

Figure 12.2 shows how Internet TV advertising may involve a mixture of general station advertising, channel advertising, and program advertising. Station advertising describes the overall values and themes that the station focuses on. Channel advertising is designed to promote media that is sent through a communication channel (such as a television channel). Program advertising communicates messages that relate to specific media programs.

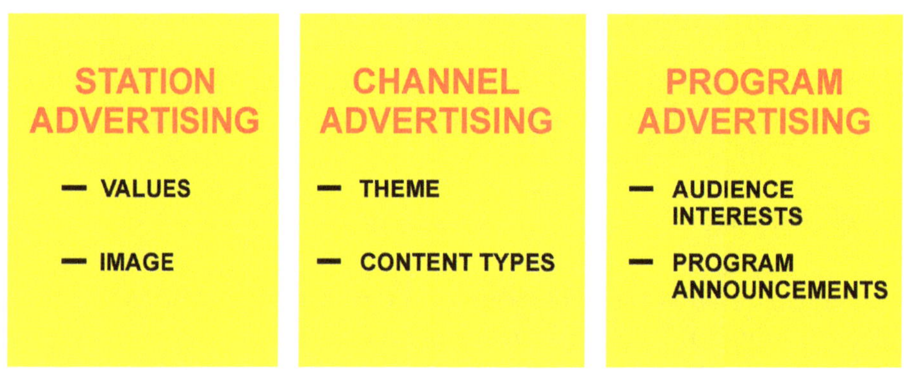

Figure 12.2, Internet TV Station Advertising

Affiliate Marketing

Affiliate marketing is a shared marketing and sales program that exists between companies that want to sell products (merchants) and companies that are willing to promote these products (affiliates) to their customers. In terms of Internet TV affiliate marketing, the affiliate merchant (the Internet TV owner) compensates affiliate partners (web site owners) for their role in communicating and promoting the station to customers (visitors). In addition to generating revenue for promoting the station and its programming, the listing of the Internet TV and summary information on a web site may attract more visitors and provide additional value (relationship building).

Affiliate Partners (Publishers)

An affiliate partner, which is also called a publisher, is an entity that sells products or services for other companies in return for receiving revenue or other forms of value.

Affiliate Promotion

Affiliate partners may promote Internet TV programming to their customers in various ways, including inserting links within episodes, listing program summary pages on their web sites, or sending promotional messages (such as email broadcasting).

Affiliate partners may place links to the Internet TV's programming on their product pages or related pages on their web site. They may create and add new program or station summary pages to their web site. Affiliate partners may also perform other types of promotion such as email broadcasts or pay per click marketing campaigns.

Affiliate Networks

Affiliate networks are companies or systems that link merchants that are looking to promote their products or services with companies that are willing to promote such products or services on their web sites.

Affiliate Content

Affiliate content is the media materials that are used to promote affiliate products or services. The affiliate merchant may provide some sample materials, such as Internet TV programming descriptions, keywords and images, which affiliate partners may use on their web sites and in their promotional messages.

When providing materials for affiliate partners to use, it is recommended to use updated content, rather than the materials that are used on the affiliate merchant's site, as duplicate content may dilute the web content value as seen by search engines.

Affiliate Guidelines

Affiliate guidelines are rules and processes that are used to define how marketing partners may use materials and promote products or services. Affiliate guidelines may include restrictions on how promotional content and Internet TV programming information may be used, how information may be presented (representation), and which types of marketing may be performed (such as email marketing and advertising programs).

Affiliate Compensation

Affiliate compensation typically consists of incentives that are provided when an account is setup, desired activity is achieved (such as new subscribers or views), or other accomplishments (such as bonuses for reaching a number of activity registrations).

Figure 12.3 shows how an Internet TV can be promoted using affiliate partners. The first step of the affiliate program is the discovery of potential affiliate partner's that can be found by searching the community or the web for specific types of companies, qualifying them as partners, and inviting them to include links to station programming on their web site. Affiliate partners may participate by including links on their web pages, adding episode summary pages to their web sites, or performing promotional campaigns (such as email broadcasting). Affiliate guidelines may be provided to affiliate partners that define how promotional content and Internet TV programming materials may be used along with the ways they can be represented. Affiliate compensation systems are created to reward affiliate partners for their promotional efforts, and may contain incentives for the registration of viewer accounts, commissions for viewing activities, and rewards (bonuses) for achieving levels of success.

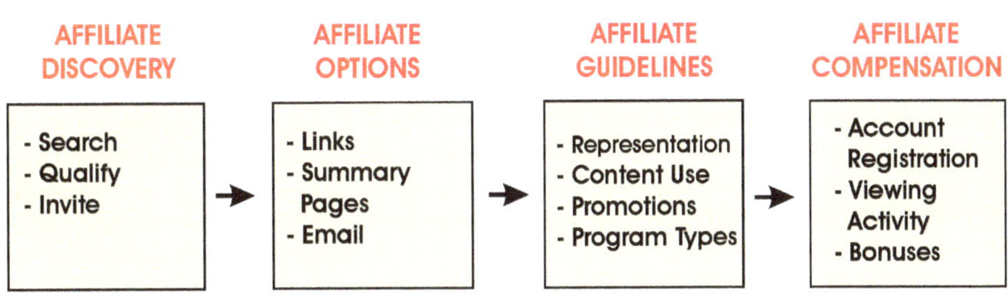

Figure 12.3, Internet TV Affiliate Promotion

Display Advertising

Display advertising is the process of inserting graphic advertising messages into media. Display advertising systems (also called banner ads) link display ad graphics to web portals (such as the Internet TV Program website) or landing pages and use link tracking systems to determine the effectiveness of the display ads. Display ads can be created by banner ad development tools and banner ad exchange networks can allow for more simplified distribution.

Display Ads

A display ad is a graphic or image that motivates that viewer to take action (to click on the banner) in anticipation of getting information promised by the graphic ad. To create effective display ads, recognizable keywords can be included, pain points enhanced, interesting images and graphics may be used, and motion (animation) can be added to help a ad to stand out from other media on the page.

It is helpful to include words that the viewer will understand and have an interest in learning more about within the text portion of the ad. Topics or issues related to the ad that cause the reader discomfort (the pain points) can be emphasized. Related images that can get the attention (colorful, conflict) can be used to generate interest. Animation can be added to display ads so they stand out from other media on the page.

Display Ad Development Tools

Display ad development tools are program functions or media services that allow users to create graphic advertisements by selecting choices (such as ad sizes), adding content (such as text and images) and choosing animation options.

One of the first steps in producing a display ad is to create a list of keywords that viewers will recognize and associate with the marketing objective of the ad. A list of discomforts (pain points) that are associated with the issue can be created. A list of images that will attract the reader (color, shape and conflict) and generate interest (initiate questions or build emotion) can be created. These elements can be combined to produce ads that can be reviewed and tested for effectiveness.

Examples of display ad development tools include www.bannerdesignerpro.com, www.bannermakerpro.com, and www.addesigner.com.

Banner Ad Networks

A banner ad network is a company or group that acts on behalf of multiple advertisers to find and place display ads on web sites that participate in the ad network program. Banner ad networks may charge fees for the insertion of ads, or operate on an ad exchange basis (we will show your ads if you show ours). When an exchange basis is used, the ad network will keep a percentage of the ad insertions for itself (that it can sell to advertisers) as a way to earn revenue on the ad exchange process. Examples of ad exchange networks include; www.exchange-it.com, www.adswap.com, and www.ebannertraffic.com.

Figure 12.4 shows how display ads can be used to promote Internet TVs. The ad creation process starts by identifying keywords, interest points and images that are associated with the promotional message. A banner development tool can be used to combine the component elements and add effects (animated banner). The ad may be published (uploaded) to web sites for use or it may be provided to ad networks that automatically place it on web sites that match the defined categories for the ad.

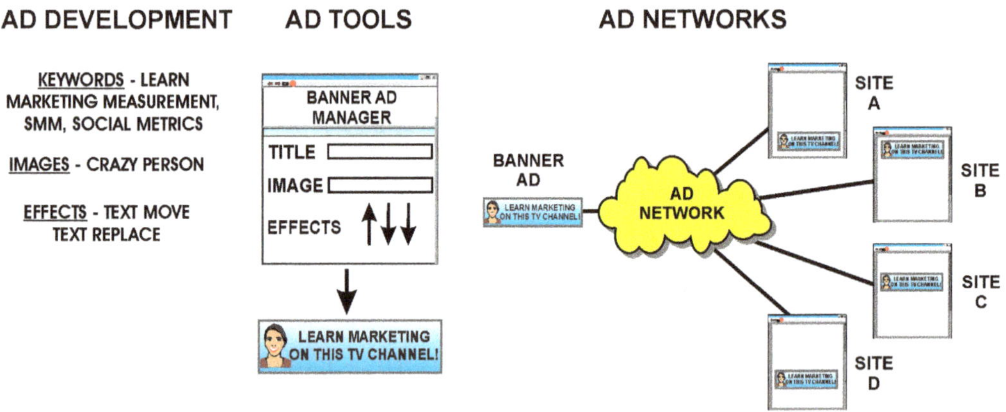

Figure 12.4, Internet TV Banner Ads

Search Pay per Click (PPC) Advertising

Pay per click advertising is an Internet marketing process that charges the advertiser only when an item is selected (clicked). While the average cost of a PPC ad click is approximately $1.31, the costs can dramatically vary based on categories and keyword bidding. In general, PPC costs are increasing as unskilled companies that do not understand the bidding process are beginning to advertise, resulting in very high bidding.

Internet TV programming offers a way to reduce or eliminate the costs of PPC campaigns, which can be an excellent tool for identifying keywords and topics that may be used in programming and promotional campaigns. For example, a PPC program may use different keywords for Internet TV programs to determine which title had the highest interest levels and conversion rates.

PPC marketing campaigns may be composed of keywords (search words), PPC ads (text ads) and landing pages (quality score). A PPC keyword list contains words that trigger the presentation of the PPC ad. The PPC ad contains words that motivate searchers to click. The landing page should contain information relative to the ad (which determines the quality score).

PPC Keywords

Keywords are identifying words or terms that relates to or is associated with an item, service or other form of information. When a keyword is matched, a bidding process may be used to determine which ad is displayed and in what order (higher bidders may be listed at the top of the list).

While some keywords may be searched often (such as show title, topic, or actor name), of key importance are converting keywords. Converting keywords are terms or phrases which are searched that result in desired actions such as download registration or even product sales. One of the best ways to determine converting keywords is to put tracking codes (hidden from the viewer) in conversion pages (such as download registration forms or product order form confirmation pages), and to alternate variations of related keywords. PPC advertising services (such as Google, Yahoo and Bing) provide these tracking codes and simple instructions on how to use them for free.

PPC Ads

Pay per click ads are promotional messages that are displayed when certain conditions exist (such as keyword matching). PPC ads may be text messages or graphic ads which may be inserted into search results (search ads), or within the content of web pages (content ads). Text ads tend to work better for search ads and graphic ads tend to work better for content ads. PPC text ads have a limited number of characters, so it is important to choose words that match the persons search and interests.

It is possible to have multiple ads which are matched to specific keywords. Split testing (an option that selects ads to display from two or more ad choices) may be used to determine which ads perform the best.

Quality Score (QS)

Quality score is a measure of the relevance or performance results of a project or campaign. An example of a quality score is the relevance of an Internet advertising message to the landing page to which the advertising message is linked. The higher the quality score, the more likely the web visitor is to interact favorably (purchase the product or service promoted in the ad). Search engines may utilize a quality score to determine the position (display ranking position) and cost (bid cost) of ads. A better quality score can result in a higher position and a lower cost.

Figure 12.5 shows sample Internet TV pay per click ads for a sports program. The process starts by identifying keywords (social media marketing, SMM Metrics, social media advertising) that people are searching for relative to the product or service that is being promoted (keyword list). Pay per click ads that match the keywords are created using keywords and key issues related to the users needs. This example shows that a display web address of the destination site is included with the ad (it is not the actual destination URL). Some search engines may use a quality score to assess the cost and display position of the ad that can be determined by matching the keyword list, keywords in the ad and keywords on the landing page.

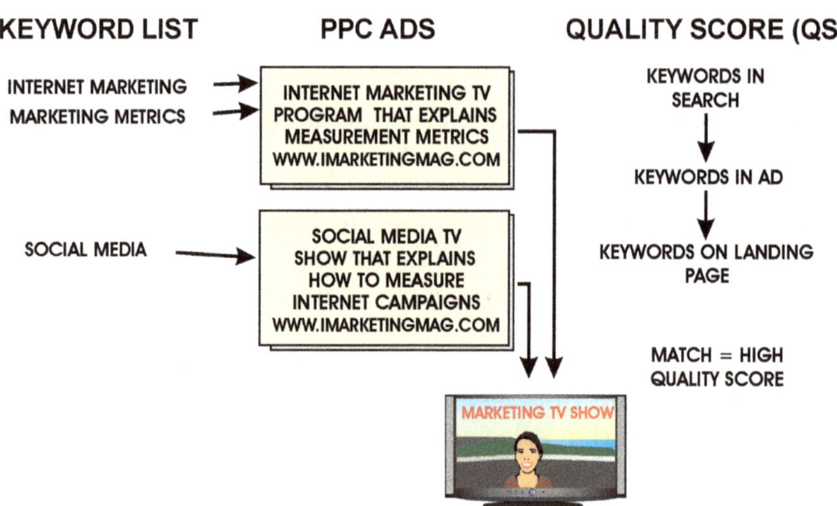

Figure 12.5, Internet TV Pay per Click Ads

Viral Marketing

Viral marketing is the process of promoting and selling products or services through the use of messages or ads that are self regenerative. Viral messages or ads include a pass-along tag line that encourages recipients to send or forward the message to other people.

Viral Content

Viral content is media that is received by people and forwarded (regenerated) to other people. Aside from added addressing text and comments, the core viral content may be regenerated many times. Good viral content may include recent news, controversial information, or highly entertaining jokes, images or video.

A good way to gather content that may be suitable for viral messages is to subscribe to newsletters, groups, blogs, bookmarking sites (to identify the most popular media), or setup alerts (such as Google Alerts - Google.com/Alerts) related to key subjects you wish to promote. After potential viral content is identified, additional research may be performed to allow for content that is enhanced with additional interesting content or factoids.

It may be helpful to include interesting images in the viral content that can rapidly get the attention of the recipient. Such images may be obtained from stock photo (small cost) or shared photo web sites (no cost in return for references).

Seed Distribution List

A seed distribution list is a group of recipients to which messages are initially distributed. The seed distribution list can come from members of social networks who already have a relationship with the sender and may, as a result, be more likely to pass on the information.

Copy Tag Line

A copy tag line is a message contained within a media item that encourages the recipient to forward the message to a friend. The copy tag line should be placed in a prominent location (hard to miss) and strongly encourage or motivate the recipient to share with their friends. For example, "Find this Very Funny", "Don't Wait", and "Be the First to Send this to Your Friends" are copy tags lines that offer motivation."

Referral Incentives

Referral incentives are reward offers given to people who recommend products or services to other people. Referral incentives can be in the form of gifts, money or discounts. As an added incentive to the referring person, the offer may include a discount that is also provided to the recipient of the referred message.

Figure 12.6 shows the basic process of viral (referral) marketing. This diagram shows that viral marketing starts with a message that contains some valuable information elements along with a referral message (viral message). The viral message is sent to people who have a likely interest in the information it contains. When people receive a viral marketing message, they are encouraged to forward the message to their friends. This example shows that it is likely that recipients will forward the message on to others who have an interest in the information. This multiplies the effect of the marketing campaign as the message is received by many more email addresses than the initial list contained.

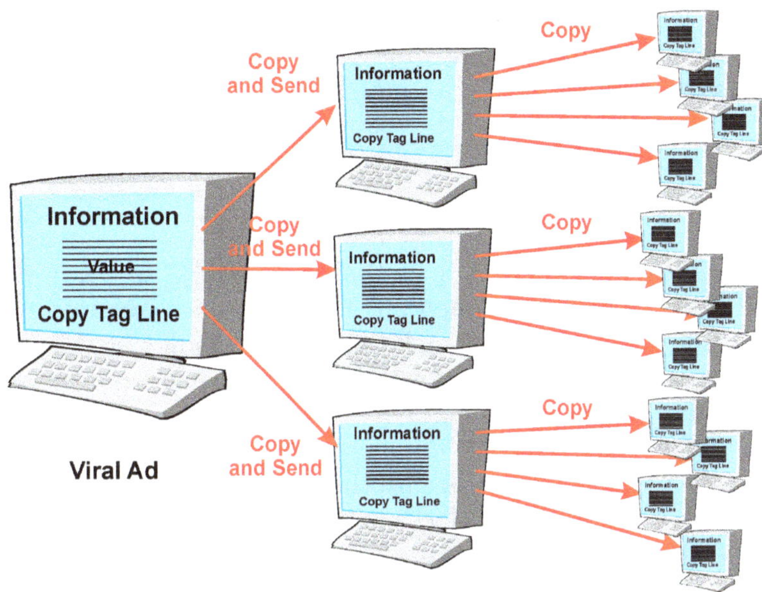

Figure 12.6, Internet TV Viral Marketing

Direct Mail Promotion

Direct mail promotion is a marketing program that sends media brochures directly to consumers through the postal (mail) system.

Direct Mail Content

The content contained in direct marking marketing campaigns may identify a hot topic, expand desires or promise a excitement that involves responding to the mailing literature. Response channels to direct mail may include web site forms, email messages or telephone numbers.

The content contained in a direct mail item may list multiple engagement opportunities related to the audience (such as fan club, events, and promotional contests), and provide a web address which guides the recipient to an online submission form that matches the options on the direct mail material. The recipient's selection from a list of multiple choices indicates which subject areas the recipient takes an interest in.

Direct Mail List

A direct mail list is a group of names that will receive any mailing materials that are sent as part of a campaign. The list may be created from existing customer contacts or an existing list of potential sales leads, or it may be rented or bartered from another source such as a magazine, newsletter or industry group.

When renting or bartering lists from other companies, a mailing house or letter shop may be used. In addition to performing the handling the mailing processes (envelope stuffing and addressing), a mailing house may keep the list renter from obtaining the list, preventing them from using the list multiple times.

Mail Stuffing

Mail stuffing is the process of inserting promotional media or items into an envelope or package that is being shipped to a recipient. Internet TV literature may be stuffed into other mailings, such as magazine subscriptions, or into packages that relate to the subject matter, such as books related to programming topics.

Tracking Codes

Direct mail literature may include tracking codes (keycodes) and links that can track responses to the promotional materials.

A key code (keycode) is a unique label that is used to identify or group items into a category or function. Keycodes may be used as part of the registration process to identify the person who is requesting a media item.

Direct mail literature may contain web addresses that can be tracked (tracking URLs), which can indicate how successful a direct mail campaign has been (such as having a media item download link).

Figure 12.7 shows a direct mail postcard that informs the recipient of the availability of a TV station that covers Internet Marketing. The recipient is provided with several popular programming choices. This card also includes a unique web address that can be tracked for this promotional campaign.

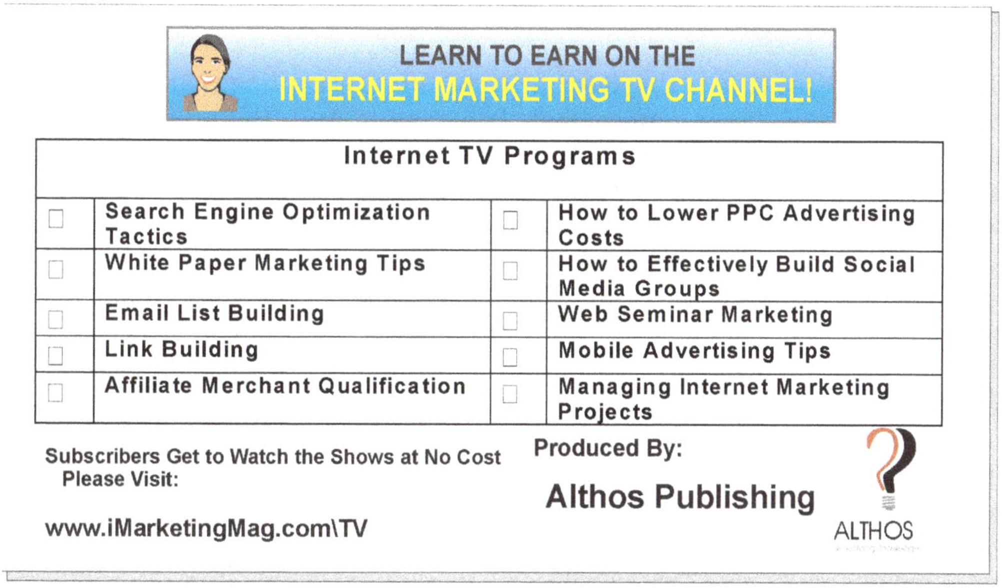

LEARN TO EARN ON THE
INTERNET MARKETING TV CHANNEL!

Internet TV Programs			
☐	Search Engine Optimization Tactics	☐	How to Lower PPC Advertising Costs
☐	White Paper Marketing Tips	☐	How to Effectively Build Social Media Groups
☐	Email List Building	☐	Web Seminar Marketing
☐	Link Building	☐	Mobile Advertising Tips
☐	Affiliate Merchant Qualification	☐	Managing Internet Marketing Projects

Subscribers Get to Watch the Shows at No Cost
Please Visit:

www.iMarketingMag.com\TV

Produced By:

Althos Publishing

ALTHOS

Figure 12.7, Internet TV Direct Mail Postcard

Publicity Programs

Publicity is information related to a person or company that appears in forms of communication (such as newspapers or television programs) which is not directly paid for by the person or company to which the information relates. Publicity programs for Internet TVs include press releases, talk shows, sponsorships, social media marketing, email broadcasts, article marketing and promotional videos.

Press Releases

An Internet TV press release is an announcement from a person or company that is issued to members of the media (writers) or companies (publishers) for use in their publications. Press releases contain detailed information about the Internet TV or of some form of content (station news, new programs or episodes). Press releases may be submitted to newswires, distributed to specific media contacts or posted at various locations on the Internet.

Press Release Title

The press release title is the descriptive heading or caption that is placed at the beginning of the announcement. It serves to grab the attention of the media person, and should contain keywords and identify the key issue and solution (not the company). Media people are in search of topics they can write about that will be of interest to their audience. Breakthroughs, new solutions and key changes are topics writers are likely to discuss. Job assignments (such as a new sales manager at the Internet TV) and company award achievements may not be on the list of important topics.

Press Release Email Subject Line

The subject line of an email that provides a press release is critical to the success of the message. It is not uncommon for magazine editors to receive hundreds of press releases each day. If each of the press releases in an editor's inbox simply said "press release", it is unlikely that they would each receive attention. Editors are looking to cover stories that relate to certain topics and issues. Subject lines that identify those topics and issues are likely to get noticed.

Press Release in Text Format

It is highly recommended to include press release information as text in an email message. Editors are looking for press releases they can use quickly. Press releases that are sent as attachments within emails are likely to be passed by rather than downloaded. Editors are forced to look at press releases that are included within email text.

Resource Links

In addition to basic press release information, it is recommended to include other media (such as images and reference documents). Images should be provided in thumbnail form along with links to medium and high resolution versions. Some the reference images may include promotional photographs of station programming actors, selected images from scenes and other supporting images such as people working on the set during the filming of station programming.

It is recommended to include links in the email instead of providing the media items as attachments. If an editor attempts to download emails that have large attachments (such as to a mobile device), it can result in significant delays and costs.

Contact Information

Press releases should have press contacts media people can use to get additional information. It is recommended to provide contact information to people who will respond within a reasonable amount of time, providing helpful information. Media people often cover multiple topics and, if they request information, it is best to try and directly help them find what they are looking for. Magazine editors, who are often burdened with deadlines, typically prefer to work with companies that offer everything they need on their web site.

Media List

Press releases can be sent to people such as magazine editors, bloggers, talk show hosts and other members of the media. It is possible to use a public relations (PR) agency to distribute press releases or build a list by identifying key media sources. Even without the use of a PR agency, it may be helpful to update media distribution lists by including key media channels within an industry.

Journalist Download Link

For press releases that are sent directly to journalists, a journalist media program download link may be included. The journalist download link provides the program without requiring registration information. Journalists may have a very limited amount of time and they may not take the extra time to register to receive media programs.

Figure 12.8 shows a press release for a new specialty program on an Internet TV covering environmentally friendly technologies. The title of the press release identifies the key topics discussed on the new program to generate interest in people who are fascinated by electrical automobiles. The subject line of the email identifies that the press release covers a new program on Eco Friendly TV. The email is sent to a media list of people who work with marketing magazines, blogs and talk shows. The press release provides links to supporting images that include promotional photos and ads, pictures of scenes from the program and the program's video trailer. This version of the press release contains a journalist download link that allows recipients to obtain access to the program without the need to register for the download.

Talk Shows

Talk shows are media programs wherein people share discussions about topics and issues. Publicity agents may be used to get scheduled interviews (bookings) on talk shows. A program manager coordinates the talk show program schedule. Talk shows are usually composed of a host who moderates the show and participants such as guests or people who call in and share. Talk shows may be aired on television, radio or the Internet (podcasts).

*** PRESS RELEASE *** PRESS RELEASE *** PRESS RELEASE ***

FOR IMMEDIATE RELEASE:
1 January 2017

Contact: Lawrence Harte
+1.919.301.0109

New Internet Marketing TV Channel

iMarketing Magazine announces the launch of ***Internet Marketing TV*** channel which allows people to relax, view, and become more successful in business.

Traditional marketing methods are not working as well for some types of business and social media seems to be the answer. Unfortunately marketing managers and business leaders do not know how to measure and prove the success of Internet marketing campaigns.

The traditional types of materials such as books, magazines, and online searches can take time and lead to the wrong answers. **Internet Marketing TV** channel was created to interview successful Internet marketing leaders and share their results in an interesting and educational format.

Some of the upcoming programs include:

Search Engine Optimization Tactics
How to Lower PPC Advertising Costs
White Paper Marketing Tips
How to Effectively Build Social Media Groups
Email List Building
Web Seminar Marketing
Link Building
Mobile Advertising Tips
Affiliate Merchant Qualification
Managing Internet Marketing Projects

To see a complete list of available Internet Marketing TV shows, go to:

www.iMarketingMag.com/TV

About iMarketing Magazine

iMarketing Magazine identifies and explains the applications, services, and technologies that allow companies and professionals to promote products or services using Internet Marketing programs. Marketing professionals and business leaders learn about the available types of Internet Marketing systems, how they operate, and effective ways to use them.

Internet Marketing TV, Althos Publishing 106 West Vance Street, Fuquay-Varina, NC 27526 USA
Telephone: 919-557-2260 Fax: 919-557-2261, **email:** success@iMarketingMag.com, **web: www.iMarketingMag.com**

Figure 12.8, Internet Press Release

Publicity Agent (PR Agent)

A publicity agent is a person or company who represents the promotional activities of another person or company, which may include booking talk shows or interviews. Publicity agents have lists of talk shows with which they often have established relationships, and provide a level of credibility for a person who wishes to secure a booking. An example of a publicity agent that specializes in getting talk show bookings is Special Guests (www.specialguests.com).

Program Manager

A program manager is a person who is responsible for identifying and managing the selection of media programs for a talk show or media channel. Program managers seek speakers for programs, such as TV or radio talk shows, and may also review show proposals. Program managers tend to be very busy people and they can be hard to reach and work with.

Talk Show Host

A talk show host is a person who performs interviews with guests. The talk show host asks questions and coordinates calls, emails or other forms of communication between listeners and guests.

Talk Show Guest

A talk show guest is a person who provides information about a topic and responds to questions from the host and from the listening or viewing audience.

Question List

While talk show hosts may have a fair understanding of the industry that their show covers, their knowledge of the specific topics or issues related to their guest may not be known. It is recommended to provide the talk show with a suggested list of questions for the interview process. The talk show host may or may not use the provided questions.

Radio Talk Shows

While a radio talk show may be initially performed live, radio talk show interviews are likely to be stored and rebroadcasted for several hours or days after the interviews.

Podcasts

Podcasts are the provision of media to multiple recipients who have registered with or belong to a podcast service.

Figure 12.9 shows how an Internet TV can be promoted on a talk show. The process may start with the use of a publicity agent who identifies talk shows that match the desired topic. The publicity agent contacts the program manager, proposes the talk show topic and, if acceptable, the program manager confirms a booking date and time for the talk show interview. The guest may prepare a question list which is provided to the publicity agent and the program manager. Shortly before the talk show interview, the guest calls in to the studio to setup the audio and/or video connections. The talk show interview is performed and recorded by the studio. The recorded talk show interview may be broadcasted again several times during the same day. It also may be made available on the broadcaster's web site for months or longer.

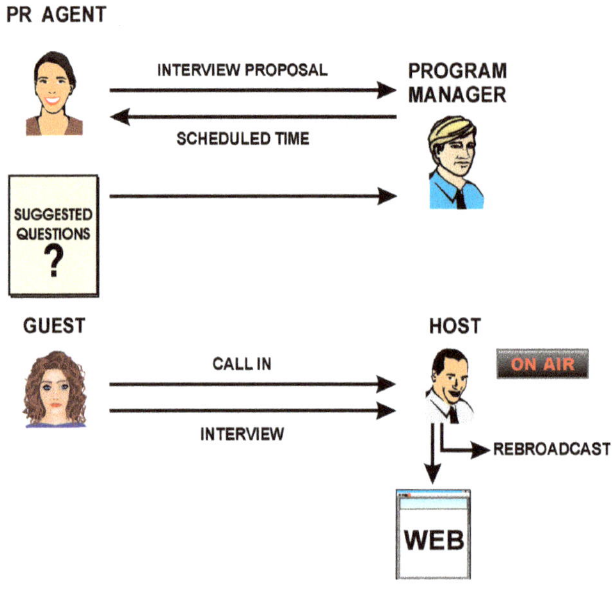

Figure 12.9, Talk Show Promotion

Sponsorships

A sponsorship is a contribution, support, or payment to a program or event by a person or company. Sponsorships commonly allow the contributor to receive some promotional value such as company references or logos on the program media materials or signs located at the events.

Events

TV stations can provide resources for events or portions of events which may include video production, literature, and staff. Events commonly ask media companies to sponsor their events to get free promotion. This means that an

Internet TV can contact local events and offer to be an event sponsor. In return for the publicity, events may be willing to provide exhibit space and include the TV station logo on their promotional literature, signage, and web pages.

Contests

Internet TVs may perform contests that give away prizes or awards to participants. Companies may donate products or services for the contests in return for including the company name and logo on the promotional event.

There may be some legal requirements for operating contests so it is recommended to check with an experienced attorney before performing contests.

Social Media Sites

TV stations may provide hosting resources and provide promotional value social media sites (such as groups or fan clubs). The social media sites may be required to display the Internet TV logo on their blog and reference them as the web site sponsor.

Figure 12.10 shows how Internet TVs can promote themselves using sponsorships. An Internet TV may sponsor events (such as a conference or club meeting) that is related to the viewing audience. Internet TVs may run contests that give away products or services to viewers who register and provide information from the Internet TV programs (the prizes may be donated by companies). Internet TVs may also provide resources for the hosting of social media sites that are related to the station image or values.

Figure 12.10, Internet TV Sponsorships

Blog Marketing

Blog marketing is the process of inserting promotional messages into blog postings. Internet TVs may provide promotional content in blogs that references to channels or programs on their TV station.

Blog posts can provide much more value than the mere presentation of information to people who follow (subscribe) to the blog. Search engines tend to highly value current blog content, and the blog posts that contain links may be highly valued by search engines.

Blog Posting

Blog posting is the process of submitting a message or media item (such as a photo) into a blog. Blog posts usually contain moderate amounts of information such as a few lines or several paragraphs of information. Blog posts may also include links, embedded images and tags (labels) that are used for categorization.

It is recommended to regularly post messages (such as weekly) when promoting a product or service using blogs. Writing good blog posts can consume a lot of time and effort. To dramatically reduce this time, short sections of a program can be rewritten to become a blog post. Typically, the script of a 30 minute show should be able to be converted into 5 to 15 blog posts.

If the program does not have a script (recorded as an interview), you can use a software program to convert the audio to text. You should be able to use portions of the text as a source for blog posts.

Blog Post Title

The blog post title is the name that references the blog message (blog post) that helps search engines and readers to find the blog post and to motivate them to select the link to connect to the blog. To do this, blog post titles may include recognizable key words, problem identifiers and solution promises.

Blog Post References

Blog posts contain information that the reader is looking for or has an interest in reading. It is important to indirectly promote products using blog messages. If possible, the blog post should identify an issue and a key area of interest. A reference to a specific channel or program may be provided at the end of the blog post.

It is recommended to include searchable and relatable words with which the desired audience is familiar. When keywords are searched, the search results show the words bolded in the body, reinforcing the reader's desire to read the blog post.

Tags

Tags are labels that are associated with a media item such as a blog post. Tags can help search engines classify the content so people may easily search for category names. In addition to subject categories, tags may also include show program names, show topics, and actor names.

Figure 12.11 shows how the script of a TV show that has been converted into several blog posts. To create the blog posts, key parts of the script are selected, summarized, and sometimes quoted. A reference tag to the TV station and channels are included in the blog post www.iMarketingMag.com/SMM. Category tags (SMM, Social Media Marketing) have been added to the blog post.

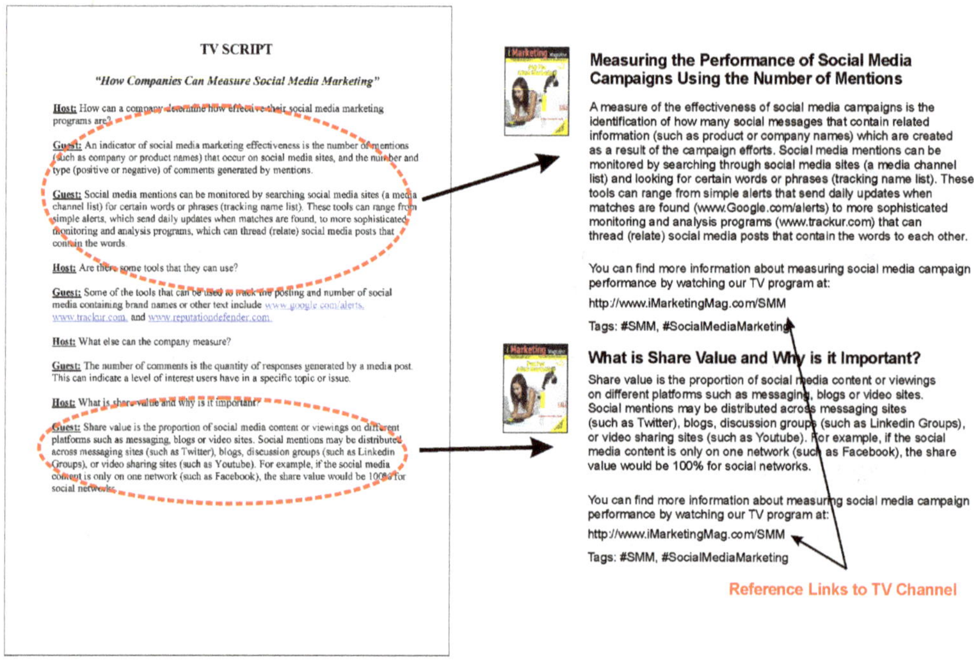

Figure 12.11, Internet TV Blog Posts

Microblogging (Tweets)

Microblogging is the contribution of small amounts of information (text messages) related to a specific subject via a shared communication medium such as a text, audio or video log on the Internet. These messages are sent to people who follow the senders on social media networks (such as Twitter).

Microblogging can provide value beyond publicity (the number of people who see the messages). Search engines and information seekers value content that is current, and tweets that contain links may be given high search engine value.

It is recommended to regularly post messages (daily or every few days) when promoting a product or service. While this may seem to be time consuming, can be efficient to create lists of multiple messages before a media items is released.

Microblog message content can range from review requests to tips and interesting factoids. Messages may be created by extracting information from the show or movie. In general, a 30 minute show or program should be able to provide 30 to 60 microblog messages (Tweets).

Account Name

If possible, the messaging identification name should be your station or channel name. If your name is already taken, create an account name that includes your name station or channel name as part of the account name.

Hashtags

Hashtags are keywords that are preceded by the # symbol. Searchers use hashtags to find messages that relate to a specific category (such as #SMM for social media marketing). When creating microblog messages, keyword hashtags that relate to the topic of the media item should be included. Search for the hashtag you created to determine if it is already in use by someone else.

Shortening URL Links

Blog posts tend to reference web addresses that can be very long. To shorten the long web address (domain name plus the file name), a link shorting service can be used. A link shortening service is a web site (usually with a short domain name) that converts a long URL into a new link that contains a shortened file name. Examples of link shortening services include www.TinyURL.com and www.bit.ty.

Some link shortening services allow for the selection of a shortened file name. When possible, it is recommended that the shortening name should include one or two keywords separated by a hyphen (dash).

Review Requests

Review requests invite people to read and evaluate programs before they are released. A link is provided to a web page that allows the person to download the draft or register to receive an advance copy. This provides advance knowledge of the upcoming TV show.

Availability Announcement

An availability announcement is a message stating that a media item is available, which also provides a link to the web page where the channel or media program can be found. Availability announcements can be sent more than once and the keywords used to describe the program can be changed.

Figure 12.12 shows some sample program promotion microblog posts on Twitter (Tweets). The first post announces a request people to review the pre-release of the show. The second post announces the release of the show. The third post identifies a topic within the program. The fourth post provides an interesting factoid about social media marketing. The messages also contain category tags (hash tags) for social media marketing (SMM) and social media optimization (SMO).

WATCH OUR NEW INTERNET TV CHANNEL
HTTP://WWW.IMARKETINGMAG.COM/TV #INTERNETMARKETING

NEW SOCIAL MEDIA MARKETING TV PROGRAM
INTERVIEWS WITH 10 SUCCESS INTERNET MARKETING LEADERS
HTTP://WWW.IMARKETINGMAG.COM/TV/SMM #SMM

SOCIAL MEDIA MARKETING TV PROGRAM - FIVE TIPS ON HOW TO
INCREASE SOCIAL MEDIA MARKETING PROGRAMS
HTTP://WWW.IMARKETINGMAG.COM/TV/SMM2 #SMM

OVER 2 BILLION SEARCHES PER DAY ON YOUTUBE
LEARN MORE SHOCKING FACTS ON THE INTERNET TV CHANNEL
HTTP://WWW.IMARKETINGMAG.COM #INTERNETMARKETING #SEO

Figure 12.12, Internet TV Microblog Messages (Tweets)

Discussion Groups

Discussion groups are forums where people can interact and exchange questions, information and suggestions. Discussion groups are typically formed around a theme or industry subject. Web based discussion groups include social network fan clubs (Facebook), groups (LinkedIn), and chat rooms.

Discussion groups can be reviewed to identify content that may be included in a TV program, submit requests for program topics, and to engage viewers so they feel part of the program.

Topic Research

Discussion groups may contain questions and commentary for which members may have a need or interest in understanding. If the discussion group is focused on a topic that is similar to a media item, a discussion with numerous comments may indicate a likelihood that it is a good topic to include in the media item.

Discussion Engagement

Discussion engagement is the amount of communication activity that is associated with the discussion topic. Some of the methods that can be used to get a high level of discussion engagement are to ask thought provoking questions in the discussion, or to ask for lists of companies that can provide products or services, since members like to list their companies as a way of getting free publicity.

A simple method for finding discussion topics that produce high levels of engagement is to find similar groups (on the same social network or other social networks) and look for discussions in those groups that generated many comments. The question can be rephrased and posted to a similar discussion group.

Earned Media

Earned media is the promotional value of content that is created by the contribution of content or services.

The way to achieve earned media is to provide the reader with relevant information or something they did not already know (reader value). This can include providing interesting factoids such as controversial statistics. The combination of multiple information sources into new summary factoids can generate significant earned media value. For example, the advertising cost for a 30 second commercial aired during the SuperBowl is approximately $3 million in 2010. Dividing this cost by the number of viewers results in a per viewer cost (impression) of 2 cents. According to the Google's financial statement in 2009, they earn approximately 54 cents per click. The comparison of these numbers (a new expression of existing information) provides for a high impact factoid about the value of targeted Internet advertising.

Internet TV Content References

Discussions may contain links to resources such as Internet TV content or video clips. While it may be possible to join groups and post many links to content, the discussion group and topic should match the Internet TV topic and the commentary should identify that the station's programming is a helpful reference, so it does not appear as a promotional message. If the discussion group leader determines that the link to the Internet TV is a promotional message, the discussion post may be removed and the member who posted the comment may be expelled from the group.

Figure 12.13 shows how a group discussion can be used to promote an Internet TV. This example shows how a provocative TV program topic may be used to spark the interests of group members. The discussion posting, measurement types, includes some value adding information (blog posts, mentions, and comments). This discussion also includes a question for group members to help motive engagement with the discussion topic (solicit comments). The discussion post also includes a reference link to the Internet TV content which can provide additional information that is relevant to the discussion topic.

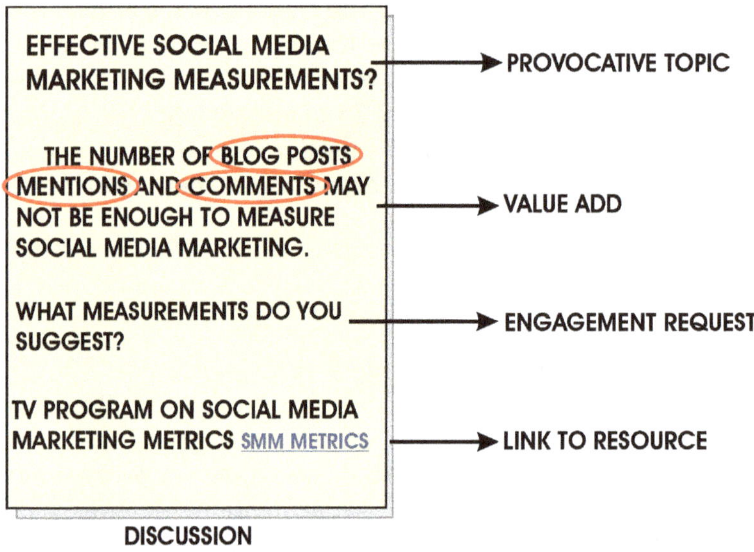
EFFECTIVE SOCIAL MEDIA MARKETING MEASUREMENTS?
PROVOCATIVE TOPIC
THE NUMBER OF BLOG POSTS MENTIONS AND COMMENTS MAY NOT BE ENOUGH TO MEASURE SOCIAL MEDIA MARKETING.
VALUE ADD
WHAT MEASUREMENTS DO YOU SUGGEST?
ENGAGEMENT REQUEST
TV PROGRAM ON SOCIAL MEDIA MARKETING METRICS SMM METRICS
LINK TO RESOURCE
DISCUSSION

Figure 12.13, Internet TV Discussion Topic

Review Programs

Review programs identify and encourage people to post reviews online and recommend TV shows or channels for others to find and view. Review systems may employ different techniques for indexing and recommending programs and channels. Some Internet TV sites prioritize the most popular programs first while others categorize and more evenly distribute the display of recommendations.

Review rating systems can be challenging as people tend to post negative reviews over positive reviews. If the program is good, the viewer may be unlikely to post a positive review. When the program is perceived as bad, the viewer may be more likely to post a negative review.

Review Ratings

Review ratings is the assignment of a value to a program or item. Review rating systems may use a number or other indicator (such as star ratings) that display feedback from viewers.

The review process may limit votes to one vote per computer to prevent the same person from submitting multiple votes. This voting control process may operate by storing a cookie on the voting computer, or it may use other identifying information, such as invalidating multiple votes that are sent from the same IP address.

Recommendations

Program recommendation is the process of providing information (text comments) that indicates the value of an item (such as a TV show) for other readers to see. The recommendation comments that are submitted should be reviewed before posting to ensure that inappropriate comments or promotional messages (comment spam) are not inserted.

Referrals

Referrals are the process of sending a recommendation message from a viewer to another person that relates to a product or services. To make it simple for people to recommend programs, share with a friend buttons may be included on program pages to allow readers to quickly connect and submit a recommendation or review.

Program Bookmarking

Program bookmarking buttons may be used to allow the viewer to store their favorite programs or to store locations within their favorite programs.

Figure 12.14 shows how a review system can be used to allow people to submit and recommend program to help other users find and view content. The review level is posted next to the program guide listing. Access to review recommendations are grouped and provided on a separate viewing page.

Recommend to a friend buttons are provided within the program. Program bookmarking options are included to allow the viewer to store the viewing selection.

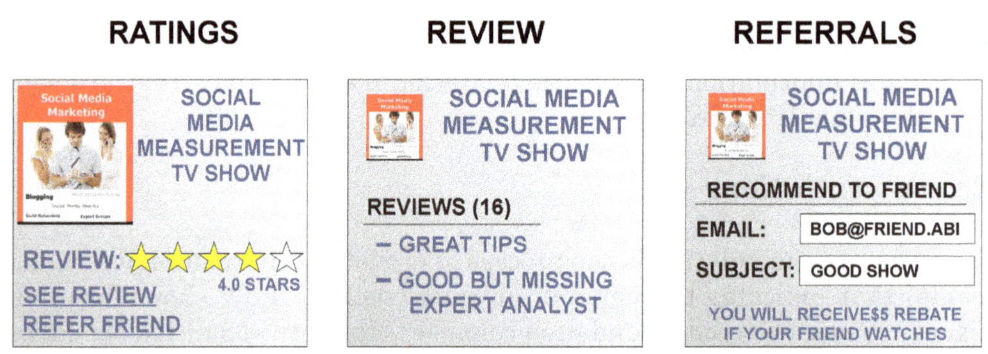

Figure 12.14, TV Program Reviews and Recommendations

Email Broadcasting

Email broadcasting is the process of sending messages to relatively similar groups of email recipients (potentially large numbers). Internet TVs can be promoted by sending programming availability email announcement messages to people who are interested in the issues or topics covered. To do this, a targeted list is obtained or leased and an announcement message is created. An email broadcast is performed, usually by an email service provider (ESP) that can track delivery and interaction with the email messages.

Targeted Lists

Email lists are groups of email addresses (called list subscribers) that are owned or rented. Email address acquisition processes can range from asking customers for email addresses when they visit a store to using newsletters and other promotional programs to get people to register their email addresses. Qualified lists can be rented from magazines, newsletters, industry associations, trade shows and other providers of focused news and content. Rented lists are commonly sent to a 3rd party such as a mailing house to prevent the user from having direct access to the list.

It is also possible to get access to qualified lists by bartering (exchanging) viewer lists for email broadcasts. If the bartered lists do not have an equal number of names, the list with fewer names may be used more than once.

Email Service Provider (ESP)

An email service provider is a company that provides email broadcasting services for other people or companies. The services provided can range from list capturing, campaign management, email broadcasting, link tracking and reporting. Some email broadcast companies include Constant Contact (www.ConstantContact.com), Topica (www.Topica.com), and Vertical Response (ww.VerticalResonse.com.

Several important government regulations must be followed when sending emails, and ESPs must strongly enforce these rules (avoiding SPAM). This can result in delays and list validation requirements before ESPs allow companies to start adding names to lists and performing email broadcasts.

ESPs commonly charge fees for hosting and/or sending (broadcasting) email messages. In 2010, it cost approximately 1 cent per email address per month to host and send email messages for small to medium size lists. This means that a list with 10,000 names would cost $100 per month to manage.

Internet TV Program Announcement Message

Internet TV program announcement messages are email alerts that inform recipients when new content that may be of interest to them are available. ESPs commonly provide templates (email messages ready for modification) and instructions that can help a person or company to setup their email messages.

Email Testing

When possible, multiple versions of announcement messages and subject lines should be tested by sending variations to small groups of similar recipients. This testing process allows for the setup and selection of the most effective email broadcast campaigns. Small variations in email messages or list selections can make a dramatic difference in the email open rates, email message interaction and ultimately in the conversion (purchase) rates.

Figure 12.15 shows how email broadcasting can be used to announce and promote an Internet TV. The email broadcasting process starts with a qualified list selection. The motivational announcement message is created along with an enticing subject line. Tracking codes are used to identify how

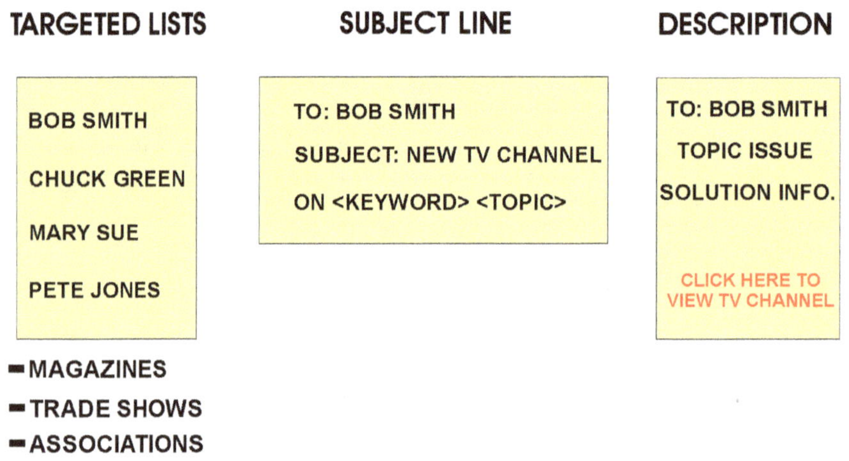

Figure 12.15, Internet TV Email Broadcasting

many people opened, interacted with and downloaded the sample Internet TV programming trailer.

Promotional Videos

Promotional videos are short media clips that provide informational and motivational messages to encourage people to make purchases, increase consumption or take some form of action. A one hour Internet TV program episode should provide enough content for 5 to 10 short videos.

Promotional videos are commonly produced by creating a sequence of scenes that are described in rough image form (storyboards). In addition to using segments of the program, promotional videos about Internet TV programs may be produced by recording people, or editing pre-existing content into short video segments, such as a trailer or episode preview.

Storyboarding

A storyboard is a group of images or media segments that describe the key elements of a media ad, campaign or program. Storyboard images may contain rough sketches of proposed images along with some captions or descriptions. Storyboards can be created from Internet TV programs by using heading sections from different segments of an episode script.

Video Production

Promotional videos for Internet TVs can be created from interviews, episode content or combined stock video.

One or more subject matter experts (SMEs) or actors may be interviewed to provide high value content. Interviews may be performed prior to the filming of an Internet TV program series, as the content derived may provide information that should be included in the programming. Interviews may be performed remotely (such as by webcam) to reduce the time and cost of recording.

If the content from the TV program can be provided in presentation format (such as a documentary), the presentation can be recorded (e.g. a web seminar) as video content. The recorded presentation video may be divided into 2 to 5 minute short video segments.

Stock video (media clips available for licensing) may be used to provide attention getting media. Stock video may contain high action content that relates to the subject matter. For example, if cooking is a key factor that relates to the programming, short clips of preparing a meal may be included in the video.

Embedded Videos

Embedded videos are media segments that may be included within web pages. Short segments of videos (such as portions of an episode) may be embedded into the Internet TV's website.

Video Titles

Promotional video titles are labels that are used to identify video content to audiences. If possible, keywords that may be used in viewer searches should be used in the video titles. This can dramatically increase the discovery of videos that may attract viewers to watch the entire video program. Video titles may also include words that serve as motivational messages that include key words and issues that are likely to interest viewers. For example "10 simple things you can do to get a pay raise!"

Video Captions

Video captions are text descriptions of the content contained in the video. Video captions should contain keywords and issues related to the video. Search engines may use video captions to help identify and categorize videos.

Video Transcriptions

Video transcription is the process of converting the audio contained within a video into text format. Including a transcription of the video can allow search engines to identify and list the video content. If possible, the script for the promotional video should contain keywords and key topics.

Shared Video Networks

Posting videos to shared video networks can allow people and search engines to find videos. Videos posted on shared video networks may include links back to other sites (such as Internet TV listing pages). Videos posted to shared video networks may be embedded into other pages (such as Internet TV programs listing pages). Setting the embedding on automatic play can increase the popularity of the video, as the shared web site will record a video view each time someone opens that web page. Examples of shared video networks include www.howcast.com, www.youtube.com, and www.eHow.com.

Promotional Video Optimization (PVO)

Promotional video optimization is the process or processes that are used to adjust the components of video programs to improve their effectiveness in achieving desired actions, such as order conversion rates or subscription rates. PVO may include testing and changing the titles, descriptions and, in some cases, the contents of videos to improve overall performance.

Figure 12.16 shows a sample video production and promotion process for an Internet TV. The process starts by creating a storyboard of scenes that qualified viewers are likely to find interesting. The production may include performing interviews (at remote locations via web cams), video recording programming, and adding interesting stock video clips. The video program is given a title that includes keywords and issues that interest the viewers. A caption is added which describes the video. The audio may be converted into text which may help search engines find the video. The video may be placed on shared video sites to allow for discovery and viewing by many people.

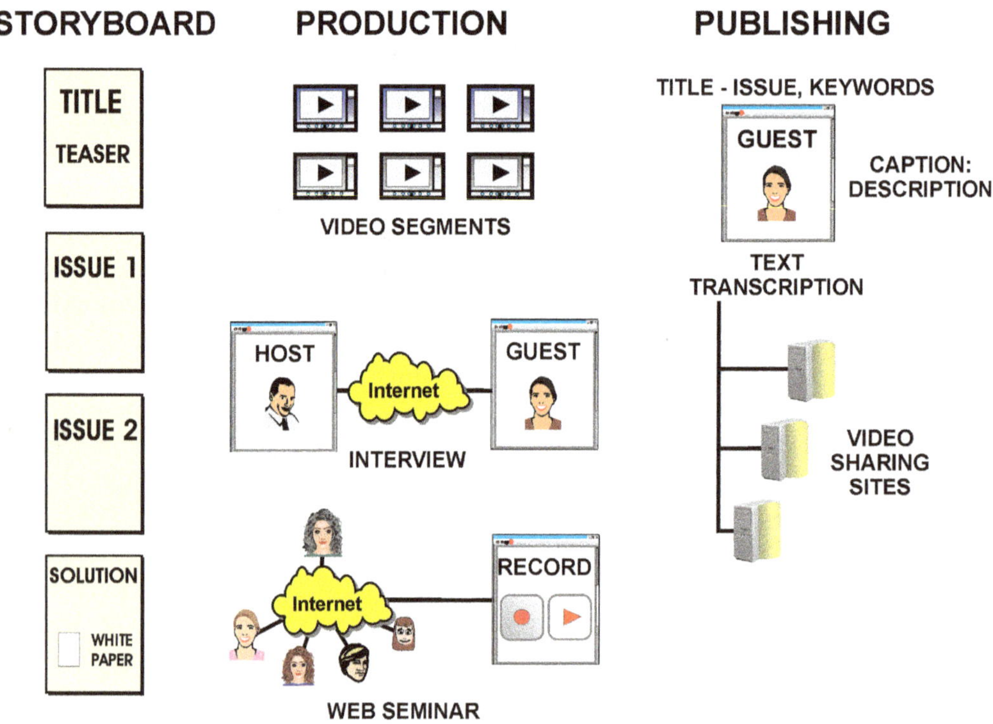

Figure 12.16, Internet TV Video Promotion

Internet TV Content Licensing

A content license is a contract that grants specific rights to the use of content in limited and specified ways. Examples of content licenses include permission to distribute a television program to users as part of a linear (24/7) channel, and permission to distribute a linear (24/7) channel service in a cable television system. There are several types of licenses that are needed to obtain and distribute content in TV systems. Great care must be taken by the licensee to ensure that the proper rights are obtained and that the content is used only in accordance with those rights.

Entertainment Law

Entertainment law refers to the practice of law pertaining to the entertainment industry. Focus is typically on the provision of services of persons with specific areas of talent, and on the licensing of intellectual property rights covered by copyright and trademarks. These rules and regulations are designed to clarify the mutual obligations of the parties with respect to the performance of certain entertainment related activities, and to clarify the respective rights of those parties to own, manage and exploit the associated intellectual property rights. Entertainment law also protects investors from excessive valuation or overstated claims of future compensation that may result from investments.

An entertainment attorney is a person who specializes in the provision of legal counsel pertaining to matters within the entertainment industry. No special degree or certification beyond that which is required to practice law is required, so long as the person is an active member in good standing of the Bar Association in the state in which they are practicing. Specialization is more a function of experience and area of practice.

Licensing Aggregator

A content licensing aggregator is a company or service that helps another company to obtain the rights from content providers to resell and distribute content through their communication systems (such as TV broadcast systems). A content licensing aggregator helps to obtain and negotiate the necessary licenses. The licensee is responsible for receiving and rebroadcasting the media from the content owner.

The content aggregator might aggregate individual items of content such as programs or program series for use as video-on-demand content or for inclusion in the line-up of a linear (24/7) channel. The content aggregator might secure a number of linear (24/7) channels for distribution over a communication system (such as TV broadcast systems).

License Types

There are several types of licenses that should be obtained for the transmission and distribution of content through TV systems. These include a Transport License and Use License.

Transport License

A Transport License gives the licensee the right to transfer the content (whether it be VOD or linear) from one location to another; usually from the source location, which may be the studio or downlink center, to the operators' headends. A Transport License is often obtained by content aggregators to enable them to deliver content to the headends of their customers; those wishing to distribute the content to subscribers.

A transport license may need to be obtained at the request of the content owner to ensure the media distribution is performed in a way that does not place the program content at risk of being altered or copy by others who may have access to the transport system. For example, a premium movie owner is not likely to agree to allow their program to be distributed through the Internet by an unprotected download link.

Use License

A Use License gives the licensee the right to use the content in a very specific manner as defined by the license. This usually involves the right to distribute the content to viewers under controlled conditions in exchange for a fee. A Use License contains specific elements that should be carefully considered by all parties prior to signing.

Figure 13.1 shows some of the key types of licenses. A Transport License authorizes the transfer of media content between locations, such as on private lines, satellite links or through the Internet. A Use License defines the rights to content usage, such as viewing, copying and editing.

License Type	Description
Transport License	Authorizes transfer on communication links such as satellite or through the Internet.
Use License	Authorizes how the media may be used. This can include limits on viewing, copying, and editing.

Figure 13.1, TV Content License Types

Type of Use

Whether a licensee is obtaining content to show as a video on demand (VOD) program on their television service, to include in an advertisement or to display on a website, they need to obtain the licensing rights that match their intended use of the content. People often tend to think that if they pay for content, they can use it however they want. However, when content is licensed, the licensee is not actually buying the content, but is purchasing the right to use the content in a very specific way. It follows then, that the licensee must exercise extreme care, both when determining where to get the content and when establishing the terms of the license.

License Scope

Once the licensee finds the proper source for the content they desire, their focus must turn to negotiating the proper Use License. Step one is to make it very clear to the content provider how the licensee intends to use the content. It will do the licensee no good to arrange a license only to find out after the fact that they used the content in a way that exceeded the scope of their license. It is better to make the intended use clear to the content owner at the beginning of the negotiation process in order to obtain the full rights that the licensee requires.

License Elements

When negotiating a license, it is important to be aware of the various elements of the license, as well as any issues that will need to be considered or addressed in the license. It is as equally important to then use the content only as allowed by the license. As with all legal issues, it is important to obtain the advice and guidance of an attorney when negotiating licenses.

Free-to-Air Content License

Free-to-Air Content is programming that is made available by the content distributor to all viewers without charge. This is mostly associated with content that is broadcast over either a terrestrial or satellite broadcast network. Typically the content distributor generates revenue from advertisements that are broadcasted along with the content. It is important to note that Free-to-Air Content is being broadcasted with an inherent license permitting people to watch the content for their own use/enjoyment. It is not permissible for people to take that content and re-broadcast it to other people for a fee. To re-broadcast Free-to-Air Content, a license is required.

Distribution Systems

There are two primary characterizations of systems that enable the distribution of content over the Internet. One characterization is based on whether the system is open (Internet broadcast) or closed (access network providers), and the second characterization is based on whether the content is delivered to Set Top Boxes or to computers including mobile devices.

Open Distribution Systems

Open TV systems are referred to as Over the Top (OTT). OTT systems deliver content to any person with a broadband Internet connection, regardless of which company provides the customer's Internet service. OTT systems are unicast systems; meaning that each individual item of content is streamed specifically to each individual viewer as they request it. This architecture provides the operator with the flexibility to deliver content almost anywhere in the world, so long as broadband is available; all from one distribution architecture.

OTT systems can deliver content to Internet Set Top Boxes (digital media adapters) for television viewing and to computers and mobile devices, such as cell phones and iPads. Each element, both the architecture and the end device upon which the content is watched, creates a different distribution architecture that must be addressed by the license.

Closed Distribution Systems

Closed systems, such as those used by Telephone Companies (Telcos), refer to distribution systems where the operator owns and manages the broadband network "pipes" that are used to deliver the content. The operator actually manages and controls the entire delivery network from the headend to the viewer and the content is delivered over that network. For this reason, distribution is limited to a specific geographic area and customers within which the network physically exists. The benefit of this architecture is that the content can be broadcast on a multicast basis; meaning that each channel can be streamed to each viewer on the network at the same time, and the viewer can simply tune to the channel they wish to watch. This results in lower operating cost.

Content owners often have very specific limitations regarding the types of systems they can use for content distribution. This can be for a number of reasons. For example, the content owner may be restricted by pre-existing agreements that exclude further licensing on certain distribution platforms. Or, the content owner may be concerned that distribution of content on an OTT system does not provide a sufficient level of security to protect the content from pirating. As a result, content owners may permit licensing in one scenario, but not another. It is important for the Licensee to identify the exact type of system they intend to use for broadcast in order to ensure that their license permits it.

Figure 13.2 shows two key types of distribution systems for content through the Internet. Open distribution systems allow the delivery of content to any viewer. Closed distribution systems limit content distribution to viewers connected through a controlled access system.

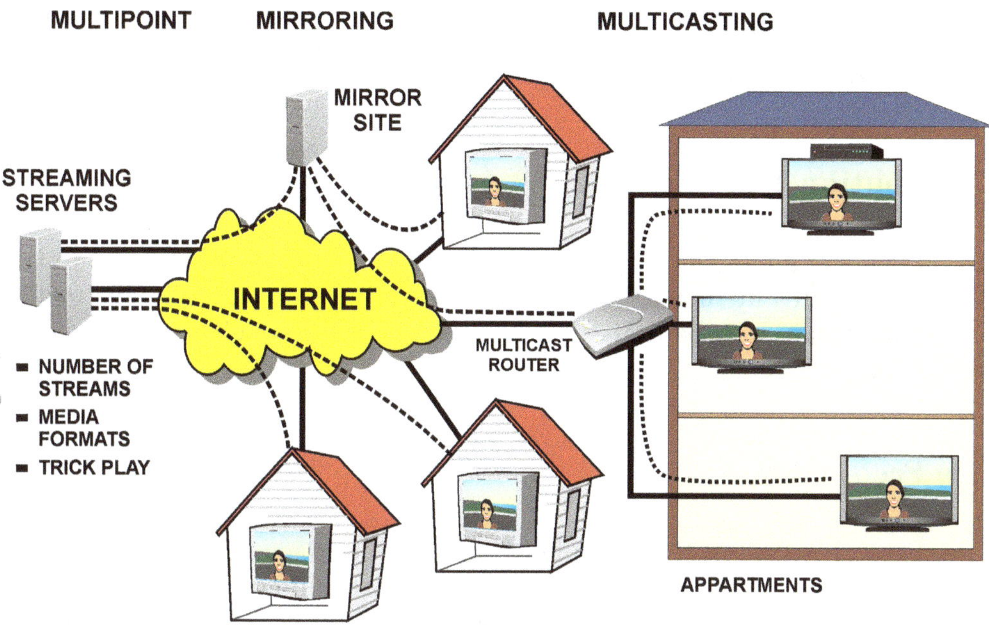

Figure 13.2, Internet TV Distribution Types

Use Period

A license to use content will last for a specific period of time. This refers to not only the dates during which the content can be used, but also the number of times it can be used during that period (frequency).

Release Windows

Content is often licensed to multiple distribution outlets, including movie theaters, DVD sales, movie rental companies like Red Box and Blockbuster, television broadcast networks and IP Television operators, such as Netflix and NextTV. The licenses granted to each of these distribution outlets will specify the time period during which content can be distributed to viewers. It is of utmost importance to both the content owners, and the other distributors, that the content be released only pursuant to the schedule, as the distribution outlets will otherwise compete with each other for viewers. Those earliest in the distribution schedule will have likely paid a premium to have access to the content first.

Distribution Time Period

An operator of a television system will want to be very clear to state in the license the dates during which the content can be distributed. The initial distribution date may be limited by the release windows chosen by the content owner.

Use Frequency

The operator will want to state how often the content can be distributed during the usage period. For example, a license might allow the content be distributed only one time as part of normal channel programming, on a specific date and time. Or, perhaps the program can be run a specific number of times over the license period.

Alternatively, the license may allow the operator to run the program as many times as the operator elects over the program period. The key is to identify the intended use and make sure that the use is permitted by the license.

When restrictions exist in the license agreement on the period and frequency that content can be distributed, the operator must put measures in place to ensure that the content is used only in accordance with the license. This control system must be verifiable to protect the operator from claims of misuse.

Geographic Limitations

Content licenses will also define where, geographically, the content can be distributed. The limitation is often specified to countries or continents, but it can be limited to any region or even a specific network.

The distribution of content in specific geographic regions will often be linked to the time period when the content can be distributed. For example, a license may allow for the distribution of content in the United States during the first and second calendar quarter, and then distribution in Europe during the third and fourth calendar quarter.

Access Network Restriction

Closed loop television operators can easily control geographic distribution as content is only delivered on their access network. So long as the license allows distribution where the network is located, they are in compliance with that element of the license.

As Over-the-Top IP television distribution systems have the potential to deliver content anywhere in the world where broadband is available, the OTT IPTV operator must be careful to ensure that they do not distribute content to areas beyond the scope of their license. The easiest way to ensure compliance is to negotiate a license without geographic limitations. However, if geographic limitations are imposed by the license, there are options to attempt compliance such as IP address geo-filtering.

Geo-Filtering

Geo-filtering enables operators to restrict the delivery of content to certain geographic locations based on the IP address ranges corresponding to certain countries. However, this approach can be circumvented if the viewer reroutes their Internet traffic to an IP address in a location where distribution is permitted. Another approach is to limit access simply by refusing to sign-up any viewer that has an address outside the licensed geographic area. However, a viewer could provide an address located within an approved geographic region, sign up for service and receive the content in an unauthorized region. As both methods can be circumvented by viewers, it is important to reach an understanding with the content owner than any restrictions on geographic distribution will be on a best-efforts basis using the technique identified.

Figure 13.3 shows how a content owner may restrict the distribution of content to specific geographic regions. This example shows how movies distributed to closed networks can limit the distribution of programs to customers that are connected to their systems. Movies that are distributed through the Internet can be limited to geographic regions by identifying the location of the Internet address that is accessing the content.

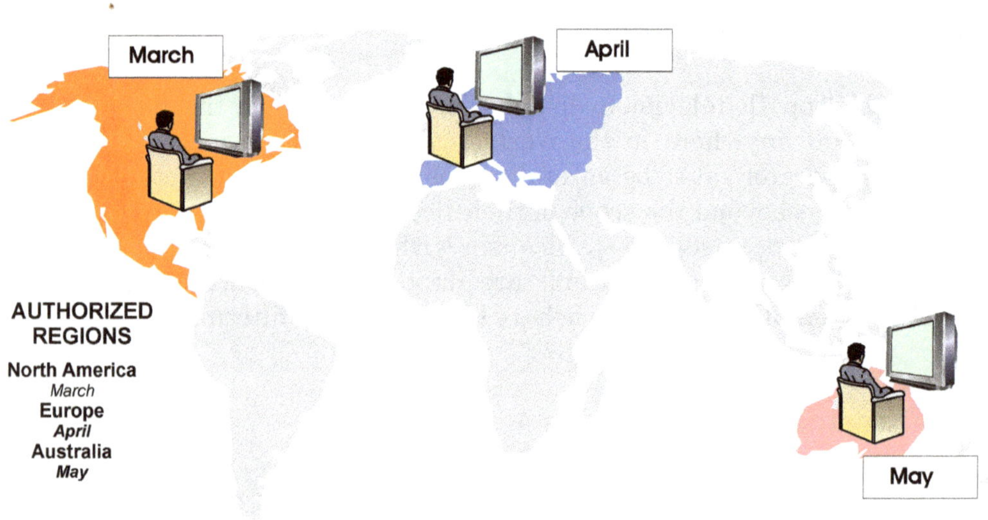

Figure 13.3, Internet TV Geographic Limitations

Authorized Media Formats

Media formats refer to the ways content can be prepared for transport and viewing. This can include the type of media compression (such as MPEG-2 or MPEG-4) used to encode and encrypt the content, as well as the parameters selected for content viewing, such as resolution (SD, HD), aspect ratio (standard 4:3 TV or widescreen 16:9), and audio formats (mono, stereo, or surround sound).

Content creators and content owners want to preserve the value of the content they license. As each showing represents the content and the brand, content owners want to ensure that minimum quality levels are maintained when their content is presented. Content owners therefore often place specific requirements in the license designed to ensure the quality of the content when viewed.

The type of encoding used, the resolution, the encapsulation and the transport bit-rate all affect the quality of the content. For example, content distributed using a 500Kbps bit-rate will have a noticeably poorer image quality than content transported at 1Mbps. Content owners may define these parameters to ensure that the content "looks good" to the viewer.

Sub-Licensing

Sub-licensing refers to the right of a licensee to further license content to a third party. Most often, a content User License only allows the licensee to play the content to the licensee's customers (the viewers).

The terms of the license will dictate how the content be used by the viewer. For example, the license may dictate whether the content can be streamed to the viewer for viewing at only a specific point in time, or whether the content can be downloaded by the viewer for viewing at their leisure.

In some circumstances, the license may allow the licensee to enter into an agreement to further license the content to a third party. This is often the case when content owners license their content to a content aggregator. In these instances, the content aggregator has the right to sub-license the content to third parties such as operators. The terms of those licenses are specifically defined, especially as they relate to how revenue from the licensing of the content is to be divided between the content owner, the content aggregator and the operator.

Fee Structures

Fee structures refer to the details of the license agreement that determine how the operator can charge the viewer for the content as well as how the content owner is to be compensated for the operator's use of the content.

A flat fee refers to a pre-determined amount that the operator will pay the content owner for the use of the content during the term of the license.

A per-use fee refers to a pre-determined amount that the operator pays the content owner each time the operator uses (plays) the content on its system. Video-On-Demand and Pay-Per-View programs are examples of per-use fee scenarios.

Revenue share refers to scenarios where the amount of payment given by the operator to the content owner is unknown at the time the license is entered into because the amount to be paid is dependent upon other criteria. For example an operator may simply give the content owner a percentage of the subscriber revenue that the operator generates, either for a service (access to a channel), or for a specific piece of content (Pay-Per-View/Video on Demand). Often times, the amount of compensation paid by the operator to the content owner will simply be a percentage of the advertising revenue generated by the operator.

Pricing scenarios can be as creative and as varied as the content owner and the operator determine.

Revenue Assurance

Regardless of the fee structure entered into by the content owner and the operator, the operator will be responsible for capturing and maintaining accurate records of all uses of the content and all revenue generated from the use of the content. The license agreement will most often impose this obligation on the operator.

License agreements may grant the content owner the right to audit the operational and financial records of the operator to ensure that the proper fee is being paid to the content owner. Alternatively, the license may grant the content owner the right to have a third party audit the records of the operator for the same purpose.

It therefore behooves the operator to have a reliable billing and records management system in place so that fees are accurately determined and compliance with the license agreement can be substantiated.

Content Protection Methods

Content protection refers to methods used by both content owners and operators to ensure that content can be accessed by viewers and third parties only in accordance with the terms of the license granted.

Content protection can also refer to the operator's obligation to store the content securely and allow access to it by others only in accordance with the terms of the license.

Content owners may specify the way content is encrypted during transport to the headend and to the viewers. Encryption is used to help ensure that unauthorized third parties cannot pirate the content. A third party encryption solution (often referred to as Digital Rights Management or DRM) is often selected by the content owner. The operator is then responsible to include that third party DRM solution in their distribution system.

Transport

Transport refers to the delivery of content from one location (often the source location such as the content owner's studio) to another location such as the operator's head-end or content delivery network (CDN). This applies to the transport of both linear channels and individual programs to the operator.

Common methods of video transport include delivery via satellite, where the content owner simply downlinks the content, either on-site or at a third party's location, using a satellite dish and receiver. This is an efficient transport and downlink method if the content is already being broadcast on satellite.

If the content is not already being broadcast on satellite, it can be transported to the operator using a dedicated broadband connection. This is an especially appealing transport option for IP Television operators as they use broadband to distribute content to their viewers so the content is often already in the correct media format and the quality of the transport solution is at least as good as the quality of the delivery solution to the end viewer.

Third party service providers, such as TVN and Comcast, can be contracted to prepare and distribute VOD content to multiple locations and multiple operators' headends.

Regardless of the content transport solution selected, it is important for the operator to determine who will incur the costs of content transporting, including the bandwidth or satellite space segment used as well as the associated hardware required.

Indemnification

Indemnification refers to one party's obligation to compensate the other party if certain events occur, such as a breach of the representations or warranties set forth in the agreement. Just as the content owner wants to make sure that the licensee will use the content only in accordance with the licensee, it is important for the licensee to know that the content owner has full authority to grant the rights given in the license. This includes the representation that the content owner actually owns or has assignable rights to the content, and that the license being granted is not in conflict with any other licenses.

The licensee will want to obtain assurances that the content owner has the authority to grant the licensee the rights that the licensee desires. The licensee will also want the content owner to indemnify the licensee, should any of those assurances appear to be un-true.

As always, an attorney should be consulted when negotiating any intellectual property right to ensure that the legal interests of both parties are protected.

Internet TV Advertising

Internet TV advertising is the insertion of promotional messages or media content into programs or surrounding media that viewers watch. Internet TV Advertising can be many times more effective than traditional broadcast ads because of targeting, customization, and built in response channels.

Internet TV ads media formats including video, images, audio, or text which is placed within, around, or on top of the delivered media. Viewers which are influenced by the messages take actions that benefit the advertiser which may be tracked by the Internet TV system. Internet TV providers can provide details on their advertising message was delivered and interacted with. Traditional TV broadcasters tend not to provide details of ad insertion, consumption, and interaction.

Advertisers

Advertisers desire to provide messages to people who are interested in their products or services. Advertisers pay media companies (such as broadcasters) to send their promotional messages. Advertisers are interested in number of viewers (reach), viewer profile (target audience), and engagement value (how viewers can respond). Advertisers coordinate the selection of broadcasters and transmission of their promotional messages using advertising campaigns.

Internet TV Broadcasters

Internet TV providers (broadcasters) operate systems that gather, organize, and provide people with content that they want to see. Internet TV broadcasters schedule or provide access to content they send through their systems.

Viewers

Viewers select programs they want to view and some of these programs contain promotional messages which motivate some of them to take actions that satisfy advertiser's business objectives.

Figure 14.1 shows how the television advertising model works. The advertiser pays money to the TV broadcaster to insert their promotional message. The TV broadcaster mixes in advertising messages with other content that the viewer wants to watch. After the viewer watches the advertising message, they performs some desired action (buy a product or subscribe to a list) which makes the advertiser money.

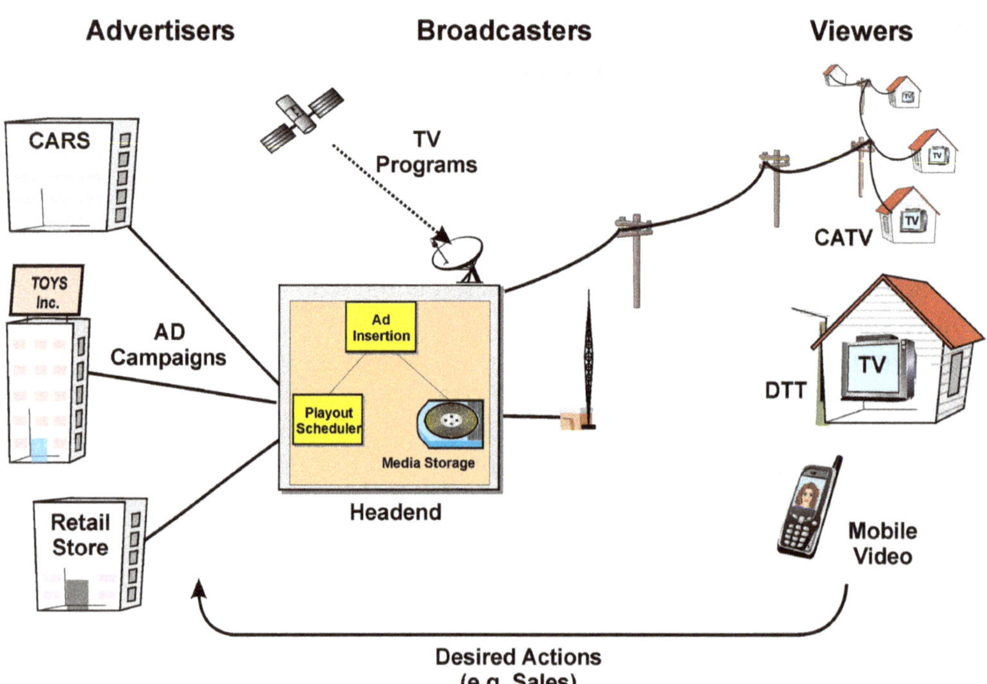

Figure 14.1, Television Advertising

Video Ad Networks

Video ad networks link advertisers and publishers through a services platform. The use of ad networks provides a simple way for Internet TV service providers to sell advertising and get ads for insertion. Advertisers select geographic areas, content types, and setup budgets. Content owners (Internet TV providers) enable insertion of ads into their programs (pre-roll, interstitial, post-roll).

Some of the companies providing ads for Internet TV services include AOL Platforms (aolplatforms.com), Adrise (adrise.com), Tremor Video (tremorvideo.com), and Tube Mogul (tubemogul.com).

Interstitial Ads (Standard TV Ads)

Standard television advertising is the insertion of promotional messages during identifiable advertising opportunities. Standard TV ads are often prescheduled media that is inserted within broadcasted programs (linear ads), tied to on demand media, or completely replace programming (long form ads).

Linear Ads

Linear advertising is the inserting of promotional messages into programs that are being transmitted in continuous form (broadcasting or streaming).

On Demand Ads

On demand ads are media segments that are merged into on demand programming. On demand ads may be inserted before content (pre-roll), after content (post-roll), within content (avails), or after media play control options.

Long Form Advertisements

Long form advertisements are promotional messages that are longer than the typical available promotional spot (over 10 minutes).

Figure 14.2 shows common types of TV advertising. Linear ads replace existing media within a broadcast channel (such as network ad avails). On demand ads can be inserted before, after, and within on demand viewing sessions. Long form ads become the program.

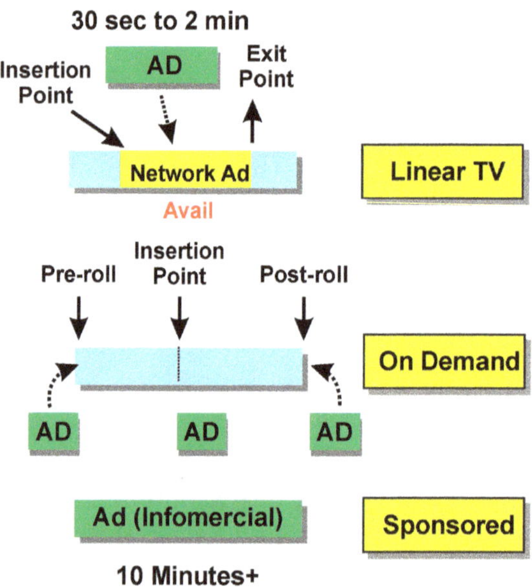

Figure 14.2, Standard TV Ads

Bumper Ads (Pre-roll and Post-roll)

A bumper is a media clip that is played before (pre-roll) or after (post-roll) a media program or video segment. Bumper ads may also be inserted during media playout commands such as pause, fast forward, or other media control processes.

Pre-roll Ads

A pre-roll is the specific amount of time that is allowed for media to run (such as a video tape) before broadcasting or editing to allow the media device to obtain normal operating speed.

Pre-roll ads tend to be fairly short (5 to 15 seconds) to reduce the amount of viewers who change channels ("click away"). The viewer may be forced to view pre-roll ads before they can gain access to the content which can guarantee advertising revenue.

Inserting pre-roll ads may be as simple as adding the pre-roll video segment to a media program that will be requested or is scheduled to be played out.

Post-roll Ads

Post-roll is a media clip that is played after another media program (typically a movie). While viewers tend to change channels after a program is completed, if the post roll ad is highly related to the previous content, more viewers may stay to watch the ad. Unlike pre-roll ads that should be very short, post roll ads can be much longer.

Pause Ads

Pause ads are media images or segments that are presented when a viewer has selected to temporarily stop the playing of the media.

Figure 14.3 shows how bumper ads may be inserted into programs. Pre-roll ads place short promotional messages (5 to 15 seconds) in front of media that the viewer has selected to watch. Post-roll ads are promotional messages that are added at the end of a media program. Pause ads are media programs that are displayed within a pause window when the viewer has selected to temporarily stop the program.

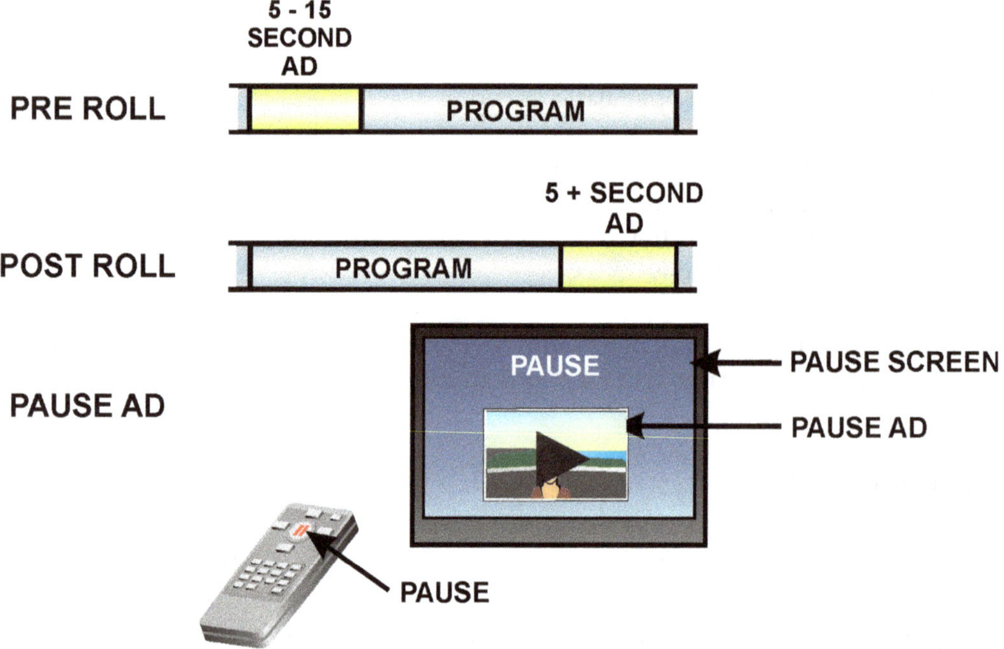

Figure 14.3, Bumper Ads

Overlay Ads

An overlay ad is a promotional message that is inserted on top of another media item. Overlay ad insertion can be the insertion of logos, images, or scrolling text. Overlay ads may be solid or transparent.

For some media types, overlay ads must be merged with the underlying media. For other media types (such as MPEG-4), overlay ads may be sent as a separate file and merged by the viewing device. Overlay ads that can be sent via a separate channel or stream may require less bandwidth and appear cleaner (less fuzzy edges).

Overlay ads can be a low bandwidth solution that may be used on any type of system and can be relatively simple and low cost addition. However, content licensing agreements may include restrictions on the modifying of programs prohibiting the use of digital overlay ads.

Logo Insertion

Logo insertion (sometimes called bugs) is placing of an image that identifies or is associated with a company, product, or service. Advertisers may pay for the time logos appear on programs or media.

Image Placement

Image placement is the process of inserting a graphic object into a display area or within a media stream such as a television program. Images may be static or they may be animated (change over time). For TV broadcasting systems, images inserts are typically inserted on programs based on their distribution networks.

Transparent Overlay

A transparent overlay is a media object such as text or images that appear on top of another media display (such as on top of a television program) where the overlay image allows some of the underlying image to bleed through.

Scrolling Text

Video text crawling is the displaying of text or image signals so they continuously move (crawl) across a video display. Scrolling text is the displaying of words or characters so they continuously move (crawl) across a display.

Figure 14.4 shows how an ad can be overlayed onto a television program. By identifying the type of program and suitable ad insertion areas (placement opportunities), ad images can be placed on top of the video display. This example shows that an ad for a pizza can be placed on top of the video display.

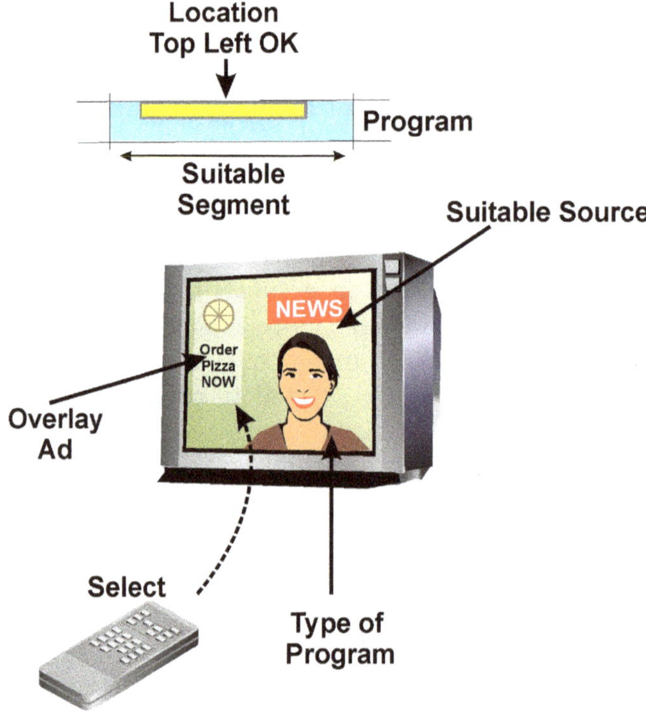

Figure 14.4, Overlay TV Ads

Squeeze Back (Squeezeback)

A squeeze back is a process that reduces the size of a video or image (such as a television display) to allow other items (such as logos, text crawls or graphics) to be inserted into the display area. Squeezeback may be used during the closing credits of a movie to introduce the viewer to upcoming content along with other promotions.

Foreground Display Resizing

The primary video source (foreground video) is selected and processed to reduce its display size for a period of time (transition period). The reduction of the foreground video exposes the underlying layer(s).

Background Video Display

The background video display contains media that can be seen when the foreground display is reduced in size. The background may contain video, images, or other content (such as text crawlers).

Figure 14.5 shows how squeeze back scales the foreground video image and exposes the background image. The underlying image in this example shows a promotional message to the viewer.

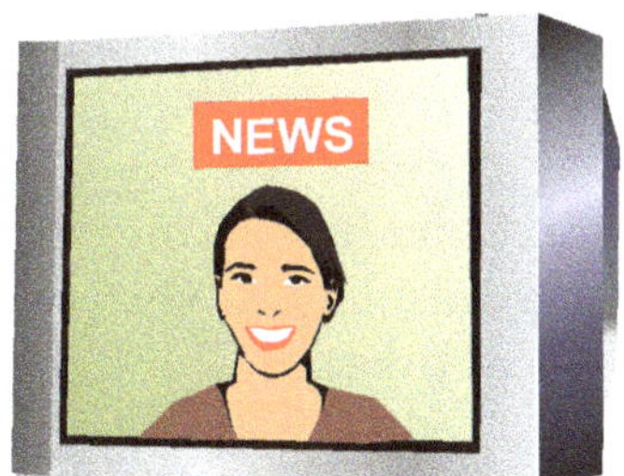

Figure 14.5, TV Squeeze Back

Product Placement

Product placement is the insertion of one or more product images within a media program Product placement options include the item appearing in the program, dynamic insertion of the product in the video (or on top), use of the product in the show (product integration), and interactive product placement (selectable items).

The sale of product placement promotion can cause conflict between creative professionals who want to maintain the look of the program and producers who want to generate more revenue.

Product Integration

Product integration involves updating the script so the product is used in the shoot. Use of the product in the program can add awareness and credibility to the product. It can be helpful to have a representative of the product manufacturer as an extra in the program as an added product placement incentive.

Dynamic Product Placement (DPP)

Dynamic product placement is the insertion of one or more product images into a media program which can be selected and controlled by other factors (such as user profile, geographic area, time of day, etc). Dynamic product placement may be performed at the media server (creating a customized stream) or overlayed on top of the video.

HTML 5 video has the capability for adding text and images on top of videos. Not all HTML 5 capable players allow overlayed images. Graphic overlay images may be blocked by platforms such as Youtube

Interactive Product Placement

Interactive product placement is the displaying of images on top of a video that can be selected by the user. Direct interactions with viewers can be highly valued by advertisers such as seeing a car commercial and being able to select a specific vehicle to get more information.

Skin Ads

TV viewer skin ads are promotional messages that appear in the area surrounding the media player window. TV viewer skins ads may be displayed to viewers who are watching the TV channel on a multimedia computer (window viewing).

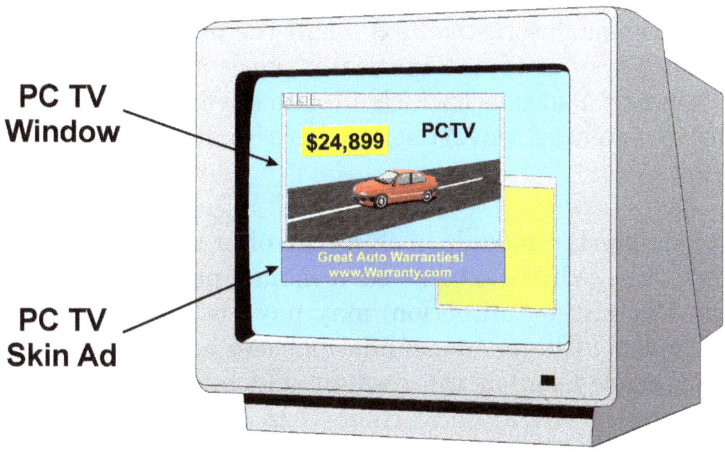

Figure 14.6, TV Player Skin Ads

Window Viewing

Some broadcasters simulcast their programming on channels through the Internet, which can be watched using a media player on a multimedia computer.

Player Skin Ads

Player skin ads are promotional messages or images that appear in the area surrounding the viewer's media player window. Skin ads may be associated with segments of content (scenes), allowing the ads to change throughout the viewing of the program. For example, if the program is about cars, ads for car wax may show when a scene shows the car in a car wash, and ads for oil may be shown if the car's engine explodes.

A simple way to insert player skin ads is to allow the insertion of text based ads (such as Google Adsense) in the area directly below the video. It is important to include some descriptive text about the program (keywords) to allow the advertising system to automatically select appropriate ads. Pay per click advertisers can also select which sites to advertise on. An Internet TV can promote to potential advertisers where to list their ads on the Internet TV site.

Inserting affiliate (co-marketing) ads in skins can offer much higher revenue potential that PPC ads. While text ads earn money pay per click, affiliate ads (such as from Commission Junction) may pay nothing unless a visitor buys something. Typical affiliate ad commissions can be $10 to $20 per sale. If the products advertised match the content and buying interests of the viewer (this can be rare), affiliate advertising can earn $500 to $1000 cpm (1-2% order rates).

Figure 14.6 shows player skin ads that are displayed in an area around the viewer's media player window. This example shows skin ads that are contextually matched to the media automotive program that the person is watching. The ads displayed around the viewing window are for automotive parts and services.

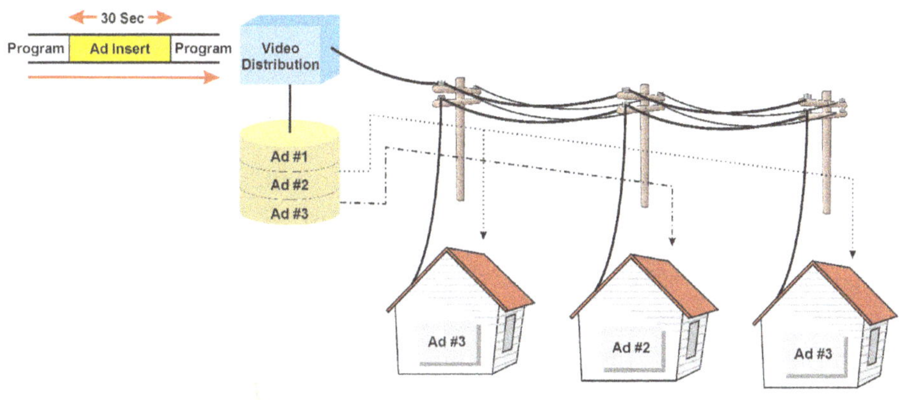

Figure 14.7, Addressable Advertising

Addressable Advertising

Addressable advertising is the communication of a message or media content to a specific device or customer based on their address. The address of the customer may be obtained by searching viewer profiles to determine if the advertising message is appropriate for the recipient. The use of addressable advertising allows for rapid and direct measurement of the effectiveness of advertising campaigns.

A key aspect of addressable advertising is the validation of the viewer. IP television systems may ask (prompt) the viewer to select their name from a list of registered users in the home when the IP television is turned on. Because of the advanced features offered by IP television such as incoming calls/emails and programming guides that remember favorite channels, viewers will typically want to select their programming name. Because the programming name has a profile (preferences), advertising messages can be selected that best match the profile.

The potential revenue for addressable advertising messages that are sent to viewers with specific profiles can be 10 to 100 times higher than the revenue for broadcasting an ad to a general audience. The ability to send ads to a specific number of viewers allows advertisers to set specific budgets for addressable advertising. It also allows the advertiser to test a number of different ads in the same geographic area at the same time.

Figure 14.7 shows how addressable advertising can be used to better match advertising messages to the wants and needs of viewers. This diagram shows that a media program (such as a television show or movie) is being

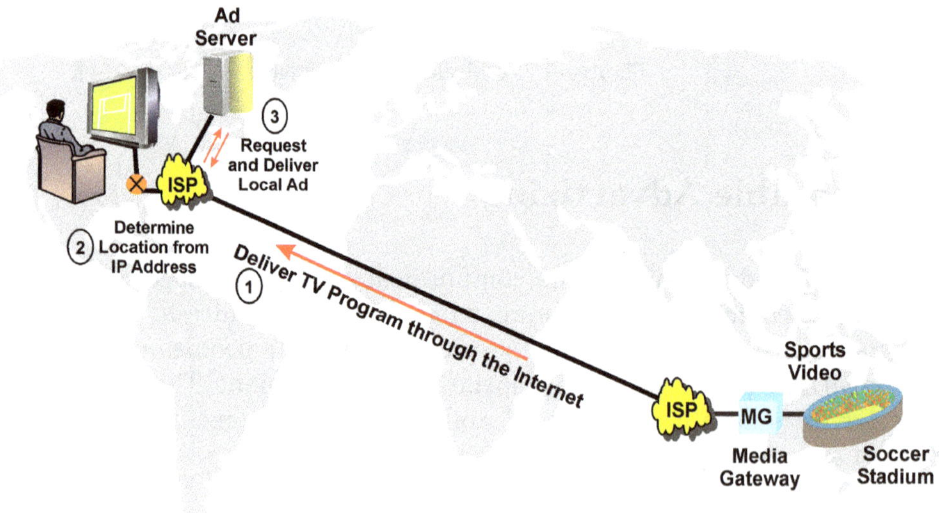

Figure 14.8, Internet TV Location Based Advertising

sent to 3 homes where the televisions in each home have a unique address. When the time for a 30 second commercial occurs, a separate advertising message is sent to each one of the viewers based on the address of the television. This allows each viewer to receive advertising messages that are better targeted to their needs and desires.

Location Based Advertising (LBA)

Location based advertising is the communication of a message or media content to one or more potential customers where the advertising message can vary based on the location of the recipient.

IP Address Geographic Coding (IP Geocoding)

IP Geocoding is the process of identifying the location of a person (or their access device) by their Internet address. Each assigned IP address is usually associated with a data routing device that has a geographic location. To obtain the location of the person or device, the IP address can be sent to an IP Geocoding service which provides back the approximate physical location.

Ad Slot Identification

Ad slot identification is the sensing of information that allows for the determination of when ad insertion opportunities occur and the duration (time) and types of ads that may be inserted. Content owners (such as TV networks) may not allow for the modification of their content. This means that indications of ad insertion opportunities may need to be sent on a separate channel or via a different process (such as image fingerprinting).

Ad Insertion

Ad insertion is the process of replacing media with another media segment or object. The source of ads may come from an ad network (such as Google) or directly from ads sales to companies.

Figure 14.8 shows how and Internet TV system may replace existing ads with promotions that are based on the local address of the viewer. This example shows that the first step is to identify the location of the viewer by using their Internet address (IP Geocoding). The next step is to identify ad insertion opportunities. This is followed by the insertion of local or localized ads (ads that are changed to match the location of the viewer).

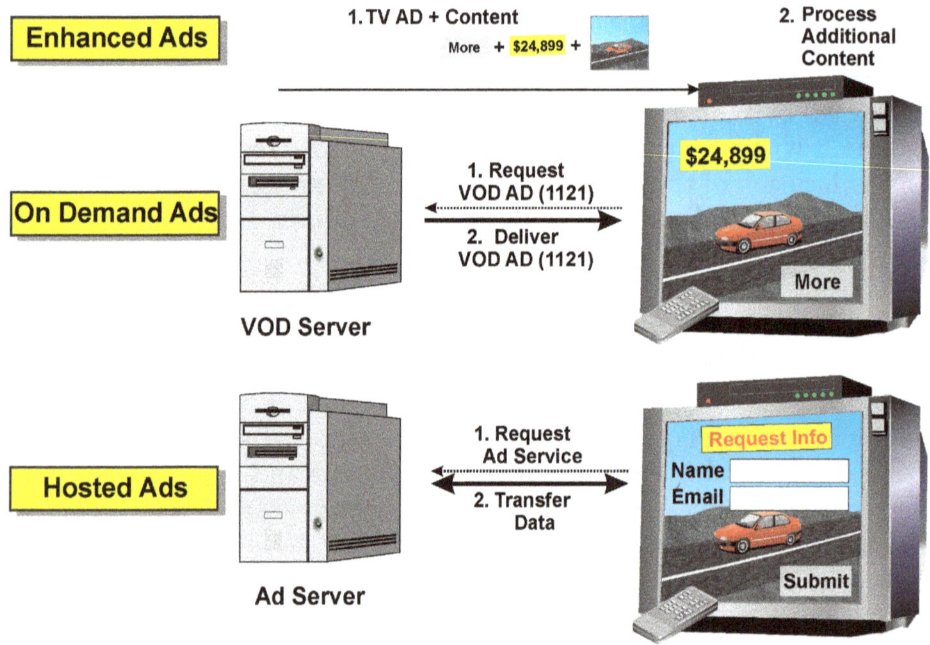

Figure 14.9, Interactive TV Ads

Interactive Advertising

Interactive ads are media communication messages that allow a viewer to influence (control) or respond to the advertising message. Interactive ads may be enhanced ads, dedicated ads, or hosted ads.

Enhanced Ads

Enhanced ads are media segments that contain additional content that may be selected and displayed to the viewer. Enhanced ads may contain images (such as sports team logos), additional video segments, or software programs that are processed on the user's device (such as the set top box). Enhanced ads may include button mapping information which can assign or associate remote control buttons to the enhanced ad features.

Dedicated Ads

Dedicated ads are promotional messages that are available for a viewer to connect and view. Dedicated ads allow the viewer to obtain extended video segments (such as long form ads). Users may be automatically directed to the dedicated ad (which may be a VOD program) when the select a button on their remote control.

Hosted Ads

Hosted ads are promotional messages that allow the viewer to interact with advertising content. Hosted ads may provide content, coordinate media flow (which media items are selected and displayed), and gather information from the viewer.

Figure 14.9 shows that interactive advertising can range from enhanced content, on demand ads, or hosted (fully interactive) advertising programs. The enhanced TV ad contains the video plus several images of a car which the viewer can scroll through using their TV remote control. The viewer can also choose to go to channel 1121 to see a 12 minute promotional message about the car "More". When the viewer selects "Request Information," their TV is connected to an ad server which present a request form that allows the viewer to enter data (name, phone, email) which is provided to the advertiser so they can send additional information.

Program Guide Advertising

Program guide advertising is the insertion of promotional messages within a directory of channels or program listings. Program guide advertising can be a combination of interstitial ads, graphic ads, or preview ads.

Interstitial Ads

Program guide interstitial ads display a promotional message to the viewer before allowing the viewer to access the program guide. Interstitial ads may be very short (1 to 3 seconds) to avoid frustrating the viewer.

Graphic Ads

Program guide graphic ads can be images that appear somewhere within the program guide. They may appear near groupings of channels of a similar theme.

Preview Ads

Preview ads are video displays that appear somewhere on the program guide. The use of preview ads allows the viewer to use the program guide while viewing the promotional message.

Figure 14.10 shows some of the ways to advertise on the program guide. Interstitial ads force the viewer to watch a promotional message before accessing the program guide. Graphic ads are images that appear somewhere within the program guide. Preview ads are video segments that play while the viewer is using the program guide.

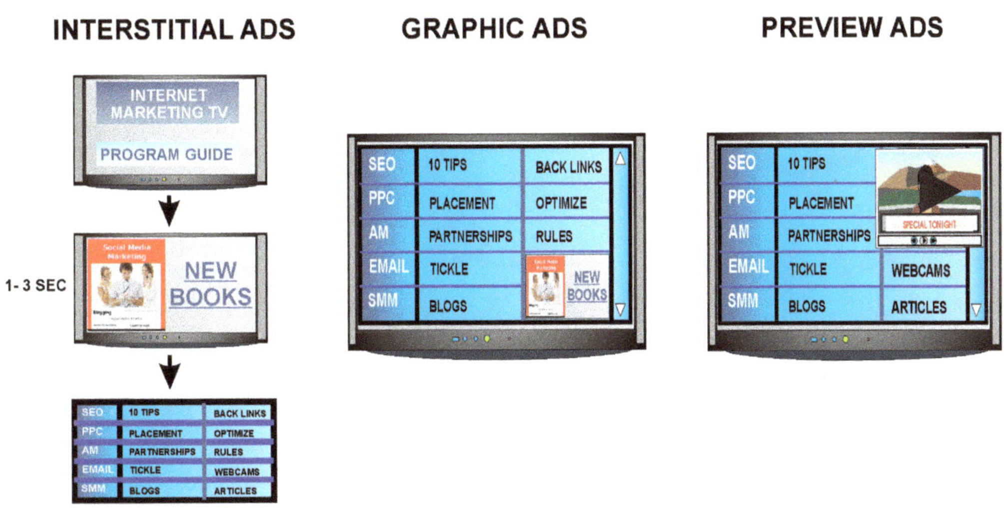

Figure 14.10, TV Program Guide Advertising

Appendix 1 - Acronyms

3DTV-Three Dimensional Television
AAAA-American Association of Advertising Agencies
AAC-Advanced Audio Codec
AACS-Advanced Access Content System
ACAP-Advanced Common Application Platform
ACR-Absolute Category Rating
Ad Agency-Advertising Agency
Ad Bookmarks-Advertising Bookmarks
Ad Campaign-Advertising Campaign
Ad Insert-AD Insertion
Ad Metrics-Advertising Metrics
Ad Package-Advertising Package
Ad Splicer-Advertising Splicer
ADC-Analog to Digital Conversion
Ad-ID-Ad Identifier
ADM-Ad Management Service
ADS-Ad Decision Service
Affiliate-Network Affiliate
AFP-Advertiser Funded Program
AIT-Application Information Table
AMBER-America's Missing Broadcasting Emergency Response
AoD-Advertising on Demand
APDU-Application Protocol Data Unit
AS-Application Server
ASF-Advanced Streaming Format
ATVEF-Advanced Television Enhancement Forum
Audio Fingerprinting-Acoustic Fingerprint
Avail-Ad Availability Slot
Avail Code-Ad Availability Code
Avails-Insertion Opportunities
BA-Broadcasting Authority
BDCP-Bi-Directional Digital Cable Product
Broadcast TV-Broadcast Television
BSA-Broadband Services Aggregator
BSAN-Broadband Services Access Node
BSR-Broadband Services Router
Cable Box-Cable Converter Box
CableLabs-Cable Laboratories, Inc.
Calls-Casting Call
CAS-Conditional Access System
CATV-Cable Television
CATV-Community Access Television
CCI-Copy Control Information
CCMS-Community Content Management System
CDK-Content Development Kit

CDN-Content Delivery Network
CGM-Consumer Generated Media
CIP-Campaign Information Package
CMS-Content Management System
Codec-Coder/Decoder
Company TV-Company Television Programming
Connected TV-Connected Television
Co-op-Cooperative Advertising
CP-Content Protection
CPE-Customer Premises Equipment
CPI-Cost per Interaction
CPM-Cost Per Thousand
CPP-Cost Per Person
CPPM-Content Protection for Prerecorded Media
CPRM-Content Protection For Recordable Media
CSM-Component Splice Mode
DAI-Dynamic Ad Insertion
Dailies-Daily Recordings
DAL-Dedicated Advertiser Location
Demos-Demonstration Reels
Dialog-Dialogue
DMA-Designated Market Area
DMA-Digital Media Adapter
DOI-Digital Object Identifier
Dongles-TV Media Stick
DRM-Digital Rights Management
DS-Docking Station
DTCP-Digital Transmission Content Protection
DTD-Document Type Definition
DTT-Digital Terrestrial Television
DTV-Digital Television
DVR Application-Digital Video Recorder Application
DWA-Digital Watermarking Alliance
EAIT-Extended Application Information Table
eBIF-Enhanced Television Binary Interchange Format
EDL-Edit Decision List
EISS-EISS Information Descriptors
EMI-Encryption Mode Indicator
Enterprise TV-Enterprise Television
EPG-Electronic Program Guide
ES-Elementary Stream
ESP-Email Service Provider
ETV-Enhanced Television
EULA-End User Licensing Agreement
FLV-Flash Video
Follow-me TV-Follow Me Television for Distribution-Program Packaging
Freeview-Free View
FTA-Free to Air
FWVGA-Full Wide Video Graphics Array
GEM-Globally Executable Multimedia Home Platform
Geoblocking-Geographic Blocking
Geocode-Geographic Code
Geocoding-Geographic Coding
Geotargeting-Geographic Targeting
Gridcasting-Peercasting
HBBTV-Hybrid Broadcast Broadband Television
HDTV-High Definition Television
HH-Households

HLS-HTTP Live Streaming
HMN-Home Media Network
HMS-Home Media Server
Hosted Ads-Hosted Advertisements
HPNA-Home Phoneline Networking Alliance Specification
HSTB-Hybrid Set Top Box
HSTB-Hybrid TV Broadcast Set Top Boxes
HUT-Homes Using Televisions
iAD-Interactive Advertisements
IAFI-Interactive Application Fulfillment Interface
IDTV-Improved Definition Television
iDTV-Integrated Digital Television Receiver
iDTV-Interactive Digital Television
IMS-IP Multimedia Subsystem
Indies-Independent Programming
Integrated STB-Integrated Set Top Box
Integrated TV-Integrated Television
Interactive CATV-Interactive Cable Television
Internet TV-Internet Television
IP Broadcast-Internet Protocol Broadcast
IP STB-Internet Protocol Set Top Box
IPG-Interactive Programming Guide
IPP-Internet Payment Processors
IPPV-Impulse Pay-Per-View
IPTV-Internet Protocol Television
IRTV-Internet Ready Television
ISAN-International Standard Audiovisual Number
ISCI-Industry Standard Commercial Identifier
ISO-International Standards Organization
ISTB-Internet Set Top Box
I-STB-Internet TV Set Top Box
ITB-Internet Television Box
ITV-Interactive Television
ITVSP-Internet Television Service Provider
LBA-Location Based Advertising
Linear TV-Linear Television
LPTV-Low Power Television
LTO-Linear Tape Open
MCSS-Master Control Switching System
MDTV-Mobile Digital Television
MG-Media Gateway
Microbrowser-Micro-Browser
MIPTV-Mobile Internet Protocol Television
MJPEG-Motion JPEG
Mobile TV-Mobile Television
MOD-Music On Demand
MP1-Moving Picture Experts Group Layer 1
MP2-Moving Picture Experts Group Layer 2
MP3-Moving Picture Experts Group Layer 3
MP3Pro-MPEG Layer 3 Pro
MP4-MPEG-4
MPEG-Moving Picture Experts Group
MSO-Multiple System Operator

MVPD-Multichannel Video Program Distributor
NCTA-National Cable Television Association
NDK-Network Development Kit
Non-Integrated STB-Non-Integrated Set Top Box
NSP-Network Service Provider
NTP-Network Time Protocol
NTSC-National Television System Committee
NVOD-Near Video On Demand
OCAP-Open Cable Application Platform
OIPF-Open IPTV Forum
OOB-Out of Band
OS-Operating System
OTT-Over the Top Television
PA-Production Assistant
Participation TV-Participation Television
PAT-Program Association Table
Pause Ads-Pause Advertising
PCR-Production Control Room
PCR-Program Clock Reference
PCs-Multimedia Personal Computers
PEID-Programmed Event Identifier
Personal TV-Personal Television
PID-Packet Identifier
PIM-Protocol Independent Multicast
PIP-Picture in a Picture
PLTV-Pause Live Television
PMT-Program Map Table
POD-Push On Demand
POIS-Placement Opportunity Information Service
PPP-Pay per Period
PPV-Pay Per View
PR-Public Relations
PR Agent-Publicity Agent
Preview Ads-Preview Advertisements
Primetime-Prime Time
Private TV-Private Television
Props-Scenic Elements
PSI-Program Specific Information
PSM-Program Splice Mode
PTM-Point to Multipoint
Publishers-Affiliate Partners
PURL-Persistent Universal Resource Locator
PVO-Promotional Video Optimization
PVOD-Push Video on Demand
PVR-Personal Video Recorder
QoS Pricing-Quality of Service Differential Pricing
QS-Quality Score
RA-Registration Authority
RC-Recurring Charge
ROAS-Return on Advertising Spend
ROS-Run of Schedule
RTP-Real Time Transport Protocol
RTSP-Real Time Streaming Protocol
SaFI-Stewardship and Fulfillment Interfaces
Script-Screenplay
Scripting-Script Writing
SCTE-Society of Cable Telecommunication Engineers
SDTV-Standard Definition Television
SDV-Switched Digital Video

SFX-Special Effects
Short Time-Nearline
SIS-Subscriber Information Service
SMATV-Satellite Master Antenna Television
SMPTE-Society of Motion Picture and Television Engineers
Soundtrack-Sound Track
Spots-Advertising Spots
SPTS-Single Program Transport Stream
Squeezeback-Squeeze Back
STB-Set Top Box
Studio-Movie Studio
STV-Subscription Television
Sublicensing-Sub-Licensing
SVGA-Super Video Graphics Array
SVOD-Subscription Video on Demand
SVS-Switched Video Service
SyncTV-Synchronized Television
Syscode-System Code
T-commerce-Television Commerce
TelcoTV-Telephone Company Television
Temporal Compression-Time Compression
Terrestrial TV-Terrestrial Television
Time Compression-Temporal Compression
Timestamp-Time Stamp
T-Mail-Television Mail
Topic Idea-Program Concept
TRP-Target Rating Points
TS-Transport Stream
TSTV-Time Shift Television
TV Ad Campaign-Television Advertising Campaign
TV Broadcaster-Television Broadcaster
TV Channel-Television Channel
TV Extender-Television Extender
TV Interviews-Television Interviews
TV Portal-Television Portal
TV Server-Television Server
TV Station-Television Station
TV Studio-Television Studio
TV Widgets-Television Widgets
TVI-Television Interference
TVOD-Transactional Video on Demand
TVoDSL-Television over DSL
TVoF-Television over Fiber
TVoIP-Television over Internet Protocol
TVoP-Television over Powerline
TVQM-Television Video Quality Metrics
TVRO-Television Receive Only
UDPC-Unidirectional Digital Cable Ready Products
UGC-User Generated Content
UMID-Unique Material Identifier
Upfronts-Upfront Advertising
UPID-Unique Program Identifier
USP-Unique Selling Proposition
UTC-Coordinated Universal Time
VBI-Video Blanking Interval
VC-1-Windows Media
VCF-Video Convergence Forum

VCPS-Video Content Protection System
Video Player Speed Control-Trick Mode
Videotrack-Video Track
VOD-Video On Demand
VOD Server-Video on Demand Server
VOD Sponsorship-Video on Demand Sponsorship
VWM-Video Watermarking
WDK-Widget Development Kit
Web TV-Web Televisions
Webinar-Web Seminar
Webisode-Web Episode
WebM-Open Web Media
WebTV-Web Television
WFM-Workflow Management
WGA-Writers Guild of America
WikiTV-Wiki Television
Wired HH-Wired Households
WVGA-Wide Video Graphics Array

Appendix 2 - Sample Release Form

PERMISSION TO RELEASE PHOTOS, VIDEO AND/OR USE NAME

I, ____ hereby
(please print)
voluntarily grant permission to ________________, Producer of ____________, and other Media Productions , the use of photographs, video tape, my name, and the company name ____________________________ recorded at this event: ____ within their media programs and publications.

I understand that by granting permission to have my activities photographs and/or videotaped, I will not be paid for the use of this material. I also understand that these materials may be used in television programs, blog posts, magazine articles that may be distributed through multiple types of broadcast and on demand television systems including cable TV, satellite TV, Internet TV, and others on a local, regional, national, or international basis.

I agree to and do hereby release ________ and agree to hold harmless the same from any and all claims for damages for libel, slander, invasion of privacy, or any other claim based on the use of said material or caused by arising from any participation and any utterance made by me or materials furnished by me in connection with any participation therein.

This agreement expresses the entire understanding and agreement of each of us and cannot be modified, waived or discharged except by written documentation executed by each of the parties thereto. It shall be governed, construed and performed according to the laws of the STATE OF ________________.

____________________________________ ____________
Signature Date

____________________________________ ____________
Media Company Date

Appendix 3 - Internet TV Marketing Plan Sample

Form
Subscriber Marketing Plan
for Linear Channel

Overview of Channel

- Content Category (Niche, Genre)
- Programming Description
- Languages
- Target Demographic
- Current Distribution
- Affiliated Companies
- Related Media (publications, websites, etc.)

Programming Highlights

- Examples of Popular Programming
  - Demo DVDs
  - Descriptive information with Pictures
- Feature Most Popular or Distinctive Programs
- Well known talent featured
- Awards or other Recognition
- Figures on viewership, popularity

Distribution Platform Strategy

- OTT
- Direct To Home (Satellite)
- Telco IPTV
- Cable Operators
- Web Delivery
- Mobile Devices

Specific Promotional Activity

- Web, On-air Announcements
  - Banners
  - Special Promotions
- Press Release/Media Coverage
  - Press Releases
  - Articles
  - Paid Announcements in trade journals and journals of interest to target audience
- Network Talent Appearances
  - Mentions of launch (on air)
  - Appearances at local events
  - Direct Mailings and Phone Campaigns using messages from the talent

Specific Promotional Activity

- Print Announcement
  - Advertisements in magazines, newspapers, billboards
- Sponsored Events
  - Sponsor events related to target market
  - Hold promotional events
- Street Promotion
  - Posters, fliers and banners in recreation centers, schools, churches, restaurants and food markets attended by the target market
- 30-second Cross-channel Spots
  - Both the Network 's and other networks' channels

Index

Abandoned Content, 40
Acoustics, 194
Activation Fee, 221-222
Ad Availability Slot (Avail), 134-135
AD Insertion (Ad Insert), 16, 128, 134, 136, 160-162, 214, 218-219, 289, 294, 296, 303-304
Ad Insertion Log, 219
Ad Insertion Order, 218
Ad Server, 136, 306
Ad Slot, 303
Ad Splicer, 135-136
Ad Spots, 27
Addressable Advertising, 134, 301-302
Advanced Audio Codec (AAC), 91-93, 117
Advertiser Funded Program (AFP), 10
Advertising Agency (Ad Agency), 219
Advertising Campaign (Ad Campaign), 180, 218, 269
Advertising Contract, 161-162, 218
Advertising Sales, 160, 162, 218-219
Advertising Splicer (Ad Splicer), 135-136
Advertising Spots (Spots), 27
Affiliate Guidelines, 236-237
Affiliate Networks, 6, 236
Agency Fees, 215
Analog Cue Tone, 135
Analog to Digital Conversion (ADC), 77
Application Platform, 48-49, 53, 66
Aspect Ratio, 81, 283
Audio Digitization, 77, 79-80
Audio Rendering, 117
Automatic Scheduling, 156
Banner Ad Network, 239
Billing Mediation, 229
Billing Service Bureau, 229-230
Blog Marketing, 256
Blog Marketing, 256
Broadcast Services, 10-11
Broadcast Television (Broadcast TV), 1, 45-46, 135
Cable Television (CATV), 52-53, 81, 138, 143, 149, 273
Campaign Management, 267
Casting Call (Calls), 31, 163, 252-253, 302
Casting, 50, 153
Channel Advertising, 233-234
Channel Lineup, 155
Closed Captioning, 123
Closed Distribution, 278
Cloud Pairing, 46
Coder/Decoder (Codec), 85, 89-90, 92-93
Community Access Television

(CATV), 52
Community Content, 21-22, 37-39, 119
Conditional Access System (CAS), 52
Connected Television (Connected TV), 54, 61-63, 66
Container Format, 85-87
Content Acquisition, 128, 149, 191
Content Aggregator, 28-29, 274, 284
Content Brokers, 28
Content Delivery Network (CDN), 151, 154, 156, 203, 286
Content Distribution, 21, 26, 29, 120, 122, 128, 203, 278
Content License, 227, 273, 275, 277
Content Licensing Aggregator, 274
Content Management System (CMS), 128, 131, 156, 168, 214
Content Management, 121, 128, 131, 154, 156, 167-169, 174-175, 198, 214
Content Protection (CP), 40, 54, 56, 285
Content Protection Methods, 285
Content Sources, 1-2, 9, 21-23, 25, 27-29, 31, 33, 35, 37, 39, 41, 43, 67, 75, 119, 121, 137, 182-183, 188
Content Storage, 129, 154
Contribution Network, 119, 121, 123-124
Core Network, 120, 137-138
Cost Per Thousand (CPM), 214, 300
Cue Tones, 135
Customer Care History, 159
Customer Support, 159-160, 163, 209
Daily Call Sheet, 195
Dedicated Ads, 305
Delivery Restrictions, 102
Demographics, 24
Demultiplexing, 115
Designated Market Area (DMA), 45
Device Capability, 145
Device Management, 145-147
Device Storage, 48
Dialogue (Dialog), 180
Digital Media Adapter (DMA), 2, 45, 47, 221
Digital Media Formats, 85, 87
Digital Rights Management (DRM), 56, 285
Digital Television (DTV), 61, 88-89
Digital Terrestrial Television (DTT), 52, 61
Direct Mail List, 246
Direct Mail Promotion, 245
Direct Sales, 9, 17-18
Discussion Engagement, 262
Discussion Groups, 261-262
Display Ad Development Tools, 238-239
Display Ads, 238-240
Display Advertising, 238
Display Resolution, 83, 146
Distribution Network, 113, 122, 127-128, 134, 137, 203
Distribution System, 119-120, 126-127, 136, 138, 154, 203, 285
Distribution Time Period, 280
DivX, 87, 90
Dolby Noise Reduction, 79
Download and Play, 14
Dynamic Product Placement, 298
Earned Media, 262-263
Electronic Program Guide (EPG),

97-98, 129
Elementary Stream (ES), 94, 249
Email Broadcasting, 235, 237, 266-268
Email Testing, 268
Embedded Videos, 270
Enhanced Advertising, 305
Enhanced Content, 306
Entertainment Law, 273
Expired Copyrights, 40
Firmware Updates, 46-47
Flash Video (FLV), 61, 87, 90
Footage, 24, 183
Foreground Display Resizing, 297
Foreign Networks, 33
Foreign Programs, 33
Foreign TV Stations, 33
Frame Rate, 81-82
Free View (Freeview), 11
Free-to-Air Content License, 277
Geo-Filtering, 281
Geographic Coding (Geocoding), 102, 303-304
Geographic Targeting (Geotargeting), 101
Global Television Channels, 22
Government Content, 40
Graphic Ads, 241, 306-307
Hashtags, 259
Headend, 119-120, 126-127, 137-138, 278, 285-286
High Definition Television (HDTV), 81, 88, 140
Home Media Network (HMN), 120, 137, 139, 141, 143
Home Media Server (HMS), 138-139
Hosted Advertisements (Hosted Ads), 305
Hosted Billing, 229-230
Hosted Internet TV, 165, 167, 169-170
Hosted Media Ingestion, 168
Human Interface Capabilities, 59
Hybrid Broadcast Broadband Television (HBBTV), 52
Hybrid Set Top Box (HSTB), 52-53
Image Placement, 295
Indemnification, 287
Independent Film, 34, 36
Independent Producers, 6-7
Independent Programming (Indies), 34, 119
Ingestion, 28, 131, 151, 167-169
Insertion Channel, 135
Insertion Event, 219
Insertion Opportunities (Avails), 134, 291-292
Insertion Orders, 218-219
Insertion Rating, 219
Insertion Reporting, 161
Integrated Internet TV, 165-166, 170-172
Interactive Advertising, 9, 305-306
Interactive Digital Television (iDTV), 89
Interactive Product Placement, 298-299
Interactive Programming Guide (IPG), 97-98
Interactive TV Ads, 304
International Programming, 32-33
International Standards Organization (ISO), 92
Internet Connection, 41, 45, 48, 52, 61-62, 64-66, 189, 200, 277
Internet Protocol Broadcast (IP

Broadcast), 203
Internet Protocol Set Top Box (IP STB), 49
Internet Protocol Television (IPTV), 2, 64, 125-126, 281
Internet Set Top Box (ISTB), 45, 47-50, 146
Internet Television (Internet TV), 1-178, 180, 182, 184-186, 188, 190-308
Internet TV Advertising, 15-17, 162, 218, 220, 234, 289, 291, 293, 295, 297, 299, 301, 303, 305, 307
Internet TV Billing, 207, 209-211, 213, 215, 217, 219, 221, 223, 225, 227, 229
Internet TV Broadcasters, 11, 21-22, 27, 29, 31, 185-186, 289
Internet TV Content Licensing, 273, 275, 277, 279, 281, 283, 285, 287
Internet TV Content Sources, 1, 21-23, 25, 27, 29, 31, 33, 35, 37, 39, 41, 43
Internet TV Content Types, 5, 7
Internet TV Distribution Systems, 2, 137, 139
Internet TV Hosting, 165, 168
Internet TV Marketing, 231, 233, 235, 237, 239, 241, 243, 245, 247, 249, 251, 253, 255, 257, 259, 261, 263, 265, 267, 269, 271
Internet TV Platform, 47
Internet TV Promotion, 233
Internet TV Service Providers, 2, 28, 45, 47, 54, 221, 291
Internet TV Services, 9, 11, 13, 15, 17, 19, 62, 64, 138, 216, 291
Internet TV Set Top Box (I-STB), 45, 47-50, 121
Internet TV System Options, 165, 167, 169, 171, 173, 175
Internet TV Viewing Devices, 2, 45, 47, 49, 51, 53, 55, 57, 59, 61, 63, 65, 67, 145
Interstitial Ad, 16
Interstitial Metadata, 97
IP Address Geocoding, 303-304
Java Scripts, 66
Leased Line, 122, 200
License Elements, 276
License Fee, 48, 228
License Scope, 276
License Types, 227, 274-275
Licensing Aggregator, 274
Lighting Requirements, 194
Linear Advertising, 291
Linear Channels, 3-4, 10-11, 286
Linear Television (Linear TV), 132
Link Protocols, 75-76
Live Broadcast Communication Links, 200
Live Broadcasting, 192, 200, 202, 204
Live Content Acquisition, 191
Live Event Preparation, 193
Live Internet TV, 191, 193, 195, 197, 199, 201, 203, 205
Live IP Broadcasting, 203
Live Media Acquisition, 195
Live Production, 193, 196, 198-199
Live Streaming, 14
Live Video Cameras, 195
Local Events, 30-31, 37, 255
Local Media, 137
Local News, 30-31
Local Programming, 21, 30, 119
Local Weather, 31-32

Location Based Advertising (LBA), 302-303
Location Preparation, 191
Location Registration, 102
Logo Insertion, 132, 295
Long Form Advertisements, 292
Lossy Compression, 69, 83
Mail Stuffing, 246
Media Capturing, 69, 204
Media Components Formats, 188
Media Decoding, 48, 56, 61-62, 66
Media Encoder, 130, 203
Media Format, 29, 85, 90, 96, 168, 203-204, 286
Media Gateway (MG), 133
Media Ingestion, 28, 167-169
Media Management, 166, 171
Media Processing, 46, 55, 61-64, 66-67, 188
Media Synchronization, 95
Media Uplink, 203
Metadata Management, 128-129
Metadata, 29, 96-98, 123, 128-129, 179
Microphones, 42, 187, 191, 195-198, 205
Microplayer, 58
Mirror Site, 112
Mirroring, 50
Mixing, 178, 186, 191, 199
Mobile Operating System, 59
Motion JPEG (MJPEG), 87, 90
Movie Studio (Studio), 5, 22-23, 120, 153, 177, 183, 185-187, 253, 274, 286
Moving Picture Experts Group (MPEG), 55, 57, 61, 64, 66-67, 70, 85, 87-95, 131
Moving Picture Experts Group Layer 1 (MP1), 91
Moving Picture Experts Group Layer 2 (MP2), 91-92, 117
Moving Picture Experts Group Layer 3 (MP3), 85, 89-93, 117
MPEG Layer 3 Pro (MP3Pro), 92
MPEG-1, 87-89
MPEG-2, 87-89, 131, 146, 203, 283
MPEG-4 (MP4), 69, 83, 87-90, 131, 146, 188, 283, 295
Multicast Routers, 112
Multicasting, 111
Multicasting, 111
Multimedia Mobile Telephone, 58
Multimedia Personal Computers (PCs), 55
Multiple Bit Rate Formats, 100
Multiple Channel Services, 150
Multipoint, 110-111, 137
National Television System Committee (NTSC), 81, 88, 97, 117-118
Nearline Storage, 129-130
Network Advertising, 233
Network Affiliate (Affiliate), 6, 18, 21, 25-26, 235-237, 300
Network Connection, 53, 61, 64, 66-67, 122, 139
Network Content Types, 26
Network Data Interface, 48
Network Feeds, 25-27, 33, 120
Network Protocols, 75
Network Television, 6, 21
On Demand Advertising, 9, 213-214, 291-292, 306

On Demand Channels, 3-4
On Demand Programming, 4, 13, 155, 291
On Demand Services, 13, 15, 214
Online Invoicing, 223-224
Open Distribution, 277-278
Operating System (OS), 55, 57-60, 62, 66
Order Processing, 17, 149, 162-163
Original Content, 43, 182-183
Original Programming, 22, 26, 41-42
Over the Top Television (OTT) , 1, 151, 277-278, 281
Overlay Ad, 16, 27, 294-295
Packet Addressing, 103
Packet Buffering, 116-117
Packet Congestion, 106
Packet Control, 104
Packet Corruption, 106
Packet Jitter, 108
Packet Losses, 105-107, 116
Packet Reception, 69-70, 115
Packet Routing, 104
Packet Sequencing, 107-108
Packet Timing, 107
Packet Transmission, 70, 103, 105, 108, 116
Packetization, 69-70
Parental Controls, 96
Pause Advertising (Pause Ads), 293-294
Pay per Period (PPP), 13-14
Pay Per View (PPV), 5, 9, 12-14, 218, 232
Payment Gateway, 224
Payment Information, 224-226
Payment Processing, 18, 207, 209, 226, 230
PC Video to TV Converter, 56
Peer Relaying, 114
Peercasting (Gridcasting), 114-115
Peercasting Protocols, 114
Pending Transactions, 223
Periodic Charges, 216
Physical Connection, 72-73
Player Skin Ads, 16, 299-300
Playout System, 3, 132-134, 167-169, 171-173, 175
Podcasts, 250, 253
Post Production, 178-179
Post-roll Ads, 293
Postroll, 291-293
PPC Ads, 240-241, 300
PPC Keywords, 241
Preauthorization, 225-226
Pre-Configured Equipment, 171
Premium Channels, 12
Preproduction Plan, 178
Pre-roll Ads, 293
Preroll, 153, 291-293
Press Release, 248-251
Preview Advertisements (Preview Ads), 306-307
Primary Channel, 135
Private Channels, 3-4
Product Integration, 298
Product Placement, 298-299
Production Console, 197-199
Production Control Room (PCR), 186
Production Crew, 193, 195, 197, 201
Production Staff, 153, 173, 183-186, 202
Production Tasks, 152
Program Advertising, 15, 234

Program Archives, 182-183
Program Development, 177, 179
Program Guide Advertising, 306-307
Program Guide, 97-98, 155, 265, 306-307
Program Metadata, 96, 98, 123
Program Packaging (for Distribution), 178
Program Schedule, 155, 250
Program Transfer Scheduling, 124-125
Programming Tiers, 12
Promotional Video Optimization (PVO), 271
Promotional Videos, 247, 269
Props, 24, 180-181, 186-187
Protocol Suites, 75-76
Public Broadcasting, 37-38
Public Channels, 3-4, 38
Public Domain, 39-41, 183
Public Relations (PR), 249, 252
Publicity Agent (PR Agent), 252-253
Publicity Programs, 247
Radio Talk Shows, 252-253
Rate Plan, 12, 208-209, 216-218
Rating System, 209
Reach, 1-2, 232, 252, 282, 289
Real Time Production, 191-192
Real Time Transport Protocol (RTP), 108-109
Recurring Billing, 225-227
Reference Key Frames, 100
Referral Incentives, 244
Release Window, 5, 21, 24, 279-280
Remote Editing, 188-189
Remote Interviews, 41-42, 185, 187
Rendering, 69, 71, 117-118, 207, 223
Resolution, 29, 33, 59, 81, 83, 88, 146, 168-169, 188-189, 249, 283
Retransmission Requests, 116
Revenue Assurance, 228-229, 285
Revenue Sharing Agreements, 208
Review Programs, 264
Review Requests, 259-260
RF Output, 118
Royalty Free, 182
Royalty Management, 227-228
Sales Commissions, 219
Sales Prospecting, 160
Sales Revenue, 61, 232
Sales Transactions, 9, 208
Satellite Link, 201, 275
Scenic Elements (Props), 24, 180-181, 186-187
Scheduling Server, 132-133
Screenings, 178
Screenplay (Script), 180-181, 184, 257-258, 269, 271, 298
Script Writing (Scripting), 65, 152-153, 180-181
Scripting, 65, 152-153, 180-181
Scrolling Text, 16, 132, 294, 296
Seed Distribution List, 243
Service Bureau, 229-230
Service Items, 213, 215
Service Provisioning, 215
Services Database, 213, 215-216
Session Protocols, 75
Set Top Box (STB), 47-49, 52-54, 64, 121, 146, 155-156, 164, 305
Shared Hosting, 167
Shared Media, 38
Shared Video Networks, 271
Shoot Plan, 193

Shortening URL Links, 260
Single Channel Services, 149-150
Single Program Transport Stream (SPTS), 95
Site Review, 193
Skin Ads, 16, 299-300
Society of Motion Picture and Television Engineers (SMPTE), 90
Soft Client, 54-55, 57
Software Versions, 146
Spatial Compression, 84
Special Effects (SFX), 25, 132, 178
Specialty Content Producers, 34
Splice In, 188
Splice Out, 188
Sponsored Programs, 10
Squeeze Back (Squeezeback), 132, 297
Station Advertising, 234
Stock Media, 177, 182-183
Store Media Applications, 66
Storyboard, 180-181, 269, 272
Storyboarding, 177, 180, 269
Stream Format, 86, 127
Streaming Control, 100
Streaming Server, 113, 132-133, 137-138, 173, 175, 192
Streaming Sessions, 47, 203
Streaming Video, 1
Striping, 114
Studio Production, 177, 183, 185
Studio Rental, 153, 186
Sub-Licensing (Sublicensing), 283
Subscriber Account, 211
Subscriber Communication History, 212
Subscriber Database, 207, 211-212
Subscriber Management, 149, 158-159, 163, 167, 169, 171
Subscriber Profile, 211
Subscriber Services, 211-212
Subscription Accounts, 12
Subscription Services, 9, 12-13, 207, 214, 217
Support Services, 165, 170-171
Surround Sound, 79, 94, 283
Switched Digital Video (SDV), 72-74
Switched Video Service (SVS), 13
Switching System, 126, 192
Syndicate, 24
Syndicates, 21, 24-25, 119
Systems Integrators, 174
Takes, 107, 205, 246
Talk Show Guest, 252
Talk Show Host, 252-253
Talk Show, 247, 249-250, 252-254
Talking Heads, 195
Target Audience, 150, 289
Television Broadcaster (TV Broadcaster), 17-18, 33, 42, 47, 52-53, 88, 161, 169, 186, 290
Television Channel (TV Channel), 1, 3, 64, 72-73, 79, 88, 110, 118, 135, 138, 232-234, 299
Television Commerce (T-commerce), 9, 17-18
Television Gateway, 110
Television Metadata, 96-97
Television Network Selection, 2, 6-7, 22, 25, 143
Television over DSL (TVoDSL), 29
Television Server (TV Server), 46
Television Station (TV Station), 31-32, 42, 166-168, 177, 232-234, 247, 255-256, 258
Television Studio (TV Studio), 186-

187
Temporal Compression (Time Compression), 84, 90
Terrestrial Television (Terrestrial TV), 52
Third Party Sales, 18, 164
Tiered Pricing, 12
Tiered Services, 12
Time Compression (Temporal Compression) , 84
Time Stamp (Timestamp), 107-109
Timeline Editing, 188
Timing Index, 100
Timing References, 95
Tracking Codes, 241, 246, 268
Transaction Rates, 216-217
Transmission Types, 110
Transparent Overlay, 295
Transport License, 274-275
Transport Stream (TS), 94-95, 97
Trick Mode (Video Player Speed Control) , 99-101
TV Ad Sales System, 161
TV Channel Types, 3
TV Media Stick (Dongles) , 45, 50-51
TV Metadata Standards, 97
TV Program Metadata, 96
Unicast Video, 110
Usage Tracking, 215
Use Frequency, 280
Use License, 274-276
Use Period, 279
User Generated Content (UGC), 7, 21
VC-1, 61, 64, 67, 83, 87, 90
Video Ad Networks, 291
Video Captions, 271
Video Components, 80
Video Compression Formats, 87
Video Digitization, 80, 82
Video Editing Systems, 188-189
Video Editing, 188-190
Video On Demand (VOD), 96, 151, 155, 274, 276, 284, 286, 305
Video Production, 179, 192, 199, 254, 269, 272
Video Rendering, 117
Video Titles, 270
Video Transcription, 271
Viewer Profile, 289
Viewership, 26, 231-232
Viewing Device, 2, 45-47, 49-51, 53, 55, 57, 59, 61, 63, 65, 67, 72-73, 75, 82, 117, 119-120, 138, 143, 145, 155, 203-204, 221, 224, 295
Viral Content, 243
Viral Marketing, 243-245
Virtual Studio, 185-187
Voice Over, 132
Web Seminar (Webinar), 41-42, 270
White Label, 167-168
WiFi Connection, 50-51, 58
Window Viewing, 299-300
Windows Media (VC-1) , 61, 64, 67, 83, 85, 87, 90
Workflow Automation, 152
Workflow Management (WFM), 128, 151, 153, 177
Workflow, 128, 151-153, 177, 191

www.ingramcontent.com/pod-product-compliance
Lightning Source LLC
Chambersburg PA
CBHW082134210326
41599CB00031B/5972
9781932813265